Praise from Job Seekers for the *Knock 'em Dead* Books

"My job search began a few months ago when I found out that I would be laid off because of a corporate buyout. By following your advice, I have had dozens of interviews and have received three very good job offers. Your excellent advice made my job hunt much easier."

—K.C., St. Louis, Missouri

"I've used *Knock 'em Dead* since 1994 when I graduated. It's the reason I've made it to VP—thank you!"

—P.L., Norfolk, Virginia

"My son called me from college last night, desperate to help a friend on her first interview. My advice? Tell her to drop everything and head to the nearest bookstore to get *Knock 'em Dead*. The book is a godsend and helped me obtain the job of my dreams eight years ago. It is by far THE best book on interviewing out there. I highly recommend it to everyone I know who asks me for help. As a Director of HR now, I know. No one should go to an interview without reading, re-reading, and re-re-reading this informative, absorbing, tremendously helpful book. It is utterly amazing. Thank you!"

—S.D., Philadelphia, Pennsylvania

"I was out of work for four months—within five weeks of reading your book, I had four job offers."
—S.K., Dallas, Texas

"I cannot tell you what a fabulous response I have been getting due to the techniques you describe in your books. Besides giving me the tools I needed to 'get my foot in the door,' they gave me confidence. I never thought I could secure an excellent position within a month!"

—B.G., Mountainview, California

"I am very grateful for your *Knock 'em Dead* series. I have read the trio and adopted the methods. In the end, I got a dream job with a salary that is almost double my previous! By adopting your methods, I got four job offers and had a hard time deciding!"

—C.Y., Singapore

"After reading your book, *Knock 'em Dead Resumes*, I rewrote my resume and mailed it to about eight companies. The results were beyond belief. I was employed by one of the companies that got my new resume and received offers of employment or requests for interviews from every company. The entire job search took only five weeks."

—J.V., Dayton, Ohio

"Your book is simply fantastic. This one book improved my yearly income by several thousand dollars, and my future income by untold amounts. Your work has made my family and myself very happy."

—M.Z., St. Clair Shores, Michigan

"After having seen you on television, I decided to order the *Knock 'em Dead* books. Your insights into selling myself helped me find opportunities in my field that would not have been attainable otherwise."

—E.M., Short Hills, New Jersey

"I just wanted to say thank you so much for your book. I can really, honestly say that it has influenced my life course!"

—P.B., London, England

"Thank you for your wonderful book! I read it before attempting to secure a position in an industry that I had been out of for fourteen years. The first company I interviewed with made me an offer for more money than I had expected."

—K.T., Houston, Texas

Praise from Job Seekers for the *Knock 'em Dead* Books

"I got the position! I was interviewed by three people and the third person asked me all the questions in *Knock 'em Dead*. I had all the right answers!"

—D.J., Scottsdale, Arizona

"I followed the advice in *Knock 'em Dead* religiously and got more money, less hours, a better hospital plan, and negotiated to keep my three weeks of vacation. I start my new job immediately!"

—A.B., St. Louis, Missouri

"Thank you for all the wonderfully helpful information you provided in your book. I lost my job almost one year ago. I spent almost eight months looking for a comparable position. Then I had the good sense to buy your book. Two months later, I accepted a new position. You helped me turn one of the worst experiences of my life into a blessing in disguise."

—L.G., Watervliet, New York

"I heard of your book right after I bombed out on three interviews. I read it. I went on two interviews after reading it. I have been told by both of those last two interviewers that I am the strongest candidate. I may have two job offers!"

—B.V., Albuquerque, New Mexico

"I read your book and studied your answers to tough questions. The first interview that I went on after doing this ended up in a job being offered to me! The interviewer told me that I was the best interviewee she'd seen! Thanks a million for writing your book. I am so thankful that I had heard about you!"

—K.P., Houston, Texas

"I just finished writing the letter I have dreamed of writing for three years: my letter of resignation from the Company from Hell. Thanks to you and the book *Knock 'em Dead*, I have been offered and have accepted an excellent position with a major international service corporation."

—C.C., Atlanta, Georgia

"I was sending out hordes of resumes and hardly getting a nibble—and I have top-notch skills and experience in my field. I wasn't prepared for this tough job market. When I read your book, however, I immediately began applying some of your techniques. My few nibbles increased to so many job interviews I could hardly keep up with them!"

—C.S., Chicago, Illinois

"It was as if the interviewer had just put the same book down! After being unemployed for more than a year, I am grateful to say that I've landed the best job I've ever had."

—E.M., Honolulu, Hawaii

"Every time I've used your book, I've gotten an offer! This book is incredible. Thanks for publishing such a great tool."

—W.Z., Columbia, Maryland

"I just received the offer of my dreams with an outstanding company. Thank you for your insight. I was prepared!"

—T.C., San Francisco, California

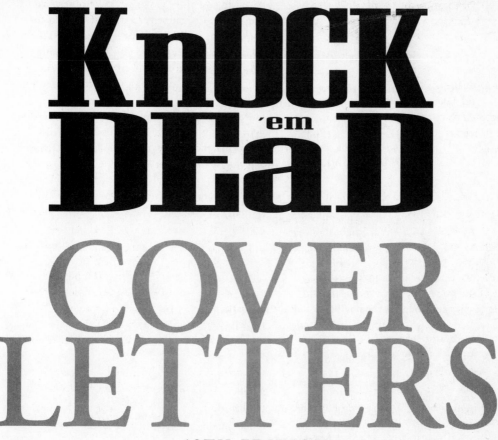

KnOCK 'em DEaD

COVER LETTERS

10TH EDITION

Cover letter samples and strategies you need to get the job you want

MARTIN YATE, CPC
New York Times bestselling author

Adamsmedia

Avon, Massachusetts

To your good fortune, that intersection of preparation, effort, and opportunity

Published by
Adams Media, a division of F+W Media, Inc.
57 Littlefield Street, Avon, MA 02322. U.S.A.
www.adamsmedia.com

ISBN 10: 1-4405-3680-5
ISBN 13: 978-1-4405-3680-9

Printed in the United States of America.

10 9 8 7 6 5 4 3 2 1

Library of Congress Cataloging-in-Publication Data

Yate, Martin John.
  Knock 'em dead cover letters / Martin Yate. – 10th ed.
    p. cm.
  Rev. ed. of: Cover letters that knock 'em dead. 7th ed. c2006.
  Includes index.
  ISBN 978-1-4405-3680-9 (pbk.) – ISBN 1-4405-3680-5 (pbk.)
  1. Cover letters. 2. Resumes (Employment) 3. Job hunting. I. Yate, Martin John.
Cover letters that knock 'em dead. II. Title.
  HF5383.Y378 2012
  650.14'2–dc23
                        2012025589

This book is available at quantity discounts for bulk purchases.
For information, please call 1-800-289-0963.

READ THIS FIRST

At every stage of the job search and hiring cycle, letters can help you make important points that can be difficult to express verbally. Use the strategies and tactics I'll show you in this book to position yourself as someone worth taking seriously.

Selling yourself with the written word is a challenge, and probably something you haven't made a priority. However, it is a greatly desired professional skill, and integrating well-crafted letters into your job search can differentiate your candidacy; it's a strategy that can get you out of that dead-end job sooner, or back to work more quickly.

Knock 'em Dead Cover Letters has helped millions of people around the world craft hard-hitting job search letters of all types that helped them land interviews, advance their candidacy, and win job offers, and it can do the same for you.

You'll find job search letters of every conceivable type here: cover letters to headhunters, hiring managers, and more; follow-up letters for after telephone and face-to-face meetings; networking, resurrection, acceptance, and rejection letters; and those jubilant (though they mustn't seem so) letters of resignation.

When you write and send a letter, for the recipient, that letter becomes *you*. It speaks for you when you aren't there to speak for yourself; it brings you back and sits you down opposite the recruiter or hiring manager; it keeps you visible and your candidacy vibrant. The letters you send during a job search give your candidacy another dimension: They give you an edge in a competitive job market. The 100-plus sample letters in this book are *real* letters that have already worked in someone's job search. I've helped people write some of these letters, while others have been sent to me by career coaches, headhunters, hiring managers, and grateful readers (I'd very much like to see yours).

> **E-MAIL AND TRADITIONAL MAIL**
> Throughout this book, the words "mail," "letter," and "e-mail," are intended to be interchangeable, unless otherwise noted. Written communications can be delivered by either e-mail or traditional mail, with the majority going by e-mail. However, you shouldn't ignore traditional mail, because when you do something other job hunters aren't doing, you stand out.

How Recruitment Works

A good cover letter and subsequent follow-up letters can speed your candidacy through the four stages all employers go through in the recruitment, screening, and selection cycle. They won't win you the job in and of themselves, but they can make a big difference in the way you are perceived, helping you stand out from the competition. The four stages are:

1. *Long-list development.* The first stage of most recruitment strategies is to develop a "long list" of 10–12 potential candidates.
2. *Short-list development.* The long list of candidates is screened for best-fit-to-the-job, reducing the long list to 4–6 candidates. Those who make the cut become the "short list," and are invited in after first passing the additional screening of a telephone interview. A folder is created for each candidate, including both print and electronic docs.
3. *Short-list prioritization.* Through a series of interviews, usually one, two, or three, the short-list candidates are ranked for ability and fit.
4. *Short-list review and decision.* Each candidate's folder is reviewed one last time before the final decision. The folder will include your resume, the employer's notes, and any cover and follow-up letters you have been smart enough to send during the interview process. These letters make additional points, clear up mistakes and omissions, and serve to brand you as a competent professional.

In each of the recruitment and selection steps you will pass through in pursuit of your next step up the professional ladder, letters have a role to play in separating you from other candidates (part of the professional branding process) and easing your passage to the next stage. Letters support your candidacy and remind employers of your relevant skills, professionalism, interest, suitability for the job, and continued existence all the way through to the offer.

Any experienced headhunter will tell you that when there are no major differences between two top candidates, the offer will always go to the most *intelligently enthusiastic*; your letters can help make that *intelligent enthusiasm* clear to prospective employers.

Each step of the hiring cycle presents you with significant opportunities to advance your candidacy. After a meeting, you can add additional information that you forgot in the heat of the moment, clear up a misunderstanding or poor answer ("I'm good at my job, but not so good at interviews, Caroline. I just haven't had that many. When we were talking about _____, perhaps I didn't make it clear that . . .").

By absorbing the *Knock 'em Dead* approach to letter writing and then mining the sample letters provided in this book, you can take a phrase from one letter and a few words from another to create original and unique letters that reflect the real you.

The different types of letters you create to advance your candidacy during the interview cycle demonstrate your writing skills, attention to detail, professionalism, and that all-important enthusiasm. Each letter adds another meaningful plus to your candidacy.

With *Knock 'em Dead Cover Letters* on your desk, you won't waste time creating letters from scratch, and once settled in a new position, you can apply these same strategies and tactics to the written communications that are an integral part of every successful career.

Read this book with a highlighter in hand so you can flag phrases or sections for later reference.

ACKNOWLEDGMENTS

Knock 'em Dead books have been in print here in America and in many languages around the world for twenty-five-plus years, and they owe their success to millions of satisfied professionals. This is only possible because books like *Knock 'em Dead Cover Letters* work. This book can be the start of significant changes in the trajectory of your professional life.

My thanks to my readers everywhere for the fun and privilege of doing this work and for bringing others in need to the *Knock 'em Dead* path. Thanks also to the Adams Media team who helps me do it, especially my editors, Peter Archer and Will Yate, and Head of House Karen Cooper.

CONTENTS

Chapter 1
COVER LETTERS: THE SECRET WEAPON OF YOUR JOB SEARCH

A recent survey of 1,000 executives revealed that 91 percent found cover letters to be valuable in their evaluation of candidates. Your cover letter can add information that isn't in your resume and help establish a communication channel between two professionals with a common interest.

You can build the greatest cover letter in the world, but if you don't learn how to use it properly, your job search will take longer, and the job you get and the money you earn may not be all you deserve. Cover letters are most effective when you develop a plan of attack that includes reaching out directly to hiring authorities. Whenever someone in a position to hire you reads your resume and cover letter, the odds of getting that interview increase dramatically, because you have skipped right over the initial hurdle—getting pulled from the resume database—and you are pitching directly to a recruiter or hiring manager.

The primary goal of every job search is to *get into conversation, as quickly and as frequently as possible, with people in a position to hire you*, because without conversations, job offers don't get made. Difficulty reaching hiring authorities with the candidate's message is one of the major reasons job searches stall. This happens when job searches involve themselves, almost exclusively, with posting resumes to resume banks and responding to job postings by uploading resumes into other resume databases.

However, when you can get your resume, personalized with a cover letter, in front of recruiters and hiring authorities, you differentiate yourself and dramatically increase your chances of landing an interview.

Recruiters and hiring managers overwhelmingly appreciate cover and follow-up letters. If all you are planning to do is load your resume into resume databases, a cover letter can help, but its main strength is in personalizing your message to a specific company, and ideally a specific person. When you develop a plan of attack for your job search that includes reaching out directly to decision makers, the personalizing touch of a letter really increases your bang.

WHO TO TARGET IN YOUR JOB SEARCH
The hiring titles to target during your job search are:

- Those titles mostly likely to be in a position to hire you. Usually this will be managers 1–3 levels above your target job.
- Those titles most likely to be involved in the selection process. Typically, this will be a manager working in a related department.

Your ideal target for direct communication is always someone who can hire you, although any management title offers opportunity for referral. Even HR contacts are valuable: They can't make the hiring decision, but the pivotal nature of their jobs means HR professionals are aware of all areas within a company that could use your skills.

Any name and title you capture in a job search is valuable. With the Internet at your fingertips, there are countless ways to identify the names of people who hold the titles you need to reach, and if a name and title is of no use to you, hold on to it anyway: It might be just the contact another job hunter needs, so it can be a valuable commodity to leverage in your networking activities. Refer to Chapter 8 for much more information on how to find the names of hiring authorities. For more on leveraging your network and general networking strategies, see the latest edition of *Knock 'em Dead: The Ultimate Job Search Guide*.

When an e-mail or envelope is opened, your cover letter will be the first thing looked at. It personalizes your candidacy for a specific job in ways that are impossible for your resume to do, given its formal nature and structure. The cover letter sets the stage for the reader to accept your resume, and therefore you, as something and someone special. It can create common ground between you and the reader, and demonstrates that you are well qualified and suitable for *this* job with *this* company.

Cover Letter Tactics

Address Your Target by Name

Your first step is to grab the reader's attention and arouse interest, so whenever possible, address the letter to someone by name.

Approaching recruiters and hiring authorities directly is one of the very best tactics for getting job offers. Whenever you can find the names of any one of these titles involved in the recruitment and selection cycle, approach them directly and address them by name. Again, see Chapter 8 for much more information on this topic.

Make Your Letter Readable

Your customer, the reader, is always going to be distracted, so your letters need to be easily readable, focused, clear, and brief. *Your letters should cut to the chase and be both friendly and respectful; they should never be unfocused, pompous, or sound like you swallowed a dictionary.*

You can also grab the reader's attention with the appearance of your letter, which should mirror the fonts and font sizes of your resume, giving you a coordinated and professional look.

Hardly anyone in a position to hire you is still young enough to comfortably read 10-point fonts. Anyone who has been staring at computer screens for ten or more years and has a dozen other priorities pressing for her attention is likely to have problems with tiny font sizes and elaborate but unreadable fonts. I recommend a minimum of 11- or 12-point font size. Applying these rules of matching font and font size to *e-mail and print* letters is easy to do and easily overlooked; but paying attention to the details pays dividends in a job search.

Emphasize Your Personal Brand

Branding is the process by which you consistently draw attention to the bundle of skills and behaviors that makes you a little different. All the job search letters you send—and yes, that includes every e-mail—are part of the packaging that captures the professional you. If your written words look good and carry a succinct, relevant, readily accessible message that shows you to be a down-to-earth professional with a clear sense of self, you're well on the road to establishing a viable professional brand. When your actions differentiate you from others, your standing as a candidate is improved.

What makes you special?

- Just being smart enough to get your resume directly under the nose of a manager, who wants to make a good hire and get back to work, makes you special.
- Getting your resume to the hiring manager in a creative way and showing that you know what you are doing makes you special. Your letter might say in part, "I sent my resume by e-mail, but thought you might appreciate a screen break, so you'll find a hard copy attached to this letter . . . ." Your e-mail might note, "As well as attaching my resume to this e-mail, in case you need a screen break, I've also sent it by traditional mail."
- Writing a strong cover letter that presents your resume and establishes connectivity between you and the manager makes you special.
- Keeping your message clear and succinct makes you special.
- Following up your meetings with thoughtful letters that continue the messaging of a consummate professional makes you special and confirms your professional brand.
- Making sure in all your e-mails and print letters that the fonts are legible and coordinated with your resume makes you special.

Continuity in Written Communication

To ensure continuity in your written communications, make a commitment to:

1. Make the font you employ for contact information and headlines in both your resume and your cover letter the same.
2. Use the same font you chose for your resume's body copy for the message in your cover letter.
3. Use the same font choices for all your e-mail communications. Smart idea: set the chosen font as your default e-mail font.
4. Make the font choices of your written communications consistent with the font choices you employ in e-mail and other electronic communications.
5. Get matching paper for resume, cover letters, and envelopes. Every office superstore has them. Sending your cover letter and resume by traditional mail when the opportunity arises is a great way to get your resume read, because most job hunters don't think to do this. Today, hiring managers get far fewer resumes by mail, but a busy manager still likes a break from the computer screen, so more time is spent reviewing your resume. You'll also need printed resumes to take to interviews.

Cut to the Chase and Stay On-Message

A good cover letter gets your resume read with serious consideration. Time is precious, which means recruiters and hiring authorities won't waste it on a letter that wanders. Your letters should always reflect a professional whose resume will have something to say.

When you can, make a specific reference to a job's key requirements. You want the reader to move from your letter to the resume already thinking, "Here's a candidate who can do the job." You can do this in either of two ways:

- Referencing a job's most important requirements.
- Referencing the issues behind the job's most important requirements.

If an advertisement, a job posting, or a telephone conversation with a potential employer reveals an aspect of a particular job opening that is not addressed in your resume (and for some reason you haven't had time to update it), use a cover letter to fill in the gaps; the Executive Briefing (you'll see samples shortly) is an especially useful tool for this job.

Brevity is important. The letter doesn't sell everything about you; it positions you for serious consideration, hoping to demonstrate that you grasp what is at the heart of the job's deliverables. Leave your reader wanting more.

End with a Call to Action

Just as you work to create a strong opening, make sure your closing carries the same conviction. It is the reader's last personal impression of you, so make it strong, make it tight, and make it obvious that you are serious about entering into meaningful conversation. Your letters should always include a call to action. Explain when, where, and how you can be contacted. You can also be proactive, telling the reader that you intend to follow up at a certain time if he or she has not already contacted you.

Every step of the job search and selection cycle offers opportunities to use letters to leverage your candidacy. A good, strong letter will get your foot in the door, differentiate you from other contenders, and ultimately help you define a distinctive professional brand. Although the majority of your communications will be e-mails, stand out by sending really important information in both e-mails and traditional letters. If nothing more, by delivering your message through two media, it gets read twice, which increases the odds of your candidacy being noticed and advanced.

Chapter 2
Six High-Mileage Cover Letters

Corporate America's wholesale adoption of the Internet as its primary recruitment vehicle has completely changed the way you need to approach your job search.

Every year, the number of resumes loaded into commercial resume databases grows exponentially. Currently, the larger databases each house more than 40 million resumes. Many individual corporate resume banks have more than 1 million resumes stored and social networking sites like LinkedIn have more than 100 million resumes and professional profiles registered. This has made life easier for recruiters, since they can usually find enough qualified candidates in the top twenty resumes from any given database, *and given the large number of potential candidates, they rarely dig deeper.*

In resume databases that allow attachments to your resume, a cover letter helps you stand out by making additional and supportive comments about your capabilities. When you send your resume directly to a recruiter or potential hiring authority by using their name and title, your resume and cover letter have even greater impact because you can differentiate yourself by addressing the hiring manager or recruiter by name and by customizing your message; and most important, you sidestepped the resume databases entirely.

Here are six types of cover letters that can help your job search momentum. Each is a composite letter I built from scouring the examples that appear later in the book, taking a word from one example and a phrase from another. In each example, I have underlined the borrowed phrases to give you an idea of how easy it is to create your own original documents with a little cutting and pasting. The six letters are:

1. The cover letter for when you do not know of a specific job, but have a name to send the letter to, or are uploading to a resume bank where you can attach your cover letter to your resume
2. The executive briefing. Always effective when you have knowledge of the job's requirements and especially so when you can address someone by name
3. A cover letter in response to an online job posting
4. A cover letter aimed at headhunters
5. A networking letter for getting the word out to the professional community about your search
6. A broadcast letter if your resume doesn't quite fit the job

A Cover Letter When You Do Not Know of a Specific Job Opening

This letter is designed to be uploaded to a database as an attachment or sent to a potential hiring manager whose name you've garnered from your research. Of course, if you are sending this letter to an individual, it should be personalized with a salutation and include references to the company, some detail of the job, or the establishment of common ground between you and the recipient.

James Sharpe
18 Central Park Street • Anytown, NY 14788
(516) 555-1212

October 2, 20—

Jackson Bethell, V.P. Operations
DataLink Products
621 Miller Drive
Anytown, CA 91234

Dear Jackson Bethell:

Recently I have been researching the leading local companies in data communications. My search has been for companies that are respected in the field and that provide ongoing training programs. The name of DataLink Products keeps coming up as a top company.

I am an experienced voice and data communications specialist with a substantial background in IBM environments. If you have an opening for someone in this area, you will see that my resume demonstrates a person of unusual dedication, efficiency, and drive. My experience and achievements include:

- The complete redesign of a data communications network, projected to increase efficiency company-wide by some 12 percent.
- The installation and troubleshooting of a Defender IV call-back security system for a dial-up network.

I enclose a copy of my resume, and look forward to examining any of the ways you feel my background and skills would benefit DataLink Products. While I prefer not to use my employer's time taking personal calls at work, with discretion I can be reached at (516) 555-1212 to initiate contact. However, I would rather you call me at _____ in the evening. Let's talk!

Yours truly,

James Sharpe

James Sharpe

JANE SWIFT
18 Central Park Street, Anytown, NY 14788
(516) 555-1212

David Doors, Director of Marketing
Martin Financial Group
1642 Rhode Island Way
Anytown, NY 01234

January 14, 20—

Dear David Doors:

I have always followed the performance of your company in *Mutual Funds Newsletter*.

Recently your notice regarding a Market Analyst in *Investor's Business Daily* caught my eye—and your company name caught my attention. Your record over the last three years shows exceptional portfolio management. Because of my experience with one of your competitors, I know I could make significant contributions.

I would like to talk to you about your personnel needs and how I am able to contribute to your department's goals.

An experienced market analyst, I have an economics background (M.S. Purdue) and a strong quantitative analysis approach to market fluctuations. This combination has enabled me to consistently pick the new technology flotations that are the backbone of the growth-oriented mutual fund. For example:

I first recommended Targus Fund six years ago. More recently my clients have been strongly invested in Atlantic Horizon Growth (in the high-risk category), and Next Wave Growth and Income (for the cautious investor). Those following my advice over the last six years have consistently outperformed the market.

I know that resumes help you sort out the probables from the possibles, but they are no way to judge the personal caliber of an individual. I would like to meet with you and demonstrate that along with the credentials, I have the professional commitment that makes for a successful team player.

Yours truly,

Jane Swift

Jane Swift

The Executive Briefing

The executive briefing is an effective form of cover letter to use *whenever you have information about a job opening*—perhaps from an online job posting, a lead, or a conversation with one of your network contacts—*and there is a good skill match.* The executive briefing gets right to the point and makes life easy for the reader. It introduces your resume, as well as customizing and supplementing it. Why is an executive briefing so effective?

1. It quickly matches job requirements against the skills you bring to the table, making analysis much easier for the reader and a successful outcome more likely for you.
2. Since an initial screener (someone who quickly sorts through cover letters and resumes to separate the wheat from the chaff) may not have an in-depth understanding of the job's requirements, the executive briefing simplifies things by matching the job's requirements point-by-point to your abilities.
3. The executive briefing allows you emphasize your skills in a particular area or fill any gaps in your resume with job-specific information.
4. If an opportunity comes along that is a slam-dunk for you, but your resume isn't current or doesn't have the right focus, the executive briefing allows you to update your work history. This very professional quick fix is a godsend when someone asks to see your resume but it isn't up-to-date.

The executive briefing assures that each resume you send out addresses the job's specific needs. It provides a comprehensive picture of a thorough professional, plus a personalized, fast, and easy-to-read synopsis that details exactly how your background matches the job description.

From: top10acct@aol.com
Subject: **Re: Accounting Manager**
Date: February 18, 2005 10:05:44 PM EST
To: rlstein@McCoy.com

Dear Ms. Stein:

I have nine years of accounting experience and am responding to your recent posting for an Accounting Manager on Careerbuilder. Please allow me to highlight my skills as they relate to your stated requirements.

Your Requirements	My Experience
Accounting degree, 4 years exp.	Obtained a C.A. degree in 2000 and have over four years' experience as an Accounting Manager
Excellent people skills and leadership	Effectively managed a staff of 24; ability to motivate staff, including supervisors
Strong administrative skills	Assisted in the development of a base reference skills–library with Microsoft Excel for 400 clients
Good communication skills	Trained new supervisors and staff via daily coaching sessions, communication meetings, and technical skill sessions

My resume, pasted below and attached in MSWord, will flesh out my general background. I hope this executive briefing helps you use your time effectively today. I am ready to make a move. I hope we can talk soon.

Sincerely,

Joe Black
Joe Black

A Cover Letter in Response to an Online Job Posting

If you are writing in response to an online job posting, you should mention both the website and any reference codes associated with the job:

"I read your job posting on your company's website on January 5th and felt I had to respond . . ."

"Your online job posting regarding a _____ on _____.com caught my eye, and your company name caught my attention."

"This e-mail, and my attached resume, is in response to job posting #145 on _____."

E-Mail in Response to an Online Job Posting

From: Helen Darvik [darviklegalpro@earthlink.net]
To: ggoodfellow@budownoble.com
Cc:
Subject: Administrator/mgmnt/mktg/cmptr/acctg/planning/personnel

Dear Ms. _____:

I am responding to your job posting on Hotjobs.com for a legal administrator of a law firm. I wrote to you on (date) about law administrator positions in the metropolitan _____ area. I have attached another resume of my educational background and employment history. I am very interested in this position.

I have been a legal administrator for two twenty-one-attorney law firms during the past six years. In addition, I have been a law firm consultant for over a year. Besides my law firm experience, I have been a medical administrator for over ten years. I believe that all of this experience will enable me to manage the law firm for this position very successfully. I possess the management, marketing, computer, accounting/budgeting, financial planning, personnel, and people-oriented skills that will have a very positive impact on this law firm.

I will be in the _____ area later in the month, so hopefully, we can meet at that time to discuss this position. I look forward to hearing from you, Ms. _____, concerning this position. Thank you for your time and consideration.

Very truly yours,

Helen Darvik
(516) 555-1212
darviklegalpro@earthlink.net

A Cover Letter to a Headhunter

Headhunters deserve your respect. They are, after all, the most sophisticated sales-people in the world—they sell products that talk back. A headhunter will be only faintly amused by your exhortations "to accept the challenge" or "test your skills by finding me a job" in the brief moment before he practices hoops with your letter and the trash can.

When approaching and working with headhunters—whether they are working for the local employment agency, a contingency, or a retained search firm—bear in mind these two rules and you won't go far wrong:

1. Tell the truth. Answer questions truthfully and you will likely receive help. Get caught in a lie and you will have established a career-long environment of distrust with someone who probably possesses a very diverse and influential list of contacts.
2. Cut immediately to the chase in your letters and conversations. For example:

    "I am forwarding my resume, because I understand you specialize in representing employers in the _____ field."

    "Please find the enclosed resume. As a specialist in the _____ field, I felt you might be interested in the skills of a _____."

    "Among your many clients there may be one or two who are seeking an experienced professional for a position as a _____."

Remember that in a cover letter sent to executive search firms and employment agencies, you should mention your salary and, if appropriate, your geographic considerations. If you want to work with headhunters productively, read the latest edition of *Knock 'em Dead: The Ultimate Job Search Guide.*

Here is an example of a cover letter you might send to a corporate headhunter:

Letter to a Headhunter

James Sharpe
18 Central Park Street • Anytown, NY 14788
(516) 555-1212

December 2, 20—

Dear Mr. O'Flynn:

I am forwarding my resume, as I understand that you specialize in the accounting profession. As you may be aware, the management structure at _____ will be reorganized in the near future. While I am enthusiastic about the future of the agency under its new leadership, I have elected to make this an opportunity for change and professional growth.

My many years of experience lend themselves to a finance management position in any medium-sized service firm, but I am open to other opportunities. Although I would prefer to remain in New York, I would entertain other areas of the country, if the opportunity warrants it. I am currently earning $65,000 a year.

I have enclosed my resume for your review. Should you be conducting a search for someone with my background at the present time or in the near future, I would greatly appreciate your consideration. I would be happy to discuss my background more fully with you on the phone or in a personal interview.

Very truly yours,

James Sharpe
James Sharpe

JS
Resume attached

Networking Letters

Nothing works like a personal recommendation from a fellow professional. It is no accident that successful people in all fields either know each other or at least know *of* each other. You get the most out of networking by being connected to your profession and the professionals within it. Networking is a topic beyond the scope of this book, so you'll want to check out networking strategies in the latest edition of *Knock 'em Dead: The Ultimate Job Search Guide.*

Here are important considerations to bear in mind with networking letters:

1. Establish connectivity. Recall the last memorable contact you had with the person, or mention someone that you have both spoken to recently. Use common past employers, membership in professional associations, interests, or a topical event as a bridge builder.

   If you are writing (and calling) as the result of a referral, say so and quote the person's name if appropriate:

   "I am writing because our mutual colleague, John Stanovich, felt my skills and abilities would be valuable to your company . . ."

   "The manager of your San Francisco branch, Pamela Bronson, suggested I contact you regarding the opening for a _____."

   "I received your name from Henry Charles, the branch manager of Savannah Bank last week, and he suggested I contact you. In case the resume he forwarded is caught up in the mail, I enclosed another."

   "Arthur Gold, your office manager and my neighbor, thought I should contact you about the upcoming opening in your accounting department."

2. Tell them why you are writing:

   "It's time for me to make a move; my job just got sent to Mumbai, India, and I'm hoping you could help me with a new sense of direction."

3. Do not talk about your ideal job. This only narrows the opportunities people will tell you about. Instead, just let contacts know your qualifications/experience and

the job title you are most likely to work under. Don't let ego cost you a valuable job lead.

4. Ask for advice and guidance:

   "What do you think are the growing companies in our industry today?"

   "Could you take a look at my resume for me? I really need an objective opinion and I've always respected your viewpoint."

5. Never ask directly, " Do you have a job opening?", "Can you hire me?", or "Can your company hire me?" Instead, ask to talk on the telephone for a few minutes. Then by all means ask for leads within specific target companies.
6. When you do get help, say thank you. If you get the help in conversation, follow it up in writing: The impression is indelible and it just might get you another lead.

Networking Letter (Computer and Information Systems Manager)

This letter was sent to follow up a meeting with a medical school dean.

DAVID KENT

1623 St. Louis Way • Honolulu, Hawaii 96813
808-555-6256 • dkent@alohanet.com

January 14, 20–

John Jones, M.D.
Dean, School of Medicine
University of Hawaii
1234 East-West Circle
Honolulu, Hawaii 96822

Dear Dr. Jones:

Perhaps you remember our chance meeting at the Bio Asia-Pacific Conference at the Sheraton Waikiki on August 18 and 19, 20–. In our brief conversation, I shared with you the idea of utilizing Web Development as an administrative tool. You expressed interest in the possibility of implementing such a system within the School of Medicine.

May I suggest a formal meeting to explore the idea?

I have some exciting and creative ideas, which may encourage you to take the next step toward realizing the positive impact a content management system would have in the School of Medicine. This would also be a great opportunity for us to discuss your goals and how an administrative intranet would help you reach them in a more timely and cost-effective manner.

In addition, there has recently been spirited discussion within the IT community on the topic of organizational continuity and its potential vulnerability due to advances in technology. I think you'll find the specific strategies I have to share with you worthy of consideration.

If you recall, my background is in Web Planning and Development, with specific skills in developing administrative intranets and public Web sites, and designing Web-based software to address the internal and external reporting needs of organizations.

Enclosed is my resume attesting to my experience and specialties. I will contact you within the next few days to discuss the possibility of meeting with you.

Respectfully,

David Kent

David Kent
Computer and Information Systems Manager

Enclosure: Resume

The Broadcast Letter

The broadcast letter acts as a brief introduction to the skills you bring to the table and is designed to be sent without a resume. You can use it when:

- You don't have a relevant resume.
- Your resume is inappropriate for the position.
- Your resume isn't getting the results you want, and you want to try something different while you are retooling it.

To be effective, the information you use in a broadcast letter must speak directly to the specific needs of a job posting or be focused on the needs of this job as you have determined them from your resume's target job deconstruction exercises (more on this shortly). This is because the intent of the broadcast letter is to *replace* the resume as a means of introduction and to initiate conversation. Keep in mind that although a broadcast letter can get you into a telephone conversation with a potential employer, that employer is still likely to ask for a resume.

While I am not a big fan of broadcast letters, people have used them effectively, so you need to be aware of them. As they pretty much require you have a name to send them to, my feeling is that, as a resume is going to be requested anyway, you should take the time to customize your resume properly. I don't advise using this kind of letter as the spearhead or sole thrust of your campaign, but you can use it as a stopgap measure when you are retooling an ineffective resume or are otherwise regrouping.

Broadcast Letter

JANE SWIFT
18 Central Park Street, Anytown, NY 14788
(516) 555-1212

October 2, 20—

Dear _____ :

For the past seven years I have pursued an increasingly successful career in the sales profession. Among my accomplishments I include:

SALES
As a regional representative, I contributed $1,500,000, or 16 percent, of my company's annual sales. I am driven by achievement.

MARKETING
My marketing skills (based on a B.S. in marketing) enabled me to increase sales 25 percent in my economically stressed territory, at a time when colleagues were striving to maintain flat sales. Repeat business reached an all-time high. I am persistent and pay attention to detail.

PROJECT MANAGEMENT
Following the above successes, my regional model was adopted by the company. I trained and provided project supervision to the entire sales force. The following year, company sales showed a sales increase 12 percent above projections. I am a committed team player, motivated by the group's overall success.

The above was based on my firmly held zero price–discounting philosophy. I don't cut margins to make a sale. It is difficult to summarize my work in a letter. The only way I can imagine providing you the opportunity to examine my credentials is for us to talk with each other. I look forward to hearing from you. Please call me at _____.

Yours sincerely,

Jane Swift

Jane Swift

Chapter 3
KNOW THE JOB, KNOW YOUR CUSTOMER

Think of potential employers as your customers. If you listen to what your customers are saying, you will find that they will tell you exactly what they want to "buy." **Understanding what is important to your customer (the employer) helps you understand what that customer wants to buy and what you need to sell.**

If you work in sales, marketing, marketing communications, or are in any way close to bringing in revenue for your employer, you will understand the importance of "getting inside your customers' heads" to find out what is important to them, because this allows you to sell the product or service based on the customers' needs. Knowing what customers want to buy makes it much easier to customize your message to meet their needs.

All the insights you need to write a good cover letter are already available to you in job postings. *All you need to do is learn how to translate it into usable information,* which is what we are going to do now.

What follows is a simple exercise called Target Job Deconstruction (TJD). *Do not skip this exercise: It can make an enormous difference to this job search and to your entire future career development.* It will tell you precisely how to prioritize the information you offer employers, and will give you examples for your letters and a new way of understanding what it is you actually get paid for. The exercise will also tell you the topics you're most likely to be asked about at interviews, and prepare you with suggestions for answers to those questions.

This exercise is geared toward:

- Determining the precise requirements of the job you want
- Matching your skill-set to those requirements
- Identifying the story you need to tell in your cover letter and resume to highlight the match between your skills and those requirements

The Target Job Deconstruction

The most difficult part of any letter is knowing what to say and how to say it, but the TJD approach ensures that the topics your letter addresses are going to be of the greatest interest to your customers, and that the words you use will have the greatest likelihood of resonating with the reader.

Step One

Collect six job postings for the job you are best qualified to do, and save them in a folder. Try to use jobs located in your target area, but if you don't have enough local jobs, collect job descriptions from anywhere. For target job deconstruction, the location of the job doesn't matter: What's important is understanding how employers *define*, *prioritize*, and *express* their needs.

Step Two

Open a new Microsoft Word document and title it TJD for *Target Job Deconstruction*. Add a subhead reading *Job Title*, then copy and paste in the variations from each of your sample job descriptions. Looking at the result, you can say, "When employers are hiring people like *me*, they tend to describe the job with these words."

From these examples, you then come up with a *Target Job Title* for your resume. You'll add this line right after your name and contact information. These words help your resume perform well in resume database searches and act as a headline, giving human eyes an immediate focus on who and what the resume is about. This again helps your resume's performance.

Step Three

Add a second subhead titled: *Skills/Responsibilities/Experience/Deliverables*.

Look through the job postings for a *single requirement* that's common to all six of your job postings. Take the most complete description of that *single requirement* and copy and paste it into your TJD document, putting a "6" by your entry to signify that it is common to all of them.

Check the other job postings for different words and phrases used to describe this same job skill, and copy and paste them beneath the entry you created. Repeat this exercise for other requirements common to all six of your sample job postings. The result will be a list of the skills/requirements that all employers feel are of prime importance, and the words they use to describe them.

Step Four

Repeat this process for requirements common to five of the jobs, and then four, and so on all the way down to those requirements mentioned in only one job posting.

When this is done, you can look at your work and say, "When employers are hiring people like *me*, they tend to refer to them by these job titles; they prioritize their needs in *this* way, and use *these* words to describe their prioritized needs." At this point you have a template for the story your resume needs to tell.

Step Five

Generate illustrative examples of your competency with the skills that employers identify as priorities. You should remember that jobs are only ever added to the payroll for two reasons:

1. To make money or save money for the company, or to otherwise increase productivity.
2. To identify, prevent, and solve the problems/challenges that occur in your area of expertise and that interfere with the company's pursuit of (1).

Working through your list of prioritized employer requirements, identify the problems that typically arise when you are executing your duties in that particular area of the job. Then for each problem identify:

- How do you execute your responsibilities to prevent this problem from arising in the first place?
- How do you tackle such a situation when it does occur? Think of specific examples.
- Whenever you can, quantify the results of your actions in terms of productivity increase, money earned, or money saved.

Step Six

Going back to the prioritized requirements you identified in earlier steps, consider each individual requirement and recall the **best** person you have ever known doing that that aspect of the job. Next, identify what made that person stand out in your mind as a true professional; think of personality, skills, and behaviors. Perhaps she always had a smile, listened well, and had good critical thinking and time-management skills.

Together with the specific technical skills of the job you have already identified, the traits of the person who stands out in your mind will give you a *behavioral profile of the person every employer wants to hire*, plus a behavioral blueprint for subsequent professional success.

Step Seven

Looking one last time at the list of prioritized requirements in your TJD, consider each individual requirement and recall the **worst** person you have ever known doing that aspect of the job. Perhaps he was passive-aggressive, never listened, and was rarely on time with projects or for meetings.

This time you will have a complete *behavioral profile of the person no employer wants to hire* and a behavioral blueprint for professional failure.

Pulling It All Together

Target Job Deconstruction will give you the insight into your target job to maximize your resume's productivity both in resume databases and with recruiters and hiring managers. The process also uncovers the areas of the job that will hold specific interest for a hiring manager and therefore likely give rise to interview questions. And because you have thought things through, you will now have answers to those questions and will be able to illustrate them with examples.

Last, but by no means least, you also have a behavioral blueprint for professional success: no small thing to possess.

Chapter 4

HOW TO IDENTIFY AND BUILD A DESIRABLE PROFESSIONAL BRAND

A resume is the primary tool that all professionals use to define and disseminate their professional brand to an ever-expanding world of contacts. Long-term success—rewarding work (without layoffs) and professional growth that fits your goals—is much easier to achieve when you are credible and visible within your profession. Creating and nurturing a professional brand as part of your overall career management strategy will help you build credibility and visibility throughout your profession, because an identifiable brand gives *you* focus and motivation, and gives *others* a way to differentiate you.

Establishing a desirable professional brand takes time; after all, you have to brand something that is worth branding, something with which your customers will resonate. It is something that evolves over years, but you need to start somewhere and you need to start now.

The greater the effort you put into working toward credibility and visibility, which over time translates into a steadily growing professional reputation in your area of expertise, the quicker you enter the inner circles in your department, your company, and ultimately your profession. And it is in these inner circles that job security, plum assignments, raises, promotions, and professional marketability all dwell.

Think of your brand as the formal announcement to the professional community of how you want to be seen in your professional world. Your resume and an accompanying cover letter will be the primary tools you will use to deliver this focused and consistent message of your brand. It's the narrative of your resume, and the complementary themes echoed in all your job search letters, that tell this story in a very particular way: by capturing your experience, skills, capabilities, and professional behavioral profile *as they relate to what your customers want to buy.*

Components of a Desirable Professional Brand

A viable professional brand must be built on firm foundations. This means you must understand what employers want and look for when they hire (and subsequently promote) someone in your profession, at your level, and with your job title. Reaching this level of understanding of how your employers think is critical for the success of this job search and for your career going forward; it's why you spent Chapter 3 learning how employers think about your work, and how they prioritize and express those thoughts . . . and by extension how they will reward those who give them what they want.

In this chapter, you'll examine some additional and equally important dimensions of the professional you; dimensions that will play into your resume, your interviews, and your success in that next step on your career path. Specifically, we'll examine something called *transferable skills,* and see how they can be used in your cover and other job search letters.

Transferable Skills and Professional Values

Over the years I've read a lot of books about finding jobs, winning promotions, and managing your career. A few were insightful and many were innocuous, but one theme that runs through them all is the absurd and harmful advice to, "Just be yourself."

"Who you are is just fine. Be yourself and you'll do fine." Wrong. Remember that first day on your first job, when you went to get your first cup of coffee? You found the coffee machine, and there, stuck on the wall behind it, was a handwritten sign reading:

YOUR MOTHER DOESN'T WORK HERE
PICK UP AFTER YOURSELF

You thought, "Pick up after myself? Gee, that means I can't behave like I do at home and get away with it." And so you started to observe and emulate the more successful professionals around you. You behaved in a way that was appropriate to the environment, and in doing so demonstrated *emotional intelligence*. Over time you developed many new ways of conducting yourself at work in order to be accepted as a professional in your field. You weren't born this way. You developed a behavioral profile, a *professional persona* that enabled you to survive in the professional world.

Some people are just better than the average bear at everything they do, and they become more successful as a result. It doesn't happen by accident; there is a specific set of *transferable skills* and *professional values* that underlies professional success: skills and values that employers all over the world in every industry and profession are anxious to find in candidates from the entry level to the boardroom. Why this isn't taught in schools and in the university programs that cost a small fortune is unfathomable, because these skills and values are the foundation of every successful career. They break down into these groups:

1. *The Technical Skills of Your Current Profession.* These are the technical competencies that give you the *ability* to do your job. The skills needed to complete a task and the know-how to use them productively and efficiently.
   These *technical skills* are mandatory if you want to land a job within your profession. *Technical skills,* while transferable, vary from profession to profession, so many of your current *technical skills* will only be transferable within your current profession.
2. *Transferable Skills That Apply in All Professions.* The set of skills that underlies your ability to execute the *technical skills* of your job effectively, whatever your job may be. They are the foundation of all the professional success you will experience in this and any other career (including dream and entrepreneurial careers) that you may pursue over the years.
3. *Professional Values.* Transferable skills are complemented by an equally important set of *professional values* that are highly prized by employers. *Professional values* are an interconnected set of core beliefs that enable professionals to determine the right judgment call for any given situation.

The importance of *transferable skills* and *professional values* led to an entirely new approach to interviewing and the science of employee selection: behavioral interviewing. These behavioral interviewing techniques (discussed in detail in *Knock 'em Dead: The Ultimate Job Search Guide* and *Knock 'em Dead: Secrets and Strategies for Success in an Uncertain World*) now predominate in the selection process because of their ability to determine whether you possess those *transferable skills* and *professional values*.

A Review of Transferable Skills and Professional Values

As you read through the following breakdown of each *transferable skill* and *professional value* you may, for example, read about *communication*, and think, "Yes, I can see how communication skills are important in all jobs and at all levels of the promotional ladder, and, hallelujah, I have good communication skills." If so, take time to recall examples of your *communication skills* and the role they play in the success of your work.

You might then read about *multitasking skills* and realize that you need to improve in this area. Whenever you identify a *transferable skill* that needs work, you have found a *professional development project*: improving that skill. Your attention to those areas will pay off for the rest of your working life, no matter how you make a living.

Certain transferable skills and professional values are seen as integral to success in every job, at every level, in every profession, everywhere in the world. The full list includes:

Communication   Motivation
Critical thinking   Determination
Multitasking   Integrity
Teamwork   Productivity
Creativity   Systems & Procedures
Leadership

There are certain key words and phrases that evoke these skills that you see in almost every job posting: communication skills, multitasking skills, works closely with others, creativity, critical thinking, motivation, integrity, and so on. They are so commonly used that some people dismiss them as meaningless. Far from being meaningless, they represent a secret language that few job hunters ever show that they understand. The ones who do "get it" are also the ones who get the job offers.

These keywords and phrases represent the skills that enable you to do your job well, whatever your job may be. They are known as *transferable skills* and *professional values* because no matter what the job, the profession, or the elevation of that job, these skills make the difference between success and failure. They factor into the successful execution of every aspect of your daily activities at work.

Take a few moments and compare this list of transferable skills and professional values against the responsibilities of your job as your "customers" have defined them (see your Target Job Deconstruction exercises), and identify which of the transferable skills helps you execute each of the job's responsibilities effectively.

A Review of Transferable Skills

The National Association of Colleges and Employers (NACE), which is made up of major corporate recruiters and university career services professionals, in agreement with the accepted thinking on these issues, has defined seven transferable skills that every professional entering the workplace must have in order to succeed. These seven include: technical, communication, teamwork, critical thinking, multitasking (time management and organization), leadership, and creativity skills.

Technical Skills

The *technical skills* of your job are the foundation of success within your current profession; without them you won't even land a job, much less keep it for long or win a promotion. They speak to your *ability* to do the job—the essential skills necessary for the day-to-day execution of your duties. These *technical skills* vary from profession to profession and do not necessarily refer to anything technical or to technology.

However, one of the *technical skills* essential to every job is technological competence. You must be proficient in all the technology and Internet-based applications relevant to your work. Even when you are not working in a technology field, strong *technology skills* will enhance your stability and help you leverage professional growth.

Some of your *technology skills* will only be relevant within your current profession, while others (Word, Excel, PowerPoint, to name the obvious) will be transferable across all industry and professional lines. Staying current with the essential *technical* and *technology skills* of your chosen career path is the cornerstone of your professional stability and growth.

Critical Thinking Skills

As I noted in the previous chapter, your job, whatever it is, exists to solve problems and to prevent problems from arising within your area of expertise. *Critical thinking, analytical*, or *problem-solving skills* represent a systematic approach to dealing with the challenges presented by your work. *Critical thinking skills* allow you to think through a problem, define the challenge and its possible solutions, and then evaluate and implement the best solution from all available options.

Fifty percent of the success of any project is in the preparation; *critical thinking* is at the heart of that preparation. In addition, using *critical thinking* to properly define a problem always leads to a better solution.

Communication Skills

Every professional job today demands good *communication skills*, but what are they? When the professional world talks about *communication skills*, it is referring to four primary skills and four supportive skills.

The primary *communication skills* are:

- Verbal skills—what you say and how you say it
- Listening skills—listening to understand, rather than just waiting your turn to talk
- Writing skills—clear written communication creates a lasting impression of who you are and is essential for success in any professional career
- Technological communication skills—your ability to evaluate the protocols, strengths, and weaknesses of alternative communication media, and then to choose the medium appropriate to your audience and message

The four supportive *communication skills* are:

- Grooming and dress—these tell others who you are and how you feel about yourself
- Social graces—how you behave toward others in all situations; this defines your professionalism
- Body language—this displays how you're feeling deep inside; it's a form of communication that predates speech. For truly effective communication, what your mouth says must be in harmony with what your body says.
- Emotional IQ—your emotional self-awareness, your maturity in dealing with others in the full range of human interaction

Communication skills also go hand-in-hand with *critical thinking skills* to accurately process incoming information and enable you to present your outgoing verbal messaging persuasively in light of the interests and sophistication of your audience so that it is understood and accepted. If you develop competency in all eight of the subsets that together comprise *communication skills,* you'll gain enormous control over what you can achieve, how you are perceived, and what happens in your life.

Multitasking

This is one of today's most desirable skills. According to numerous studies, however, the *multitasking* demands of modern professional life are causing massive frustration and meltdowns for professionals everywhere. The problem is NOT *multitasking*; the problem is the assumption that *multitasking* means being reactive to *all* incoming stimuli and therefore jumping around from one task to another as the emergency of the moment dictates. Such a definition of *multitasking* would of course leave you feeling that wild horses are attached to your extremities and tearing you limb from limb.

Few people understand what *multitasking* abilities are built on: sound *time management* and *organizational* abilities. Here are the basics:

Establish Priorities

Multitasking is based in three things:

1. Being organized
2. Establishing priorities
3. Managing your time

The Plan, Do, Review Cycle

At the end of every day, review your day:

- What happened: A.M. and P.M.?
- What went well? Do more of it.
- What went wrong? How do I fix it?
- What projects do I need to move forward tomorrow?
- Rank each project. A = Must be completed tomorrow. B = Good to be completed tomorrow. C = If there is spare time after A and B priorities.
- Make a prioritized To Do list.
- Stick to it.

Doing this at the end of the day keeps you informed about what you have achieved, and lets you know that you have invested your time in the most important activities today and will do so again tomorrow. That peace of mind helps you feel better, sleep better, and come in tomorrow focused and ready to rock.

Teamwork

Companies depend on teams because the professional world revolves around the complex challenges of making money, and such complexities require teams of people to provide ongoing solutions. This means that you must work efficiently and respectfully with other people who have totally different responsibilities, backgrounds, objectives, and areas of expertise. It's true that individual initiative is important, but as a professional, much of the really important work you do will be done as a member of a group. Your long-term stability and success require that you learn the arts of cooperation, team-based decision-making, and team communication.

Teamwork demands that a commitment to the team and its success come first. This means you take on a task because it needs to be done, not because it makes you look good.

As a team player, you:

- Always cooperate.
- Always make decisions based on team goals.
- Always keep team members informed.
- Always keep commitments.
- Always share credit, never blame.

If you become a successful leader in your professional life, it's a given that you were first a reliable team player, because a leader must understand the dynamics of teamwork before she can leverage them. When teamwork is coupled with the other *transferable skills* and *professional values, it results in greater responsibility and promotions.*

Leadership Skills

Leadership is the most complex of all the *transferable skills* and combines all the others. As you develop teamwork skills, notice how you are willing to follow true leaders, but don't fall in line with people who don't respect you and who don't have your best interests at heart. When others believe in your competence, and believe you have everyone's success as your goal, they will follow you. When your actions inspire others to think more, learn more, do more, and become more, you are becoming a leader. This will ultimately be recognized and rewarded with promotion into and up the ranks of management. Here's how other transferable skills factor into leadership skills:

- Your job as a leader is to help your team succeed, and your *teamwork skills* give you the smarts to pull a team together as a cohesive unit.
- Your *technical* expertise, *critical thinking,* and *creativity skills* help you correctly define the challenges your team faces and give you the wisdom to guide them toward solutions.
- Your *communication skills* enable your team to *buy into* your directives and goals. There's nothing more demoralizing than a leader who can't clearly articulate why you're doing what you're doing.

- Your *creativity* (discussed next) comes from the wide frame of reference you have for your work and the profession and industry in which you work, enabling you to come up with solutions that others might not have imagined.
- Your *multitasking skills*, based on sound *time management* and *organizational* abilities, enable you to create a practical blueprint for success. They also allow your team to take ownership of the task and deliver the expected results on time.

Leadership is a combination and outgrowth of all the *transferable skills* plus the clear presence of all the *professional values* we are about to discuss. Leaders aren't born; they are self-made. And just like anything else, it takes hard work.

Creativity

Your creativity comes from the frame of reference you have for your work, profession, and industry. This wide frame of reference enables you to see the *patterns* that lie behind challenges and so connect the dots and come up with solutions that others might not have seen. Others might be too closely focused on the specifics of the issue —thus, they don't have that holistic frame of reference that enables them to step back and view the issue in its larger context.

There's a big difference between *creativity* and just having ideas. Ideas are like headaches: We all get them once in a while, and like headaches they can disappear as mysteriously as they arrived. *Creativity*, on the other hand, is the ability to develop those ideas with the strategic and tactical know-how that brings them to life. Someone is seen as creative when his ideas produce tangible results. Other transferable skills complement *creativity. Creativity* springs from:

- Your *critical thinking skills*, applied within an area of technical expertise (an area where your *technical skills* give you knowledge of what works and what doesn't).
- Your *multitasking skills*, which, in combination with your *critical thinking* and *technical skills,* allow you to break down your challenge into specific steps and determine which approach is best.
- Your *communication skills*, which allow you to explain your approach and its building blocks persuasively to your target audience.
- Your *teamwork* and *leadership skills*, which enable you to enlist others and bring the idea to fruition.

Creative approaches to challenges can take time or can come fully formed in a flash, but the longer you work on developing the supporting skills that bring *creativity* to life, the more often they *will* come fully formed and in a flash. Here are five rules for building creativity skills in your professional life:

1. **Whatever you do in life, engage in it fully.** Commit to developing competence in everything you do, because the wider your frame of reference for the world around you, the more you will see the patterns and connectivity in your professional world, delivering the higher-octane fuel you need to propel your ideas to acceptance and reality.

2. **Learn something new every day.** Treat the pursuit of knowledge as a way of life. Absorb as much as you can about everything. Information exercises your brain, filling your mind with information and contributing to that ever-widening field of vision that allows you to overcome challenges. The result is that you will make connections others won't and develop solutions that are seen as magically creative.

3. **Catch ideas as they occur.** Note them in your smartphone or on a scrap of paper. Anything will do so long as you capture the idea.

4. **Welcome restrictions in your world.** They make you think, they test the limits of your skills and the depth of your frame of reference; they truly encourage *creativity*. Ask any successful business leader, entrepreneur, writer, artist, or musician.

5. **Don't spend your life glued to Facebook or TV.** You need to live life, not watch it go by out of the corner of your eye. If you do watch television, try to learn something or motivate yourself with science, history, or biography programming. If you go online, do it with purpose.

Building *creativity skills* enables you to bring your ideas to life; and the development of each of these seven interconnected *transferable skills* will help you bring your dreams to life.

Professional Values

Professional values are an interconnected set of core beliefs that enable professionals to determine the right judgment call for any given situation. Highly prized by employers, this value system also complements and is integral to the *transferable skills*.

Motivation and Energy

Motivation and *energy* express themselves in your engagement with and enthusiasm for your work and profession. They involve an eagerness to learn and grow professionally and a willingness to take the rough with the smooth in pursuit of meaningful goals. *Motivation* is invariably expressed by the *energy* you demonstrate in your work. If you're motivated, you always give that extra effort to get the job done right.

Commitment and Reliability

These words represent your dedication to your profession and the empowerment that comes from knowing how your part contributes to the whole. Your *commitment* expresses itself in your *reliability*. The *committed* professional is willing to do whatever it takes to get a job done, whenever and for however long it takes to get the job done. Doing so might include tackling duties that don't appear in your job description and that might be perceived by less enlightened colleagues as "beneath them."

Determination

The *determination* you display with the travails of your work speaks of a resilient professional who does not back off when a problem or situation gets tough. It's a *professional value* that marks you as someone who chooses to be part of the solution.

The *determined* professional has decided to make a difference with his or her presence every day, because it is the *right* thing to do.

She is willing to do whatever it takes to get a job done, and she will demonstrate that determination on behalf of colleagues who share the same values.

Pride and Integrity

If a job's worth doing, it's worth doing right. That's what *pride* in your work really means: attention to detail and a *commitment* to doing your very best. *Integrity* applies to all your dealings, whether with coworkers, management, customers, or vendors. Honesty really *is* the best policy.

Productivity

A true professional always works toward *productivity* in her areas of responsibility, through efficiencies of time, resources, money, and effort.

Economy

Remember the word "frugal"? It doesn't have to be associated with poverty or shortages. It means making the most of what you've got, using everything with the greatest efficiency. Companies that know how to be frugal with their resources will prosper in good times and in bad, and if you know how to be frugal, you'll do the same.

Systems and Procedures

This is a natural outgrowth of all the other *transferable skills* and *professional values*. Your *commitment* to your profession in all these ways gives you an appreciation of the need for *systems* and *procedures* and their implementation only after careful thought. You understand and always follow the chain of command. You don't implement your own "improved" procedures—or encourage others to do so—without first talking them over with the group and getting proper approvals. If ways of doing things don't make sense or are interfering with efficiency and profitability, you work through the system to get them changed.

Developing Skills Is Worth the Effort

Development of *transferable skills* and *professional values* supports your enlightened self-interest, because your efforts will be repaid with better job security and improved professional horizons. The more you are engaged in your career, the more likely you are to join the inner circles that exist in every department and company, and that's where the plum assignments, raises, and promotions live.

Anyone seen to embody these *transferable skills* and *professional values* will be known and respected as a consummate professional.

That you have these admirable traits is one thing; that *I* know you have them, well, that's another matter. You need to:

- Develop these skills and values.
- Make them a living dimension of your professional persona.
- Understand how each enables you to do every aspect of your job just that little bit better.
- Reference them subtly in your resume and other written communications.
- Reference them appropriately in your meetings with employers as the underlying skills that enable you to do your work well.

Examples of your application of these skills or the impact of these values on your work can be used in your resume, cover letters, and as illustrative answers to questions in interviews. But most importantly, these skills must become a part of you, for they will bring you success in everything you do.

Identifying Your Competitive Difference

To win job offers, you need to differentiate yourself from other candidates. The following questionnaire will help you identify all the factors that help make you unique. Each of these is a component of your professional brand.

You aren't going to discover anything earth shattering here, just a continuum of behaviors and beliefs you've always had—but the value of which you've perhaps never understood. It'll be a series of those, "Of course, I knew that" moments.

COMPLETE THE COMPETITIVE DIFFERENCE QUESTIONNAIRE ONSCREEN

An expandable version of this questionnaire is available in Microsoft Word at *www.knockemdead.com* on the resume advice page under the title: The Competitive Difference Questionnaire.

THE COMPETITIVE DIFFERENCE QUESTIONNAIRE

List and prioritize the transferable skills, behaviors, and values that best capture the essence of the professional you.

_____

_____

_____

_____

Which of the transferable skills, behaviors, and values have you identified for further professional development? What are you going to do about it?

_____

_____

_____

_____

What skills/behaviors/values or other characteristics do you share with top performers in your department/profession?

_____

_____

_____

_____

What have you achieved with these qualities?

_____

_____

_____

What makes you different from others with whom you have worked?

_____

_____

_____

What do you see as your four most defining transferable skills and professional values and how does each help your performance?

_____

How do your most defining professional traits help you contribute to the team?

1. _____

2. _____

3. _____

4. _____

How do your most defining professional traits help you contribute to your departmental goals and/or help you support your boss?

1. _____

2. _____

3. _____

4. _____

Why do you stand out in your job/profession?

_____

_____

_____

If you realize you don't stand out and you want to, explain in a few sentences why the people you admire stand out. What plans do you have for change?

_____

_____

_____

In what ways are you better than others at your workplace who hold the same title?

_____

_____

What excites you most about your professional responsibilities?

_____

_____

What are your biggest achievements in these areas?

_____

_____

What do your peers say about you?

_____

_____

What does management say about you?

_____

_____

_____

What do your reports say about you?

_____

_____

_____

What are your top four professional skills?
    Skill #1: _____
    Quantifiable achievements with this skill:_____
    Skill #2: _____
    Quantifiable achievements with this skill:_____

Skill #3: _____

Quantifiable achievements with this skill:_____

Skill #4: _____

Quantifiable achievements with this skill:_____

What are your top four leadership skills?

Skill #1: _____

Quantifiable achievements with this skill:_____

Skill #2: _____

Quantifiable achievements with this skill:_____

Skill #3: _____

Quantifiable achievements with this skill:_____

Skill #4: _____

Quantifiable achievements with this skill:_____

What do you believe are the three key deliverables of your job?

1. _____

2. _____

3. _____

What gives you greatest satisfaction in the work you do?

_____

_____

_____

What *value* does your combination of transferable skills, professional values, and achievements enable you to bring to your targeted employers?

_____

_____

Now compile endorsements. Looking at each of your major areas of responsibility throughout your work history, write down any positive verbal or written commentary others have made on your performance.

_____

_____

_____

After rereading your answers, make three one-sentence statements that capture the essence of the professional you and your competitive difference.

_____

_____

_____

Take these three statements and rework them into one sentence. This is your competitive difference.

_____

Once you have completed the Competitive Difference Questionnaire and identified what your competitive difference is, you'll feel a new awareness of the *professional you*. The next step is to weave this new awareness and your competitive difference into all your job search communications and, in the process, give form to your brand.

A True and Truthful Brand

You have to be able to deliver on the brand you create. It must be based on your possession of the *technical skills* of your profession, those *transferable skills* that you take with you from job to job, and the *professional values* that permeate your approach to professional life.

It is all too easy to overpromise, and while an employer might initially be attracted by the pizzazz of your resume, whether or not you live up to its value proposition decides the length and quality of the relationship.

If a box of cereal doesn't live up to the brand's hype, you simply don't buy it again; but if you sell yourself into the wrong job with exaggerations or outright lies, it is likely to cost you that job—plus you risk the possibility of collateral career damage that can follow you for years.

Benefits of a Defined Professional Brand

Understanding the skills and attributes demanded for professional success might be the most immediately recognizable benefit of a defined professional brand, but your professional brand is also extremely valuable for your long-term survival and success. Knowing who you are, what you offer, and how you want to be perceived will differentiate you from others. And because you understand yourself and can communicate this understanding, you will have a professional presence.

Your Professional Brand and the Long Haul

Globalization has made your job less secure than ever, yet you are a financial entity that must survive over what will be at least a half-century of work life. So while you develop an initial professional brand as part of your job search strategy, you don't want to shelve it once you've landed a new job.

In this new, insecure world of work, it makes sense to maintain visibility within your profession. It is nothing more than intelligent market positioning for the *professional brand* that you begin to define in this job search through your resume, cover letters, and other job search communications. This gradually evolving professional brand should become an integral part of the professional profile you show to the world on LinkedIn and other professional networking sites. Your brand raises your credibility and visibility within your profession as well as within the recruitment industry, making you more desirable as an employee and increasing your options.

The professionals who survive and prosper over the long haul are always people who do that little extra to make sure that they achieve their goals. When you complete the work in this chapter, you will have achieved a greater sense of self-awareness than you have ever had before. You will know exactly what you have to offer the professional world, and when you know where you stand and where you want to get in life, you can form the roadmap that will guide you on your journey to your destination.

Chapter 5

ELEMENTS OF A GREAT COVER LETTER

There is a fine line between pride in achievement and insufferable arrogance when writing about your experiences and who you are as a professional.

Now that you have a clearer idea of what makes you different, and you have captured that in a personal branding statement, you're ready to reflect this in your cover letters and all the other types of letters you use to differentiate your candidacy during the job hunt. Incidentally, you're also ready to reflect that understanding in your resume; but for that story, see the latest edition of *Knock 'em Dead Resumes*.

Differences Between Electronic and Print Cover Letters

Today's workplace can demand fifty or more hours weekly from busy, multitasking professionals. Everyone is busy; everyone is distracted. Corporate executives often base decisions on whether to return a call or respond to an e-mail on the first few words of the message. They figure that if you can't cut to the chase, they shouldn't have to waste their time: Your communication inadequacies aren't their problem. Your cover letter and resume, whether sent by e-mail or snail mail, compete for the attention of this audience. The key to successful communications is to construct clear, well-ordered, compelling, cut-to-the-chase letters.

A cover letter is a narrative of sequenced sentences organized around a single goal: to build a bridge of connectivity between you and the recipient and get your resume read with serious attention.

While you will likely need to create more than one type of cover letter, start by creating one general letter first. You can then use this letter as a template to cut, paste, and otherwise adapt to create other letters for different purposes. It should be brief and focus on the employer's needs, the "must haves."

Cover Letter Ingredients

Your letters will be most effective when you do each of the following:

1. Address someone by name—whenever possible, find someone involved in the recruitment and selection cycle, ideally a hiring manager: as noted, typically 1–3 management levels above your title.
2. Mention something you have discovered in common between you and the recipient, the job, or the company.
3. Explain why you are writing, tailoring the letter to the reader/job/company as much as is practicable.
4. Include information relevant to the job you are seeking. If you completed the TJD exercise earlier in this book, you will recognize that this is possible even when you do not have a job posting.
5. Show concern, interest, and pride in your work; the branding exercises from the previous chapter will help you with this.
6. Maintain a balance between professionalism and friendliness.
7. Ask for the next step in the process clearly and without apology or arrogance.

Before discussing formatting, let's take a minute to talk in more detail about some of these issues.

What Makes a Cover Letter Work?

Your first step is to grab the reader's attention. Whenever possible, your letter should start with a personalized greeting. E-mail has increased the ease of written communication and relaxed a number of letter-writing rules, but you must always use a greeting/salutation to open your letter and set a professional tone. If you do not start your letter with a greeting, you are immediately seen as someone who does not have a grasp of business communication or basic social graces. Because written communication is so important in today's workplace, a lack of salutation can get your letter ignored. That's why you want to open the letter by using a person's name, spelled correctly and using one of the following forms:

- Dear Mr. Yate, (standard)
- Hello, Mr. Yate, (more casual, but still okay; not as acceptable in the professions of law, medicine, and education)
- Dear Martin Yate, or Hello, Martin Yate, (acceptable if you are an experienced professional, but not so much if you are at the entry level or in your first two or three years in the professional workplace)

Do not use first names (Hello, Martin or Dear Carole) when you haven't communicated with the reader before. First names are okay once you have spoken and you have been encouraged to use first names, when you are of similar age and professional standing. If you are younger, and even if you might have been encouraged to use first names, only do so in person; in writing, use a more formal address. It is a sign of respect that is invariably appreciated.

Starting the Letter

Everything you need to say must be short and to the point so that your copy never exceeds one page. At the same time, you want to find common ground with your reader and present yourself in the best way. Use the first paragraph to introduce yourself with conviction and establish your reason for writing, perhaps integrating a phrase that foreshadows the opening brand statement from your resume.

Here are a few examples:

"Our mutual friend Carole Mraz over at C-Soft told me to say hello. You and I haven't spoken before, but Carole thinks we might have an interesting conversation, especially if you anticipate the need for an industrious young marketing acolyte who comes equipped with a great education, two ears and one mouth, and a great desire to start at the bottom learning from an acknowledged master in the field."

"Our mutual colleague, John Stanovich, felt my skills and abilities would be valuable to your company . . ."

"The manager of your San Francisco office, Pamela Bronson, suggested I contact you regarding the opening for a _____."

"I received your name from Henry Charles, the branch manager of Savannah Bank, last week, and he suggested I contact you. In case the resume he forwarded is caught up in the mail, I enclose another."

"Arthur Gold, your office manager and my neighbor, thought I should contact you about the upcoming opening in your accounting department."

"A colleague of mine, Diane Johnson, recommended your recruiting firm to me, as you recently assisted her in a strategic career move. I understand that your firm specializes in the consumer products industry."

"I met you briefly at the import/export symposium last _____ and your comments about productivity being pulled down by sloppy communications really resonated with me. As I am looking to harness my _____ years of logistics expertise to an organization with a major role in global distribution . . ."

When You Have No Referral and No Job Posting

"I have been researching the leading local companies in _____, and the name of _____ Products keeps coming up as a top company. This confirms an opinion I've developed over my three years as a committed distance-learning educator."

"Right after my mentor mentioned _____ as one of the top companies in our industry, I saw you speak at the association meeting last year. I really resonated with your comments about productivity, and as I am looking to harness my _____ years of logistics expertise to a major player, I felt this was the right time to introduce myself."

"I understand you are a manager who likes to gets things done, and who needs competent, focused, goal-oriented employees . . ."

"I'm focused on finding the right boss to bring out the best in a consistently top-producing _____ . I am a highly motivated producer who wants to make a contribution as part of the hard-driving team of the industry leader."

"I thought the best way to demonstrate my drive and creativity was to get you my resume in this priority mail envelope. I also sent it to you by e-mail and uploaded it to your company resume bank, but sales is all about stacking the odds . . . and I also knew you'd appreciate a break from the computer screen."

*"I've been meaning to contact you ever since I attended/read/heard about
_____. It encouraged me to do a little research, which has convinced
me that you are the kind of company I want to be associated with, and that I
have the kind of analytical focus coupled with creative drive that can be successfully applied to your current projects."*

"I have been following the performance of your company in Mutual Funds
Newsletter. *With my experience working for one of your direct competitors in the
critical area of customer service, I know I could make significant contributions
. . . I am detail-oriented, a problem solver, and am used to working with varied,
often frustrated customers."*

*"Recently, I have been researching the local _____ industry. My search
has been focused on looking for companies that are respected in the field and that
prize an employee's commitment to professional development. I am such an individual and you are clearly such a company. I bring sound technical skills, strong
business acumen, and sound management skills for complex technical projects in
a fast-paced environment."*

*"Although I am currently employed by one of your major competitors, I must
admit that I was captivated by your company's mission statement when I visited
your website."*

*"Within the next few weeks, I will be moving from New York to _____.
Having researched the companies in _____, I know that you are the
company I want to talk to because . . ."*

*"The state of the industry in _____ changes so rapidly that it is tough
for most professionals to keep up. The attached resume will demonstrate that I am
an exception and am eager to bring my experience as a _____ to work
for your company."*

When You Are Responding to a Job Posting

*"Your job posting #23567 cited the need for drive and creativity. I thought a
good way to demonstrate my drive and creativity was to get you my resume in
this priority mail envelope. Of course, I sent it to you by e-mail as well, but*

marketing communications is all about psychology and results . . . so I knew you'd get the message, appreciate the contrarian thinking, and enjoy a break from the computer screen."

"I read your job posting on your company's website on January 5th and felt I had to respond . . ."

"Your online job posting regarding a _____ on _____.com caught my eye, and your company name caught my attention."

"This e-mail, and my attached resume, is in response to your job posting on _____."

"I read your advertisement in the Daily Gotham *on October 6th for a _____ and, after researching your company website, felt I had to write . . ."*

"Reference job #C/AA 5670. As you compare your requirements for a _____ with my attached resume, you will see that my entire background matches your requirements exactly."

"This letter and attached resume are in response to your posting in _____."

"I was excited to see your opening for the accounting vacancy (job #S9854) on _____.com. As my attached resume demonstrates, the open position is a perfect match for my fifteen years' payroll, general ledger, and accounts receivable experience."

"While browsing the jobs database on _____.com, I was intrigued by your Regional Sales Manager job posting."

Presenting Yourself

If you haven't managed to build the reason for writing into your opening, as you just read in some of the above examples, introduce it now and go on to identify something desirable about the *professional you*.

"I am writing because . . ."

"My reason for contacting you . . ."

". . . you may be interested to know . . ."

"If you are seeking a _____, you will be interested to know . . ."

"I would like to talk to you about your staffing needs for _____ and how I might be able to contribute to your department's goals."

"If you have an opening for someone in this area, you will see that my resume demonstrates a person of unusual dedication, efficiency, and drive."

You then go on to define the kind of work you do with a brief statement and/or 2–3 statements that highlight your capabilities. With a short paragraph or a couple of bullets, you might highlight one or two special contributions or achievements. These can include any qualifications, contributions, and attributes that brand you as someone with talent and energy to offer.

You can also use this part of the letter to address an aspect of a particular job opening that is not addressed in your resume, and for some reason cannot be addressed there at the moment.

Or you can use the cover letter to emphasize a priority requirement from the posting.

"In my resume you will find proof points for my PR acumen, including:
- *"Demonstrated track record of strategic communications and influential public relations*
- *"Accomplished media relations and story placement, from* ABC World News Tonight *to* ZDNet
- *"Team, account, budget, client, and C-level executive management*
- *"Client loyalty and satisfaction*
- *"Knowledge of high-tech industry and players*
- *"New business success*
- *"Self-motivated team player"*

"Although I am currently employed by one of your competitors, I have kept my eye open for an opportunity to join your organization. Over the past year I have:

- "Built a sales force of seven reps, reduced turnover, and increased individual productivity an average of 14 percent
- "Implemented a customer service plan that successfully reduced client turnover by 18 percent
- "Initiated warranty tracking, increasing upsell by 7 percent
- "Increased revenue by $4.3 million"

"As a Marketing Director with twelve years of experience in consumer products, I have:

- "Doubled revenues in just eighteen months
- "Introduced a new product that captured a 38 percent market share
- "Successfully managed a $5 million ad budget"

"I have an economics background from Columbia and employ cutting-edge quantitative analysis strategies to approach cyclical fluctuations. This has enabled me to consistently call all major peaks and valleys in the last twelve years."

"I noticed from your posting that training experience in a distance-learning environment would be a plus. You will see in my enclosed resume that I have five years' experience writing and producing sales and management training materials in new media."

"You are looking for a database administrator with experience in Intranet implementation and management. As my attached resume demonstrates, I have done this type of work for six years with a regional organization on a platform of 15,000 users:

- "Desk technology upgrades
- "Responsible for hardware and peripheral selection
- "Coordinated installation of workstations
- "Trained users
- "Full upgrade achieved under budget and within deadline. Savings to company: $25,000"

You want the reader to move from your letter to the resume already primed with the feeling that you can do this job; the reference to a job's key requirement does just that. Since you want the reader to move quickly to your resume, brevity is important. Leave your reader wanting more; the letter doesn't sell you—that's the resume's job—but it should position you for serious consideration. Whet the reader's appetite, no more.

Make It Clear to the Reader That You Want to Talk

Explain when, where, and how you can be contacted. You can also be proactive by telling the reader that you intend to follow up at a certain point in time if contact has not been established by then. Just as you worked to create a strong opening, make sure your closing carries the same conviction. It is the reader's last personal impression of you, so make it strong, make it tight, and make it obvious that you are serious about entering into meaningful conversation.

Useful phrases include:

"It would be a pleasure to give you more information about my qualifications and experience . . ."

"I welcome the opportunity to discuss your specific projects and explore the possibility of joining your team."

"I look forward to discussing our mutual interests further . . ."

"I prefer not to use my employer's time taking personal calls at work, so instead you can reach me at _____."

"I will be in your area around the 20th, and will call you prior to that date. I would like to arrange . . ."

"I have pasted and attached my resume for your review and will call you in the next couple of days to discuss any openings for which your firm is currently conducting searches."

"I hope to speak with you further, and will call the week of _____ to follow up."

"The chance to meet with you would be a privilege and a pleasure, so to this end I shall call you on _____."

"I look forward to speaking with you further, and will call in the next few days to see when our schedules will permit a face-to-face meeting."

"May I suggest a personal meeting where you can have the opportunity to examine the person behind the resume?"

"My credentials and achievements are a matter of record that I hope you will examine in depth when we meet. You can reach me at _____."

"I look forward to examining any of the ways you feel my background and skills would benefit [_____]. I look forward to hearing from you."

"Resumes help you sort out the probables from the possibles, but they are no way to judge the caliber of an individual. I would like to meet you and demonstrate that I have the professional personality that makes for a successful _____."

"I expect to be in your area on Tuesday and Wednesday of next week, and wonder which day would be best for you. I will call to determine. In the meantime, I would appreciate your treating my application as confidential, since I am currently employed."

"With my training and hands-on experience, I know I can contribute to _____, and want to talk to you about it in person. When may we meet?"

"After reading my resume, you will know something about my background. Yet you will still need to determine whether I am the one to help you with current problems and challenges. I would like an interview to discuss my ability to make meaningful contributions to your department's goals."

"You can reach me at [_____] to arrange an interview. I know that your time investment in meeting with me will be repaid amply."

"Thank you for your time and consideration; I hope to hear from you shortly."

"May I call you for an interview in the next few days?"

"A brief phone call will establish whether or not we have mutual interest. Recognizing the demands of your schedule, I will make that call before lunch on Tuesday."

Some people feel it is powerful in the closing to state a date—"I'll call you on Friday if we don't speak before"—or a date and time—"I'll call you on Friday at 10 A.M. if we don't speak before" when they will follow up with a phone call. The logic is that you demonstrate that your intent is serious, that you are organized, and that you plan your time effectively, all of which are desirable behavioral traits and support the brand of a goal-oriented and consummate professional.

A complete idiot of a resume writer once said that an employer would be offended by being "forced" to sit and await this call. In more than thirty years of involvement in the hiring process, as a headhunter, as a hiring manager, as an HR executive, and as a writer on these issues who speaks to executives all over the world, I have never met anyone who felt constrained to wait by the phone for such a call. What sometimes *does* get noticed, though, is the person who doesn't follow through on a commitment to call as promised. Therefore, if you use this approach, keep your promise: It's part of the value proposition in your professional brand.

Now that you have a frame of reference for the factors that impact cover letters and any other job search letters, let's move on to the nuts and bolts of making them work. Later in the book you'll find examples of different types of cover letters: follow-up letters; networking letters; thank-you letters; resurrection letters; and acceptance, rejection, and resignation letters. You'll also find ready-to-use Microsoft Word job search letter templates in the eBook version of this book at *www.knockemdead.com*.

A Question of Money

Recruitment advertisements sometimes request salary information—either current salary, salary requirements, or salary history. Over the years, this issue has taken far more of people's attention than it deserves.

Recruiters and hiring managers ask about your salary for two principal reasons:

1. *Because all jobs have an approved salary range* and no matter what your skills, it is hard to win an exception to an approved salary range.
2. *Because it tells about your salary trajectory*, the offer you are likely to accept, and the raises you are used to.

There are other considerations as well:

- Interviews take precious time, and managers are reluctant to waste it on candidates who could never be hired because of their salary needs.
- In a down economy, when money is tighter and companies have more candidates to choose from, it is known as a "buyer's market" and employers have far less incentive to negotiate beyond the approved salary.
- If there is an exception, it is when you are in a hot job within an in-demand professional area or you have a unique skill set that gives you a competitive edge.

Writing that your salary is "negotiable" annoys HR people. They already know salary is negotiable, and the reply doesn't answer the question they need answered.

With an in-demand job in a good economy, "negotiable" is rarely grounds for refusing to talk to a candidate, but in a buyer's market, "negotiable" might not always have the desired result.

Given this understanding, if you have the skills and you are in the approved range you'll get an interview. If you aren't . . . well, then your energies are probably better invested in finding other opportunities, but make the pitch anyway; you have nothing to lose.

When your salary requirements are requested, don't restrict yourself to one figure; instead, give yourself a range. All job openings have an approved salary *range*, so providing your own range dramatically improves your chances of fitting into the salary range that is authorized for every position.

HOW DO I DETERMINE MY SALARY RANGE?

For more on how to determine the salary range you should be sharing with employers, see the negotiation chapter in this year's edition of *Knock 'em Dead: The Ultimate Job Search Guide.*

If you are asked about your current salary and choose to answer, be honest. This isn't something you can ever fudge on. It can and does get verified. Any discrepancies can result in your being dismissed with cause, and such an event will dog your career for years. Here is one way to address the topic of money in your cover letter. You will find other examples later in the book.

> *"Depending on the job and the professional development environment, my salary requirements are in the $_____ to $_____ range, with appropriate benefits."*

Address this issue in the cover letter or in a document attached to the cover letter but never in the resume itself. This is because your resume may be kept in a database for years and your salary range may typecast you as, say, an entry-level professional in the eyes of that company's computer. Here is an example of a salary history attachment.

Salary History Attachment

PAUL QUARN

86 Concord Street, Apt # 232 • Charlotte, NC 46776

Home (555) 555-1234 • Mobile (555) 555-1234 • me@email.com

SENIOR OPERATIONS/PLANT MANAGEMENT PROFESSIONAL

Continuous Improvement/Lean Six Sigma/Start-Up & Turnaround Operations/
Mergers & Change Management/Process & Productivity Optimization/HR/
Logistics & Supply Chain

SALARY HISTORY

UNITED STATES MARINE CORPS AIR STATION, Cherry Point, NC—2008 to 2010

Chief Operations Officer/*** Training School Officer in Charge**

Salary—$95,309

UNITED STATES MARINE CORPS AIR STATION, Futenma, Okinawa, Japan—2005 to 2008

********** Maintenance Chief—General Operations Manager/Plant Manager**

Starting Salary—$64,484/Ending Salary—$97,500

UNITED STATES MARINE CORPS AIR STATION, Beaufort, SC—2001 to 2005

Plant Manager/Senior Operations Manager

Starting Salary—$49,507/Ending Salary—$64,484

UNITED STATES MARINE CORPS RECRUITING STATION, Jacksonville, FL—1998–2001

Recruiting Manager

Starting Salary—$42,545/Ending Salary—$49,507

Contact Information

With an e-mail, your return address is built into your communications and you can add a telephone number beneath your signature. A printed letter should include address, telephone number, and e-mail address. Once you have determined a primary contact number for your job search, you must ensure that it will be answered *at all times*. There is no point in mounting a job search campaign if prospective employers can never reach you. Using your cell phone means that calls will usually get answered, but can you guarantee the voicemail and your live greeting will always be professional? If not, and you have a landline, your telephone company offers you multiple numbers and voice mails. Take advantage of this and dedicate one line exclusively to your career. Your voicemail message is important when you miss calls, or when taking a call simply isn't appropriate. Keep the message businesslike and, once recorded, replay it and listen carefully to the message for clarity, tone of voice, and recording quality. Does it present you as a clear-spoken, confident professional? Does it reflect the professional image you'd like to show to the world? Never use your company telephone or e-mail for any job search activities, ever.

If you're sending out cover letters by e-mail with resume attachments, be sure to hyperlink the e-mail address in your resume. That way, anyone can send an e-mail back to you with one click of the mouse, directly from your resume. Remember, it's all about making it easy for recruiters and hiring managers to contact you. The less work you make them do, the better your chances of success.

Chapter 6
HOW TO BUILD A KILLER COVER LETTER

There are six steps to organize the building blocks of your cover letter into a coherent, effective whole.

Step One: Identify Your Target Job

Your job search—and the resume and letters that go with it—will be incalculably more productive if you begin by clearly defining a target job that you can land and in which you can be successful. Start by identifying this target job title.

Step Two: Research the Target Job

Any evaluation of your background must begin with an understanding of what potential employers will be looking for when they come to your cover letter and resume. Collect six job postings that carry this target job title. Once you have a selection, deconstruct them as described in the Target Job Deconstruction exercise in Chapter 3.

Step Three: Review Your Most Recent Work History

When you know what your customers are looking for, and therefore what they will respond to, it's time to walk through your work history with an eye to those facets of your experience that will be of particular interest to such customers. *Knock 'em Dead Resumes* and *Knock 'em Dead: The Ultimate Job Search Guide* walk you through this process in detail. We can't do that here, but knowing what your customers want to buy (through your TJD) and how to illustrate your ability to deliver on their needs, is part of the story. For now, consider the following components, culled from the more comprehensive treatment in the other two books:

A. **Current or most recent employer:** Identify your current or most recent employer by name and location, and follow it with a brief description (five or six words) of the company's business/products/services.
B. **Duties:** Make a prioritized list of the duties/responsibilities/deliverables of this position.
C. **Skills:** What special skills or knowledge did you need to perform each of these tasks well? Which *transferable skills* and *professional values* helped you execute each of these tasks successfully?

- What educational background and/or credentials helped prepare you for these responsibilities?
- For each area of responsibility (deliverable), consider both the daily problems that arise and the major crises. Recall how you executed your job's responsibilities to prevent these problems from arising in the first place, and the analytical processes, subsequent actions, *transferable skills*, and successful solutions you implemented to reach successful outcomes when, despite your best efforts, these problems did arise. (More on this in Step Four.) There is a four-step technique called PSRV that you will find useful here:

> **P.** Identify the *project* and the problem it represented, both from a corporate perspective and from the point of view of your execution of duties.
>
> **S.** Identify your *solution* to the challenge and the process you implemented to deliver the solution.
>
> **R.** What was the *result* of your approach and actions?
>
> **V.** Finally, what was the *value* to you, the department, and the company? If you can, define this in terms of meaningful contribution: time saved, money saved, or money earned. This is not always possible, but it is very powerful whenever you can employ it.

Step Four: Consider *Transferable Skills* and *Professional Values* Used

Which *transferable skills* and *professional values* helped you succeed with this particular task? Come up with examples of how you used each particular skill in the execution of each of your major duties at this job. The examples you generate can be used not only in your job search letters, but in your resume and as illustrative answers to interview questions.

Step Five: Add Your Earlier Work History

Now repeat Step Three, the problem-solving nature of your work, and Step Four, how you used the *transferable skills* and *professional values* in your work, with each of your previous jobs. Do not skimp on this process. Everything you write might not go into the final version of your first cover letter, but all your effort will be rewarded by using the information in another letter, in your resume, or in response to an interview question. This exercise identifies the building blocks of what it takes to be successful in your profession, and the information you need at your fingertips to explain what you do objectively. The ultimate payoff is more and better job offers and a more successful career.

Step Six: Compile Endorsements

Looking at each of your major areas of responsibility throughout your work history, write down any positive verbal or written commentary others have made on your performance. As you will see in some of the sample letters in Chapter 10, praise for you that comes from someone else often has a much greater impact than anything you could come up with yourself.

Now, these compliments don't always happen that often, and you might sometimes push the accolades away. That's okay, lots of people do; but from now on, make a point of capturing them for use in the future.

QUESTIONS TO ANSWER

Comments that answer questions like these make for great endorsements: How did you work productively with coworkers, reports, and management? What different levels of people do you have to interact with to achieve your job's deliverables? What have you learned about productivity and communication from these experiences, and what does this say about you? Don't have any endorsements? Then evaluate yourself in these same areas with the Competitive Difference Questionnaire from Chapter 4, and use the results in letters, your resume, or at job interviews.

Create Punchy Sentences

Ultimately, any letter is only as good as the individual sentences that carry the message. Your goal is to communicate an energizing message and entice the reader to action. Concise, punchy sentences grab attention.

Verbs always help energize a sentence and give it that short, cut-to-the-chase feel. For example, one professional—with a number of years at the same law firm in a clerical position—had written:

"I learned to manage a computerized database."

Sounds pretty ordinary, right? Well, after looking at her job as an ongoing problem-solving exercise, certain exciting facts emerged. By using verbs and an awareness of employer interests as they relate to her target job, she was able to charge up this sentence and give it more punch. Not only that, but for the first time the writer fully understood the value of her contributions, which greatly enhanced her self-confidence in interviews:

"I analyzed and determined need for comprehensive upgrade of database, archival, and retrieval systems. Responsible for selection and installation of 'cloud-based' archival systems. Companywide archival system upgrade completed in one year."

Notice how the verbs show that she made things happen and put flesh on the bones of that initial bare statement. Such action verbs and phrases add an air of direction, efficiency, and accomplishment to every cover letter. Succinctly, they tell the reader what you did and how well you did it.

As you recall information that will contribute to your cover letter, rewrite key phrases to see if you can give them more depth with the use of action verbs. While a cover letter is typically one page, or one screen shot, don't worry about the length right now; you can shorten it later. The process you go through helps you think out exactly what you have to offer and also creates the language and ideas you will use to explain yourself during an interview.

Vary Sentence Structure

As noted in the previous section, your letters will be most effective when they are constructed with short, punchy sentences. As a rule, try keeping your sentences under about twenty-five words; a good average is around fifteen. If your sentence is longer than the twenty-five-word mark, change it. Either shorten it through restructuring, use semicolons to save space instead of all the words needed to start a whole new sentence, or make two sentences out of one. At the same time, you will want to avoid choppiness, so vary the length of sentences when you can.

You can also start with a short phrase ending in a colon:

- Followed by bullets of information
- Each one supporting the original phrase

These techniques are designed to enliven the reading process for readers, who always have too much to read and too little time. Here's how we can edit and rewrite the last example.

Analyzed and determined need for comprehensive upgrade of database, archival, and retrieval systems:

- *Responsible for software selection and compatibility issues*
- *Responsible for selection and installation of "cloud-based" archival systems*
- *Trained users, from managing partner through administrators*
- *Achieved full upgrade, integration, and compliance in six months*

Partner stated, "You brought us out of the dark ages, and neither you nor the firm missed a beat!"

K.I.S.S. (Keep It Simple, Stupid)

Persuading your readers to take action is challenging because many people in different companies and with different agendas see your letters and make different judgments based on those agendas. This means you must keep industry jargon to a reasonable level (especially in the initial contact letters—covers, broadcast, and the like); the rule of thumb is to use only the jargon and acronyms used in the job posting. Some readers will understand the intricacies and technicalities of your profession, but many more will not.

Within your short paragraphs and short sentences, beware of name-dropping and acronyms, such as, "I worked for Dr. A. Witherspoon in Sys. Gen. SNA 2.31." Statements like these can be too restricted to have meaning outside the small circle of specialists to whom they speak. Unless you work in a highly technical field and are sending the letter and resume to someone by name and title who you know will understand the importance of your technical language, be sure to use such phrases with discretion.

While you want your letters to have the widest possible appeal, they also need to remain personal in tone, so they don't sound like they're from Publishers Clearing House. You are trying to capture the essence of the *professional you* in just a few brief paragraphs. Short words in short sentences help make short, gripping paragraphs—good for short attention spans!

Person and Tense

Whether you use the first or the third person for different letters depends on a few important factors:

- Getting a lot said in a small space
- Packaging your skills and credentials for the target job
- Being factual
- Capturing the essence and personality of the *professional you*

There is considerable disagreement among the "experts" about whether to write in the first or the third person, and each option has both champions and detractors. The most important point is that, whichever one you use in your letters, you must be consistent throughout that letter. For example, bullet points in all types of cover letters can be shortened and given a more immediate feel, by omitting pronouns such as *I, you, he, she, they*:

> *I analyzed and determined the need for comprehensive of upgrade of database*
> can be replaced with:
> *Analyzed and determined the need for comprehensive of upgrade of database*

In fact, many authorities recommend dropping pronouns as a technique that both saves space and allows you to brag about yourself without seeming boastful. It gives the impression of another party writing about you. Some feel that to use the personal pronoun—"I analyzed and determined the need for comprehensive upgrade of database . . ."—is naive, unprofessional, and smacks of boasting.

Still others recommend that you write in the first person because it makes you sound more human.

In short, there are no hard-and-fast rules—they can all work, given the many unique circumstances you will face in any given job search. It is common in resumes to cut personal pronouns, but given the personal nature of a letter, there is a danger of the message sounding too choppy without pronouns. Use whatever style works best for you and for the particular cover letter you are writing. If you use the personal pronoun in your letters, try not to use it in every sentence; it gets a little monotonous, and it can make you sound like an egomaniac. The mental focus should be not on "I" but on "you," the person with whom you are communicating.

A nice variation is to use the first person throughout the letter, and then end with a final few words in the third person. Make sure these final words appear in the form of an attributed quote, such as an insight into your value:

"Partner stated, 'You brought us out of the dark ages, and neither you nor the firm missed a beat!'"

Don't confuse professionalism in your job search letters with stiff-necked formality. The most effective tone is one that mixes the conversational and the formal, just as we do in our offices and on our jobs. The only overriding rule is to make the letter readable so that the reader can see a human being and a professional shining through the page.

Length

As I indicated earlier, the standard length for a cover letter is usually one page, or the equivalent length for e-mails; typically this is as much as you can see on your screen without scrolling. Subsequent letters stemming from verbal communications—whether over the telephone or face-to-face—should strive to keep to the one-page rule, but can run to two pages if the complexity of content demands it.

Yet, in many cases, with conscientious editing over a couple of days, that two-page letter can usually be reduced to one page without losing any of the content, and at the same time it will probably pack more punch. As my editor always says, "If in doubt, cut it out."

Having said this, I should acknowledge that all rules are made to be broken. Occasionally a two-page letter might be required, generally in one of the following instances:

1. You are at a level, or your job is of such technical complexity, that you cannot edit down to one page without using a font size that is all but unreadable.
2. You have been contacted directly by an employer about a specific position and have been asked to present data for a specific opportunity.
3. An executive recruiter who is representing you determines that the exigencies of a particular situation warrant a dossier of such length. (Often such a letter and resume will be prepared exclusively—or with considerable input—by the recruiter.)

You'll find that thinking too much about length considerations will hamper the writing process. Think instead of the story you have to tell, and then layer fact upon fact until your tale is told. Use your words and the key phrases from this book to craft the message of your choice. When that is done, you can go back and ruthlessly cut it to the bone.

Ask yourself these questions:

- Can I cut out any paragraphs?
- Can I cut out any sentences?
- How can I reduce the word count of the longer sentences?
- Where have I repeated myself?

Whenever you can, cut something out—leave nothing but facts and action verbs! If at the end you find too much has been cut, you'll have the additional pleasure of reinstating your prose.

Chapter 7

HOW TO POLISH AND EDIT YOUR LETTERS FOR MAXIMUM IMPACT

Any job search letter is only as good as the individual sentences that carry your message. The most grammatically correct sentences in the world won't necessarily get you interviews, because they can read as though every breath of life has been squeezed out of them. Your goal is to communicate an energizing message and entice the reader to action.

A cover letter typically consists of 3–5 carefully constructed paragraphs. That's plenty of space to get your message across—and a second page simply won't get read.

Just as you would limit a printed cover letter to one page, you should try to keep an e-mail cover letter to one screen: that's as compact as possible. If you cannot get your entire letter into one screen view, at least make an effort to be certain that the meat of your pitch is on that first full screen.

The amount of e-mail traffic is growing exponentially, so hit your main points quickly and with clarity or lose your reader's attention. A good subject line grabs attention, but if the first two sentences don't succinctly state your purpose and maintain that initial attention, the reader has little reason for wasting any more precious time on the rest of your message.

Your professional business correspondence should demonstrate your written communication skills with powerful messaging that omits extraneous information and delivers the message in a format that is a model of clarity: easily accessible to both the eye and the mind.

Readability

Whether delivered by e-mail or in an envelope, your resume and letter will typically arrive on a reader's desktop with a dozen other priorities. You can expect your letter to get *a maximum five-second scan to see if it is worth reading*; this will cover the subject line/opening sentence, spelling of the recipient's name, and general readability. If it passes the scan test, you probably have *thirty seconds* to make your point, and that's assuming your letter cuts to the chase and speaks to the reader's needs.

Mistakes to Avoid

Letters that never get read have four things in common:

- They have too much information crammed into the space and are difficult to read—clearly the customer doesn't come first.
- The layout is unorganized, illogical, and uneven; it looks shoddy and slapdash—and no one wants an employee like that.
- The recipient's name is misspelled—that's disrespectful.
- The letter contains typos—not acceptable in an age of spell-checkers.

Get Your Head Into Communication Mode

Your resume and cover letter will always compete for the attention of a consistently distracted audience. The good news is that while your cover letter has a difficult job to do, if you apply just a few simple tactics, you can create one that dramatically increases the impact of your accompanying resume.

Advertising copywriters, with their ability to entertain and sell us stuff we absolutely don't need in a thirty-second commercial, are arguably society's most effective communicators. They all share one common approach to their work: They get inside, and stay inside, the customer's head throughout the writing process. They focus on what features their product possesses and which benefits are most likely to appeal to the customer.

With your Target Job Deconstruction in hand, you know with considerable accuracy what your customer wants to hear about. From the Competitive Difference Questionnaire, you know what unique features and benefits you have to offer. With this self-knowledge, you have everything you need to polish the draft letters you have just created.

How Long Should It Be?

Long enough to make your point and not a word longer. The standard length for a cover letter is less than one page (or fewer than 300 words); with an e-mail, the equivalent is typically as much as you can see on your screen without scrolling. They can also be much shorter. Here is a cover letter that gets to the point in seventy-one words:

> *"Your colleague, Bill Jacobson, suggested that I send you my resume. He mentioned that your department is looking for a database administrator with experience in intranet implementation and management. As my attached resume demonstrates, I have done that type of work for six years with a regional organization on a platform of 15,000 users. I welcome the opportunity to discuss your specific projects and explore the possibility of joining your team."*

With conscientious editing (spread over a couple of days to give you an objective distance), you can get any letter down to 300 words. The result will be a tighter letter that packs more punch.

Avoid Acronyms and Professional Slang

Every profession has its acronyms and professional slang/jargon, but there will be people in the recruitment and selection cycle who don't get it all. The acronyms and jargon have their place in your resume, but try to keep them under control in your letters.

The rule of thumb is that if the professional slang is used in the job posting, you can use it in your cover letter, because the employer is pretty much guaranteed to understand it. If not, find another way of saying it.

Give Action to Your Statements with Verbs

The focus of your letter echoes the prioritization of keywords identified in your TJD and the results of your Difference Questionnaire. These keywords are invariably nouns, but simply listing them doesn't make for an interesting story. Use verbs that show you in action.

- Responsible for all Accounts Payable
- Reduced Accounts Payable by . . .
- Streamlined Accounts Payable by . . .
- Managed all Accounts Payable . . .

Verbs always help energize a sentence and give it that short, cut-to-the-chase feel. Verbs show you in action: They give the reader a point of view, a way to see you. Verbs are an important part of creating your professional brand because they bring an air of direction, efficiency, and accomplishment to your written communications. Succinctly, they tell the reader *what* you did and *how well* you did it, and by implication anticipate you performing to the same standards when on the reader's payroll.

To help you in the process, here are more than 175 action verbs you can use. This list is just a beginning. Just about every word-processing program has a thesaurus; you can type any one of these words into it and get more choices for each entry.

accomplished	compiled	educated	indoctrinated	oversaw
achieved	completed	eliminated	influenced	performed
acted	composed	enabled	informed	persuaded
adapted	computed	encouraged	initiated	planned
addressed	conceptualized	engineered	innovated	prepared
administered	conducted	enlisted	inspected	presented
advanced	consolidated	established	installed	prioritized
advised	contained	evaluated	instigated	processed
allocated	contracted	examined	instituted	produced
analyzed	contributed	executed	instructed	programmed
appraised	controlled	expanded	integrated	projected
approved	coordinated	expedited	interpreted	promoted
arranged	corresponded	explained	interviewed	provided
assembled	counseled	extracted	introduced	publicized
assigned	created	fabricated	invented	published
assisted	critiqued	facilitated	launched	purchased
attained	cut	familiarized	lectured	recommended
audited	decreased	fashioned	led	reconciled
authored	delegated	focused	maintained	recorded
automated	demonstrated	forecast	managed	recruited
balanced	designed	formulated	marketed	reduced
budgeted	developed	founded	mediated	referred
built	devised	generated	moderated	regulated
calculated	diagnosed	guided	monitored	rehabilitated
catalogued	directed	headed up	motivated	remodeled
chaired	dispatched	identified	negotiated	repaired
clarified	distinguished	illustrated	operated	represented
classified	diversified	implemented	organized	researched
coached	drafted	improved	originated	restored
collected	edited	increased	overhauled	restructured

retrieved	set	streamlined	tabulated	upgraded
revitalized	shaped	strengthened	taught	validated
saved	solidified	summarized	trained	worked
scheduled	solved	supervised	translated	wrote
schooled	specified	surveyed	traveled	
screened	stimulated	systemized	trimmed	

Fonts

The font you choose has a big impact on the readability of your work. Stay away from script-like fonts, and use only those accepted as suitable for professional communication. A script may at first seem to be more visually appealing, but it can be tedious to read, and the goal is accessibility for a reader who is plowing through stacks of resumes when she gets your message.

The font(s) you choose must be used in a size legible for hiring managers. Anyone who has been staring at computer screens for ten or more years is likely to suffer from eyestrain and have problems with ten-point fonts; eleven- or twelve-point fonts are recommended.

Your branding message stays strong and consistent by using the same font choices (and paper) for your letters as you use for your resume.

The font you used for contact information and headlines in your resume is the same font you will use for your letterhead on your cover letter. The font you chose for your resume's body copy is the same as you will use for the message in your letters.

Good Fonts for Headlines/Contact Information/Signature
Arial
Times
Century Gothic
Verdana
Gill Sans
Lucida Sans

Good for Body Copy of Letters
Bodoni
Garamond
Georgia
Goudy Old Style

Note: Copy written in all capital letters, in any font, is harder to read. Use sparingly, if at all.

How to Brighten the Page

Once you decide on a font, *stick with it*. Apart from headlines and contact information, more than one font on a page can look confusing. You can do plenty to liven up the visual impact of the page within the variations of the font you have chosen.

All the recommended fonts come in regular, bold, italic, underlined, and bold italic, so you can vary the impact of keywords with *italics*, underlined phrases, and **boldface** for additional emphasis. For example, when you are sending a cover letter and resume in response to an Internet job posting or recruitment advertisement, you can bold or italicize those words used by the employer in the recruitment copy, emphasizing your match to their needs.

You should stay away from exclamation points and emoticons. In the samples section you will find little variation on the font choice beyond an occasionally italicized or bolded word. In the end, it's your judgment call. Just don't overdo the typographic pyrotechnics.

CLIP ART ALERT
Another no-no is the use of "clip art" to brighten the page. Those little quill pens and scrolls may look nifty to you, but they look amateurish to the rest of the world.

E-Mail Considerations

Do not include your e-mail address in the cover letter, because contact information for the medium and the date and time of your communication are entered automatically. If you are attaching a resume, your e-mail address will be seen in the contact information there.

Subject Line

Provide a revealing and concise subject line. It should allow the receiver to know immediately who you are and what you want.

The use of a powerful subject line can mean the difference between someone opening your e-mail and hitting the delete key. Think of it like a magazine cover, which uses splashy headlines to grab the reader and draw him into the stories inside. With e-mail, your subject line is your headline; it draws the reader into your e-mail. Your subject line needs to be intriguing and it also needs to be professional.

Do not use a subject line that states the obvious, like "Resume" or "Jim Smith's Resume." If you are responding to a job posting, the job title and job posting number are necessary, but just a start. Combine this factual information with a little intriguing information, such as:

Financial Analyst #MB450—CPA/MBA/8 yrs' exp.

Posting 2314—MIT Grad is interested

Job #6745—Top Sales Professional Here

Or, if there is no job posting to refer to:

IT Manager—7 yrs IT Consulting

Benefits Consultant—Nonprofit Exp in NY

Referral from Tony Banks—Product Management Job

You can also try longer subject lines, for example,

Your next Reg HR Manager—EEOC, FLSA, & ADA exp.

A message in your inbox will typically reveal a maximum of 60 characters (the above example is just 56 characters), and an opened message will show up to 150 characters. To be safe, try to get the most important part of your headline in the first 30 characters:

Your next Reg HR Manager—EEOC, FLSA

but feel free to use all this extra headline space; this example is just 144 characters:

Your next Reg HR Manager—EEOC, FLSA, ADA, OSHA. 10 years' exp. includes arbitration, campus, executive recruitment, selection, compensation, T&D

Greeting

It is unprofessional to start an e-mail (or any business communication) without a salutation. There are basic professional courtesies that you must recognize. Don't address the recipient on a first-name basis unless you are already familiar with him.

Begin your messages:

Dear Tiffany Carstairs,

Or refer to a specific job, followed by salutation

Ref Job #2376

Dear Ms. Carstairs,

Or with one of the other appropriate greetings we mentioned in Chapter 5.

Sign Off

End your e-mails with your name followed by contact information:

Thomas Torquemada

516.555.9374

Although there is a reply button built into every e-mail program, some people add a hyperlinked (live) e-mail address here because it encourages a response. If you decide to do so, place it before the telephone number:

Thomas Torquemada
ThomasTorquemada@hotmedia.com
516.555.9374

You could also finish with a signature in a script-like font:

Thomas Torquemada
ThomasTorquemada@hotmedia.com
516.555.9374

When you receive an e-mail that contains what appears to be a real signature, it makes an impression. However, *you should never use your real signature*; with the littlest bit of technical expertise anyone could copy it, and electronic signatures can have the same legal validity as a written signature. Don't risk your online security for the sake of style. Instead, use one of the more legible script fonts. It's a nice touch that most people don't use, and it becomes part of the branding process that differentiates you. But only do this when everything else about your resume and letter package is complete and consummately professional.

Custom Stationery

A number of e-mail programs now support the creation of customized stationery for your e-mails. This is a "nice to have" look when you are sending directly to an individual and all other aspects of your resume and letter are perfect. There is little point in having fancy e-mail stationery if the wording of your letter is sloppy. It sends entirely the wrong message about who you are as a professional and works against your brand.

If you pursue the option of creating e-mails that look more like traditional business letters, you will follow the same rules for font choice, layout, and page color as you would sending traditional mail communications.

Paste and Attach

It is normal when sending resumes without a prior conversation to attach a Microsoft Word or PDF version of your resume and to paste an ASCII version of your resume into the e-mail after your signature. You do this because some employers will not open attachments from people they do not know, for fear of viruses. With PDF documents, the layout is fixed and will appear exactly as you send it. With Microsoft Word, the formatting sometimes gets altered in transmission. Both ways are acceptable, and some people even attach their resume in both formats to give the reader a choice. Because of the layout issues with Microsoft Word docs, I am leaning toward using PDF.

Your cover letter will address this by saying, perhaps toward the end of your message:

"I have attached my resume in Microsoft Word [or PDF] and also pasted it below the signature in ASCII for your convenience."

MAIL MERGE ALERT FOR E-MAIL AND TRADITIONAL MAIL

If you are crafting a cover letter for mass distribution, beware using the mail merge feature of a word-processing program. All too often, the program will fill in the blanks: "Dear _____" with *italics* (Dear *Fred Jones*) or ***bold italics*** (Dear ***Fred Jones***). This detracts from all your efforts to be seen in a positive light; all you've achieved is to make it clear that this is a form e-mail, probably sent to thousands of people.

Spell-Checking Options

You can and should set your e-mails to check spelling before each and every message is sent, but never forget that *automatic spell-check is not completely reliable*.

Before you send any online or print resume, cover letter, or any other job search communication, remember to proofread and get additional outside help in proofreading. Ask family and friends to review your deathless literary prose looking for typos and errors in formatting and wording to make sure that what you believe you are sending is received in the way you intended. If you want a professional editor to review your work, we offer an editing service on the resume services page at *www .knockemdead.com*.

Traditional Mail Still Works

Whenever you send your resume by more than one communication medium, it greatly improves your odds. With e-mail as the standard communication medium, most managers get far less traditional mail than they used to, so when you send an e-mail cover letter and also one by traditional mail, you at least *double* your chances of getting your resume read by someone in a position to interview and hire you. We all like to open the mail; it helps us get started at the beginning of the day and fills in those gaps before lunch and as we are winding down at the end of the work day.

Coordinate Your Stationery

Letter stationery should always match the color and weight of your envelopes and resume. Sending a white cover letter—even if it is your personal stationery—with a cream resume detracts from the statement you are trying to make. As for colors, white, cream, and gray are all acceptable. Do not use pastel shades unless your target job involves interaction with the very young, aged, or infirm, where your color choice may then speak to a personal sensitivity that is relevant in such professions.

Paper Quality

The quality of the paper you use matters because it affects the way others perceive you. It tells the recipient something about your values and the importance you attach to the message. Coordinating paper and quality deserves proper attention as an integral part of establishing your professional brand.

All the office supply superstores carry good-quality matching resume paper and envelopes. When you print out resumes, print some letterhead at the same time.

Consistency

Contact information on your letters should be the same as the contact information on your resume, and should use the same font. Likewise, the body copy of your letters will use the same font as the body copy on your resume: Matching paper and coordinated and complementary fonts speak of a person who proceeds with intent in her professional life. It is another subtle way in which you establish a professional brand.

All subsequent letters (follow-up letters after interviews, for example) should be on the same matching paper and envelopes, using the same matching fonts in the same or similar font sizes.

Your written communication is likely to be filed in a candidate dossier. Prior to the hiring decision, a hiring manager will review all the written materials from all the short-list candidates. A thoughtfully packaged written-communication aspect of your job search campaign will paint the picture of a top-notch professional, and the sum of your letters will become a powerful and expressive component of the total *professional you*.

What goes on the envelope affects the impact of the message inside. Over the years, I've spoken with countless managers and human resources professionals about the appearance of the envelopes they receive. Did it affect the likelihood of the letter being read and, if so, with what kind of anticipation? Here's what I heard:

"I never open letters with printed pressure-sensitive labels; I regard them as junk mail, and I simply don't have the time in my life for ill-targeted marketing attempts."

"I never open anything addressed to me by title but not by name."

"I will open envelopes and read letters or e-mails addressed to me by misspelled name, but I am looking with a jaundiced eye, keen for other examples of sloppiness."

"I always open correctly typed envelopes that say 'personal' and/or 'confidential,' but if they're not, I feel conned. I don't hire con artists."

"I always open neatly handwritten envelopes. What's more, I open them first, unless there's another letter that is obviously a check."

This last comment is especially interesting in an age when just about all correspondence is printed. In an entirely unscientific test, over a two-week period, every letter I had to send I sent with a hand-addressed envelope. About 50 percent of the recipients actually commented that they had not seen a handwritten envelope in ages.

If your letter is going by traditional mail and is more than one page, it should be paginated with contact information on every page, the pages stapled together with one staple in the top left-hand corner. Remember, never use company e-mail or telephone number as contact information unless your current employer understands that you are leaving and you have permission to use company time and equipment for your search.

NEAT TRADITIONAL MAIL TACTIC

I once received an intriguing resume and cover letter. Both letter and resume had a circular red sticker attached to the top right-hand corner. It worked as a major exclamation point; I was impressed. I was even more impressed when I realized that once this left my hands, no other reader would know exactly who attached the sticker, but they *would* pay special attention to the content because of it.

Appearance Checklist

Remember that the first glance and feel of your letter can make a powerful impression. The letter's appearance should go hand in hand with its professional-sounding, clear content. Before you seal the envelope, go through this checklist:

Appearance and Formatting

❑ Does the paper measure 8½" × 11", and is it of good quality with a nice weight?

❑ Have you used white, off-white, cream, or pale gray paper?

❑ Did you use only one side of the page?

❑ Is contact information on every page?

❑ If there is more than one page, have you paginated your letter?

❑ If there is more than one page, are the pages stapled together? One staple in the top left-hand corner is the accepted protocol. Resume should *not* be stapled to cover letter.

❑ Did you spell-check, grammar-check, and then proofread carefully just to make sure everything's correct?

Content

❑ Does your letter state why you are writing?

❑ Is the letter tied to the target company?

❑ Does it refer to a specific job or job posting code when this is relevant?

- ❏ Is it focused on a target job's duties whenever possible?
- ❏ Does it include a reference to relevant *transferable skills* and *professional values*?
- ❏ Does it use verbs to show you in action, making a difference with your presence?
- ❏ Are your most relevant and qualifying experiences prioritized to lend strength to your letter?
- ❏ Have you avoided wasting more space than needed with employer names and addresses?
- ❏ Have you omitted any reference to reasons for leaving a particular job? Reasons for making a change might be important at the interview, but they are not relevant at this point. Use this precious space to sell, not to justify.
- ❏ Unless they have been specifically requested, have you removed all references to past, current, or desired salaries?
- ❏ Have you removed any references to your date of availability?
- ❏ Do you mention your highest educational attainment only if it is especially relevant, and do you mention your major only if it adds credence to the message?
- ❏ Have you avoided listing irrelevant responsibilities or experience?
- ❏ Have you given examples of your contributions/achievements, when possible?
- ❏ Have you avoided poor focus by eliminating all extraneous information?
- ❏ Is the letter long enough to whet the reader's appetite for more details, yet short enough not to satisfy that hunger?
- ❏ Have you let the obvious slip in, like heading your letter "Letter of Application" in big bold letters? If so, cut it.
- ❏ Do you have complete contact information—name, address, zip code, telephone number, and e-mail address? Omit your current business number unless it is absolutely necessary and safe to include it. This will only be the case if your employer understands that you are leaving and you have permission to use company time and equipment for your search.

Proofing and Printing

It simply isn't possible for even the most accomplished professional writer to go from draft to print, so don't try it. Your pride of authorship will blind you to blemishes you can't afford to miss.

You need some distance from your creative efforts to give yourself detachment and objectivity. There is no hard-and-fast rule about how long it should take to come up with the finished product; if you think you have finished, leave it alone, at least overnight. Then come back to it fresh. You'll read it almost as if it were meeting your eyes for the first time.

Before you e-mail or print your letters, make sure that your writing is as clear as possible. Three things guaranteed to annoy cover letter readers are incorrect spelling, poor grammar, and improper syntax. Go back and check all these areas. If you think syntax has something to do with the IRS, you'd better get a third party involved; we have affordable proofreading services at *www.knockemdead.com*.

Chapter 8
USE COVER LETTERS TO GET FOUR TIMES THE INTERVIEWS

Great cover, broadcast, and follow-up letters won't get you a job if they sit on your desk like rare manuscripts. You have to do something with them.

In *Knock 'em Dead: The Ultimate Job Search Guide*, I spend more than 150 pages showing you the best ways to execute a job search, including a dozen different networking strategies. I'm going to dip into just a few tactics from that book to show you some of the ways to find names and titles of hiring authorities so that you can contact them directly.

Responding to job postings is a big part of most job searches, so while there are many other effective job search strategies, this chapter will focus on tactics that can double, triple, and quadruple your chances of getting interviews from job postings by identifying and approaching the people most likely to be in a position to hire you.

Online Job Postings

Whenever you see a job you can do, respond to the posting in the requested way. In addition, compile all contact information for the company, including website and mailing address. Whenever you can find the names and titles of managers likely to hold authority over the ultimate hiring decision (I'll show you how), you can approach them directly in three different ways, each approach increasing your chances of getting an interview:

1. E-mail your resume directly to that manager with a personalized cover letter, doubling your chances of an interview.

2. Send a resume and personalized cover letter by traditional mail to that manager, tripling your chances of an interview.
3. Make a follow-up telephone call to that manager first thing in the morning, at lunchtime, or at 5 P.M., quadrupling your chances of an interview.

How to Find Names of Hiring Authorities

The more frequently you speak with managers whose job titles signify that they have the authority to hire you, the faster you will land that new position. By approaching hiring managers directly, you skip waiting to have your resume pulled from a resume database, you sidestep the recruiter's evaluation process, and you have the attention of a hiring manager and can make a direct and personal pitch.

Your target for direct approach is always someone who can hire you, although any management title offers opportunity for referral. For example, while HR people won't have the authority to hire you, the pivotal nature of their work makes them aware of all areas within a company that could use your skills.

Getting a resume to the "right someone" by name and making a personalized pitch gives you a distinct advantage; this is never more important than when the economy is down or in recovery. At such times, your competition is fierce, and employers always recognize initiative and motivation as differentiating factors in your candidacy.

Who to Target in Your Job Search

I am going to tell you the hiring titles to target during your job search. As you read, make a list of the specific titles that apply in your professional world, because if you have a list of the high-value titles that specifically apply to your opening, you will be more likely to find the names that go with them.

1. Those titles most likely to be in a position to hire you are usually the management titles one, two, and three levels above you.
2. Other titles likely to have knowledge of an opening include:
    *   Management titles 1–3 levels above you in departments that have ongoing interaction with your department.
    *   Peers holding similar titles (a little less desirable).
3. Titles of people who are most likely to know those involved in the selection process, and are able to refer you. These titles might be employees of a target company, or employees of a company or organization that does business with such a company.

- Management titles 1–3 levels above you in any department
- Internal recruiters and HR professionals

Any name is better than no name, and with the Internet at your fingertips, there are endless opportunities to identify the names of people who carry the appropriate hiring titles for your needs.

Internet Research Tactics for Finding Names

With a little work you can find the names, titles, and contact information for a lot of the people who have the ultimate authority to hire someone like you. I'm going to start you on the right road in this chapter, but for a thorough guide on how to do this, study the job search chapters in the first 150 pages of the latest edition of *Knock 'em Dead: The Ultimate Job Search Guide*.

For a start, try keyword searches for your target hiring titles on Google, Bing, and other search engines. They are all likely to deliver names, and they'll all get different results.

For example, a professional in pharmaceutical sales looking to make direct contact with potential hiring authorities for a job at a specific company in the Pittsburgh area could try all the following keyword searches and gather new useable information on each search.

- Pharmaceutical sales (company name)
- Pharmaceutical sales (company name) Pennsylvania
- Pharmaceutical sales (company name) Pittsburgh
- Pharmaceutical Mgr sales (company name) Pennsylvania
- Pharmaceutical Mgr sales (company name) Pittsburgh
- Pharmaceutical Director sales (company name) Pennsylvania
- Pharmaceutical Director sales (company name) Pittsburgh
- Pharmaceutical VP sales (company name) Pennsylvania

Now take these additional steps:

- Repeat all without "pharmaceutical"
- Repeat all without company name
- Repeat with just the job title
- Repeat with separate searches for target title plus: hired, resigned, or deceased

Drill down, and you will come up with people holding these titles at this and other target companies in your area.

USE GOOGLE NEWS

When you have completed each of these searches first as a standard Google search, redo each one as a Google News search; this looks for mentions of your keywords in media coverage. Click on "News" above the standard Google search box.

When you do a Google news search for news about a company or a title within a company and find relevant intelligence, you can use it as an opener for your cover letter. Refer to the article and its relevance in your letter. Then copy and paste a URL to the reference if you're sending e-mail, or enclose a copy of it with a traditional letter.

Try all the keyword combinations of job title, profession, location, and company phrases. You will come up with more job openings and job sites with most of them. When you drill down beyond the first couple of pages of results, you will come up with names to go with your target hiring titles for both your target company and for other companies.

Also check out the following resources:

- *Company websites.* On the "about us" pages, you can find names and sometimes contact information for management titles.
- *Biographical Directory/Database.* This is maintained by Standard and Poor's. It's a database of executives by name and title with contact information. Higher-level target hiring titles will be identifiable here or through one of the following options.

The following online resources are also useful for compiling a list of contacts to whom you can send your letter and resume:

www.onesource.com/businessbrowserus.aspx
Twelve major resources for locating executives by name.

www.knowx.com
Lists company owners, officers, and affiliations. Find out almost anything for about $60 a month.

www.jigsaw.com
An extensive database of contact information. It charges $1 a name, but give them two names they don't have and you get credited a dollar.

www.privateeye.com/?from=p31702&vw=background&Input=Name&piid=44
Offers personal details and contact information.

www.lambresearch.com/CorpsExecs.htm
Provides lots of links for finding names and titles. An excellent research site.

www.business.com/directory/advertising_and_marketing/sales/selling_techniques/lead_generation/
This page has links for lead-generating tools.

Names and Titles Increase Your Options

Sometimes, to alert all the right people at a target company that you're available, you might approach half a dozen different managers. For example, let's say you are a young engineer crazy for a job with Last Chance Electronics. It is well within the bounds of reason that you would submit a cover letter and resume to any or all of the following people, with each letter addressed by name to minimize its chances of going straight into the trash:

- Company president
- Vice president of engineering
- Chief engineer
- Engineering design manager
- Vice president of Human Resources
- Technical engineering recruitment manager
- Technical recruiter

Think through all the titles likely to be of use to you based on the above criteria, and keep all these titles in mind when you go looking for names to attach to them: The more options you have, the more results you will get.

Networking

One of the best ways to find names and get introductions to hiring authorities is to talk to people. *And because speaking with the people who can actually offer you a job is the only way you are going to get hired, the more ways you have to get into these conversations, the more successful you are going to be.*

When they are integrated into your job search, networking strategies deliver incredible results. Here are some effective ways to build relevant professional networks almost instantly.

Social Networking

Social networking has now become an integral part of cutting-edge job search and career-management strategies. It revolves around social and/or professionally oriented online networks that help you reach out to people you know, once knew, or would like to know. You can leverage your professional reach through connecting with others in your field, as well as through people with whom you share common experiences or interests.

Here's an example: A soldier who was cycling out of the military sought my help in her search for a new civilian career. First, to find other individuals with a similar background, I plugged in the word *army* at *www.linkedin.com*, perhaps the premier professional online networking site. I got more than 4,000 profiles of people who shared her military experience. (That was six years ago; with the same search today, I got 539,000: This growing connectivity is a big argument for joining LinkedIn.) We then tried a search using the phrase "*information technology*" (for her desired career change) and got 39,000 profiles (today it is well over one million). Both these potential networks would have relevance to her job search, but it got even better when we combined both the keywords: "*information technology* and *army*." This pulled up 908 profiles (today over 26,000) of people who shared her life experience and who had already made the transition into her desired profession. Such a degree of initial connectivity ensured she could hold helpful conversations with an enormous number of people, each of whom is relevant to her job search.

Corporate recruiters and headhunters often visit social networking sites, so you should shape the information you make available about yourself. For the professional in a job search, this will start with your resume (simply cutting and pasting your resume into your official profile) and possibly end there too. You make yourself visible, but because this is a social networking site and not a resume bank, you do it without an "I'm for sale" sign, which is useful when you are employed and looking for a new position.

HOW MANY SOCIAL NETWORKS ARE THERE?

There are just too many social networks to list, and the more these sites proliferate, the more specialized they become. It is probably a good idea to have a presence on two of the biggest, LinkedIn and Facebook. Beyond this, go to *www.wikipedia.org* and key in "social networks" for a complete listing. You'll find networking sites by special interests, languages, sex, race, and more.

Social networking can get you useful introductions to people throughout your profession, the country, and the world—people who might know of jobs at their own companies or who can introduce you to people at companies that have openings. This new application of technology enables you to reach out into an almost limitless community of like-minded professionals.

It works simply: You join a social networking site and find people you have worked with in the past. Then expand your network by joining the discussion groups that exist on all social networking sites and connect with other members of those groups.

For employers and recruiters, networking sites constitute a reliable pathway for recruiting qualified candidates, while for a job hunter they constitute a reliable pathway to jobs through the people connected to them. You can search a site's database by zip code, job title, company, or any keywords of your choice. The database will pull up the profiles of people who match your requirements and allow you to initiate contact directly, through your common membership in groups, or through the chain of people who connect you.

CAN SOCIAL NETWORKING HELP CAREER TRANSITION?

You will find social networking sites especially important when you are involved with or are planning a career transition. If you know you are cycling out of one profession and into another, you can use social networking sites to build a network of people who do the target job in your chosen profession and, whenever possible, people who have made a similar transition. If you are involved in a job search that involves career change, go to www.knockemdead.com and read the "Stepping Stones" article.

Professional Associations

One of the best things you can do for this job search and your long-term career success is to become an active member of one or two professional associations. You'll get job leads and an awesome network immediately, and such organizations provide great vehicles for increasing your credibility and visibility in the profession. In fact, if you have heard disgruntled job hunters mutter, "It's not what you know, it's who you know," it probably means they don't understand networking, and are probably not members of a professional association.

Associations have monthly meetings in most major metropolitan areas, plus regional and national get-togethers every year. The local meetings are of immediate interest, and unless you work on a national level, membership in the local or state chapters of a national association will be quite adequate for your needs—and cheaper, too. When you join a local chapter of a recognized national association and attend the local meetings, you get to know and be known by the most committed and best-connected people in your profession within your target marketplace. Your membership will help you stay attuned to what is going on in your profession, as associations offer ongoing training that makes you a more knowledgeable and therefore a more desirable employee.

The professional association is a new "old boy/old girl" network for the modern world. Your membership becomes a link to millions of colleagues, almost all of whom will gladly talk to you, based on your mutual connectivity through the association.

All industries and professions have multiple associations, any of which could be valuable depending on your needs. For example, if you are in retail, you could join any of some thirty national associations and fifty state associations. Together these associations represent employees of more than 1.5 million retail organizations, which in turn provide employment for more than 14 million people. Most other associations offer similarly impressive networking potential.

If you fit the profile of a special interest or minority group, you will also find professional associations that cater to another dimension of the *professional you*. These include—but are by no means restricted to—associations for African Americans, Latinos, Asian Americans, professionals with disabilities, and women. If you can find a niche association that's a fit, join it: It represents another, even more finely tuned network.

A good place to start online is the Wikipedia professional associations page, or the library, where you can check out the *Encyclopedia of Associations* (published by Gale). Alternatively, you can try a Google search for relevant keywords. For example, "legal association" will generate listings of associations for the legal profession.

LOOK FOR NICHE ASSOCIATIONS

If you belong to any identifiable minority, use that in your Google searches as well. For example, "Asian legal association" will generate a listing of local associations for Asian professionals working in the legal field.

When you join an association, you'll benefit greatly from attending the meetings, because this is where you will meet other professionals in your field. But don't just attend the meetings; get involved. Associations are largely volunteer organizations and always need someone to set out chairs or hand out paperwork and nametags. The task itself doesn't matter, but your visible willingness to be an active participant most certainly does, and will get you on a first-name basis with people you would probably never meet otherwise. Given the nature of association membership, you don't have to go straight from introductions to asking for leads on jobs. In fact, it can be productive to have initial conversations where you do not ask for leads or help in your job search, but where you make a contribution to the group; this is always preferable, because others are more likely to help you when they see you making an effort toward the common good.

It is easier to get to know people than you might think, because all professional association members are there, at least in part, to advance their careers through networking. Once you have the lay of the land, volunteer for one of the many committees that keep associations running. It's the best way to meet people and expand your sphere of influence, as you can reach out to others as you engage in your volunteer association activities. Committee involvement doesn't take much time because they invariably employ the "many hands make light work" approach; they are structured to function with the help of full-time professionals like you, with mortgages to pay and families to support.

There is a good argument that, from a networking point of view, the bigger the committee, the better. Membership and program committees are among the best to join. However, involvement in any committee will serve your needs, because being on one will enable you to reach out to those on other committees. If you join the conference or event committee, you can initiate contact with just about anyone in your professional world: "Hi, Bill Parsons? I'm Becky Lemon with the conference committee of the local association. I'd like to invite you to a meeting we are having next week on . . . ."

Don't join committees for which you lack the experience to be a productive member, unless you make it clear that the reason you want to become a part of that team is for professional development—if this is the case, expect to become the designated water carrier, at least initially.

If you volunteer and become active in an association, the people with whom you come into contact will begin to identify you as a team player, and this perception can be instrumental in landing that new job and surging ahead in your career.

Use the Association Database or Directory

The association directory, which comes with your membership package, provides you with a superb networking resource for telephone and e-mail networking campaigns. You can feel comfortable calling any other member on the phone and introducing yourself: "Hi, Brenda Massie? My name is Martin Yate. We haven't spoken before, but we are both members of the Teachers' Federation. I need some advice; can you spare a minute?"

Your mutual membership, and the commitment to your profession that it bespeaks, will guarantee you a few moments of anyone's time, a courtesy you should always return.

You can also use your association membership directory to generate personal introductions for jobs you have heard about elsewhere. For example, you might have found an interesting job posting on *www.careerbuilder.com*, or perhaps on a company website, with the request that you upload your resume. This is where your networking can pay big dividends. Apply just as the website where you found the job requested, then return to your membership directory and find people who work for that company. A judicious call or two will frequently get you a personal referral and some inside information on the opening: You have just *doubled your chances of landing that interview.* Once you have an interview scheduled, these same contacts can help you prepare for the interview with insider knowledge about the company, the department, and the hiring manager.

Professional associations all have online newsletters, and many have a jobs section on the website linked to the newsletter, where companies advertise because of the always qualified response. So you will see job postings here that often don't appear anywhere else. In down economic times, a savvy corporate recruiter will use an association website to skim the cream of available talent while screening out the less committed. You will also notice that association members write all the articles in the newsletters; as everyone likes to have their literary efforts appreciated, telling a member you have read an article that he has written gives you a great introduction to a networking call or letter.

Active association membership puts you on the radar of all the best qualified and best connected professionals in your area. You can also list it at the end of your resume under a Professional Affiliations heading. This is guaranteed to get a second glance, as it signifies professional awareness. Employers and headhunters will sometimes use words like *association*, *club*, and *society* in their keyword searches, so association membership will also help get your resume pulled up from the databases for investigation by human eyes.

How to Make Networking Work

Professional associations are just one of a dozen approaches to networking, all of which can be tremendously beneficial to your job search and overall career success if you nurture them.

Think of networking as professional connectedness, because becoming properly connected to your profession is the activity that will generate the widest range of relevant contacts for your job search.

You may well discover that your network is not as comprehensive as you might have wished, and that to be effective, your networking requires more than shooting the breeze with old cronies on the telephone. A successful outcome demands you move beyond the comfort level of inadequate personal networks.

Besides, just because you worked with someone five years ago doesn't mean she still regards you as a friend, especially if you haven't spoken to her since then. Surveys show that we all respond in these understandable ways:

- *To those requests from people I didn't know,* I asked for a resume (of course, if they had an introduction or were fellow members of an association, things would be different). If I received it in good time with a thoughtfully prepared accompanying letter, I would give that person help if I could.
- *To those requests from people with an introduction from someone I liked and respected,* I gave time and consideration and, whenever possible, assistance.
- *To those requests from friends, people I had worked with at one time* and who had kept in touch since we had worked together, I provided leads and even made calls on their behalf.
- *To those requests from people who regarded themselves as friends* but who had not maintained contact, or who had only re-established contact when they wanted something, for some reason I was unable to really help. I wished them the best of luck. "Sorry I couldn't help you. If something comes to mind, I'll be sure to call."

Nothing works like a personal recommendation from a professional colleague—and you get that by being a colleague, by being connected to your profession and the professionals within it, *and by being known as someone who cares and who shares.* It is no accident that successful people in all fields know each other; they helped each other become successful because they stayed in touch, through good times and bad, and helped each other whenever they could.

If you are going to use business colleagues and personal friends in your job search, don't mess up and do it halfheartedly. We live in a mobile society, so in addition to family, friends, and the colleagues you naturally know, it is *a smart long-term career-management strategy to establish yourself as a member of your professional community.*

A Very Smart Networking Idea

Intelligent networking encourages you to form relationships with people in your profession and industry at many levels. Almost anyone in your industry or location can be useful regardless of title or experience, but the people of most interest will likely fall into these categories:

1. Those who are 1–3 title levels above you and who might hire you, now or in the future. With this group, you can initiate contact by sending an e-mail to introduce yourself and ask them to look at your profile. If this proceeds to a conversation and interviews, fine; if not, you can ask your contact to connect you to others.
2. Those at or below your level but with similar professional experience.
3. Those who work in related areas within the same profession or industry.

It's best to build a relationship by finding common ground. You can initiate relationships by asking for advice; many people will give you a few minutes of their time. You will develop the best relationships, though, by reaching out to others with help and advice, because when you offer good things, forging a relationship with you becomes important to the other person. It is easy to do this by taking an active part in special-interest groups and searching the social sites for people in your profession who are actively looking for jobs.

The challenge then becomes how to help, advise, or make a gesture that will encourage a relationship that shares introductions and job leads. The answer is logical and painless: Use the job leads you hear about that are inappropriate for your own use.

It's a not-so-funny thing about the job search: When you are fresh out of school, no one is hiring entry-level workers; they all want you to call back in five years. Five years later, when you are once again looking for a job, they now only want someone fresh out of school or with ten years' experience.

In your job search activities, you are constantly coming across positions that aren't right for you, but that could be just what someone else is aching to hear about. Offer these leads to others as part of your introduction. Here's how it can work: Sometimes you have to send an e-mail stating why you want to make contact, and sometimes you can communicate immediately—it depends on a number of variables. In the first instance, you send an e-mail simply stating that you have a job lead that the contact might find interesting. This is a nice gesture and will get you lots of introductions.

In the second instance, where you are actually in direct e-mail communication, state your business: "I am involved in a strategic career move right now, and I have come across a job that isn't right for me, but that could be perfect for you. If you'd like to talk, let's exchange telephone numbers. I'll be happy to pass the lead on, and perhaps you have heard about something that would suit me . . . I am cycling out of the army and into the private sector and have been looking for jobs in IT in the South . . . ."

DON'T TALK ABOUT YOUR IDEAL JOB

If you are serious about getting back to work quickly, never talk about what you want in that ideal next job when you are networking. It reduces the odds of someone telling you about an opening. Instead, talk about what you can do.

Your job search has you scouring the job sites for job leads, and now you have a use for all those positions that aren't quite right for you. Build your own database of the jobs that are not suitable for you and pass them on to all those people above and below you in your profession who will make perfectly symbiotic networking partners.

How Social Networks Expand Your Approach Options

When you find suitable job postings, you are usually faced with uploading your resume into a corporate or headhunter database, but now, along with your professional association memberships, social networks give you additional approaches.

On your social networking sites, look for people who work at that target company now or have in the past. Search for them, using the target company name in your keyword search, then look for job titles one, two, and three levels above your own, and then those at the same level or one or two beneath you.

NETWORKING AND GROUP DISCUSSION POSTS

All the social networking sites—LinkedIn, Facebook, etc.—have special-interest groups that are used by recruiters (be sure to connect with me). It is becoming increasingly common for job hunters to post pitches about themselves in the discussion groups. This helps you become visible to recruiters. This is done very effectively with the Subject Line technique we discussed in Chapter 7. At 133 characters, this subject line does double duty as a "signature resume" for group discussions:

Reg HR Manager—EEOC, FLSA, ADA, OSHA. 10 years' exp includes arbitration, campus, executive recruitment, selection, compensation, T&D

The more you reach out, the better your reputation becomes and the more others will reach out to you. You will find much more on social and other networking approaches in the latest edition of *Knock 'em Dead: The Ultimate Job Search Guide.*

Networking Letters

When you write networking e-mails and letters, use these guidelines for your structure; you can also use the same guidelines as frameworks for networking conversations:

1. Establish connectivity: something or someone in common, or information likely to be of interest.
2. Use your common membership in professional associations as a bridge builder to other members.
3. Let contacts know what you can do. They will invariably want to help, but you have to give them a framework within which to target their efforts. DO NOT tell them about your dream job, or the promotion you always hoped for; don't get too specific, or allow your ego to get in the way of leads for jobs you really could do. You want to be specifically vague: "I'm looking for something in operations within the medical devices area" gives the listener the widest possible opportunity for coming up with leads.
4. Tell whomever you are writing or calling, "It's time for me to make a move" or "My job just got sent to Mumbai, and I'm hoping I could pick your brain."
5. Don't ask specifically, "Can you hire me?" or "Can your company hire me?" Ask for advice and leads. Then ask for guidance: "Could I send you my resume?"
6. By all means, ask for leads within specific target companies, but don't rely on a contact with a particular company to get you in.
7. When you do get help, say thank you. And if you get the help verbally, follow it up with a thank-you note in writing. The impression is indelible, and it just might get you another lead.

When you write networking letters and make the follow-up calls, you might be surprised to find who your friends are: Someone you always regarded as a real pal won't give you the time of day, and someone you never thought of as a friend will go above and beyond the call of duty on your behalf.

More on Referrals

Most people have horribly inadequate networks. The professional association strategy is just one of a dozen approaches you can learn to begin building and expanding them. You can learn much more about networking for referrals, finding names and titles of hiring authorities, making verbal presentations, recognizing and responding to "buy signals," and overcoming objections in the latest edition of *Knock 'em Dead: The Ultimate Job Search Guide*.

Chapter 9
SENDING OUT COVER LETTERS

A successful job search needs an integrated overall plan that includes all the most practical job search strategies.

On a call-in radio show during this last recession, I took a call from a woman who had "done everything and still not gotten a job." She explained that she had sent out almost 300 letters and still wasn't employed. After I asked her a couple of questions, I learned that she had been job-hunting for almost two years and had responded to two or three job postings a week. When I asked, she told me that as an accountant, there were probably some 2,000 companies for whom she could work. This means she was engaged in a job search that used only one largely passive approach to finding a job (responding to job postings) when there are at least five practical ways to find jobs, and where she only managed to approach about 15 percent of her customers in two years. *Two employer contacts per week will not get you back to work*—or even on the right track with the kind of job that can help you advance toward your chosen work-life goals.

Just sending out letters and resumes in response to job postings, without integrating them into more productive job search approaches, is a sad excuse for a job campaign. E-mail and traditional mail initiatives should be integrated into every aspect of your job search. They should be a vital part of your job search strategy. You will then need to maintain a balance among the *number* of e-mails and letters you send out on a daily and weekly basis, the *types* of e-mails and letters you send out, and how you follow up on them by making telephone calls to initiate the conversations that must take place to win job offers.

A Plan for a Direct Approach to Hiring Authorities

A professionally conducted campaign will include the ongoing identification of the names that go with "most-likely-to-hire" target job titles at target employers and use both e-mail and traditional mail for initial approach, and then follow up with a phone call. This approach really works; you'll find step-by-step tactics laid out in the latest edition of *Knock 'em Dead: The Ultimate Job Search Guide*.

As you discover names to go with the priority job titles, send a personalized cover letter and resume via e-mail and traditional mail and schedule a follow-up telephone call in your week's agenda.

Subsequently, send further resumes and personalized cover letters through e-mail and traditional mail as you come up with the names of people who hold other "most-likely-to-hire" target job titles within that company. You might also consider book-marking desirable companies so you can regularly check in on their job openings.

This Is Not Your Last Job Search

This is probably not the first or the last job search you will ever do, so save all your job search letters within a career management folder where you can find them again when you need them.

Develop electronic documents or paper file folders containing all the relevant information for each company. You'll want to keep the company's website and a list that includes the names of the company's executives and all other management names and titles that you have identified as relevant to your job search. Whenever you find other interesting information, copy it into the company folder. For instance, you might come across information on growth or shrinkage in a particular area of a company, or you might read about recent acquisitions the company has made; you can use the website, Google, and Google News to these track company activities.

All this information will help you target potential employers and stand out in different ways. Your knowledge will create a favorable impression when you first contact the company: that you made an effort is noticed and sets you apart from other applicants who don't bother. The combination says that you respect the company, the opportunity, and the interviewer; combined, these perceptions help differentiate your candidacy.

All your efforts have an obvious short-term value in helping you generate job interviews and offers. Who would *you* interview and subsequently hire? The person who knows nothing about your company, or the person who knows everything and shows enthusiasm with that knowledge?

Your efforts also have long-term value, because you are building a personalized reference library of your target industry/specialty/profession that will get you off to a running start the next time you wish to make a job change.

Following Up: A Cautionary Tale

Although you will get calls from your mailing, if you sit there like Buddha waiting for the world to beat a path to your door, you might wait a long time.

A pal of mine placed a posting for an analyst. Within a week, he had received more than 100 responses. Ten days later, he'd received 50 more and was still plowing through them when he received a follow-up call (the *only* one he received) from one of the candidates who'd tracked down his name. The candidate's resume was "in the tank" with all the others, but the follow-up phone call got it discovered. The job hunter was in the office by the end of the day and returned the following morning, and she was hired by lunchtime. This is not an isolated incident: Candidates who make themselves visible get hired.

MAKE IT EASY FOR THE HIRING MANAGER

If you are not already successful in management, you need to know one of the success principles outlined in my book for managers titled *Hiring the Best*: "The first tenet of management is getting work done through others." Managers are always on the lookout for competent professionals in their field for today and tomorrow. BUT, they hate recruiting and interviewing; they just want to find the right person, hire her, and get back to work. All you have to do is help them by packaging yourself professionally and using the strategies and tactics learned in this book to make them aware of your existence.

Follow-Up Calls Work!

You'll notice that examples in the following letter section mention that the applicant will follow up with a phone call. This allows the writer to explain to any inquisitive receptionist that Joe Schmoe is "expecting my call" or that it is "personal," or, "it's accounting/engineering/customer service business."

It's surprising that so many people are nervous about calling a fellow professional on the phone and talking about what they do for a living. *Don't worry so much.* In this unsettled world there is an unwritten credo shared by the vast majority of professional people: You should always help one another if it isn't going to hurt you in the process. Everyone out there has been in your situation and knows it can happen at any moment. Because of this, almost everyone you speak to will be sympathetic to your cause and help you if they can and, of course, if you ask the right questions.

No manager will take offense at a call from a professional colleague, and this is what you are. To know exactly how to make the call and what to say, look at the chapters on making contact and telephone interviews in the latest edition of *Knock 'em Dead: The Ultimate Job Search Guide*.

Use a Contact Tracker

To ensure that you keep track of your mailings and the follow-up phone calls, I recommend that you create a Contact Tracker on a spreadsheet program like Microsoft Excel. Create columns for the company name, telephone number, e-mail address, and contact name. As a rule of thumb, an e-mail sent today is ripe for follow-up within twenty-four to forty-eight hours; a mailing sent today is ripe for follow-up three to five days later.

Cover Letters: The Key to Your Job Search

Nine out of ten hiring managers prefer a cover letter with a resume, so a great cover letter will guarantee your resume gets read with serious attention. It will set you apart from other candidates and increase your interviews. You'll even have more productive and successful interviews, because the hiring manager will have a better idea of who you are professionally and who you are as a person.

The sample section that follows includes many types of job search letters that you can use throughout your search to help your candidacy stand out. Hope to see you soon at *www.knockemdead.com*, and join me every day on the Secrets & Strategies group on LinkedIn for more discussion and live workshops.

Chapter 10
SAMPLE LETTERS

Here's the real meat and potatoes of the book—the sample letters you can use as models for your own.

Apart from the sender's name and address (the personal stationery aspect), all letters adhere to Houghton Mifflin's *Best Writer's Guide* specifications. To those who might notice these things, it is important that we present an impeccable attention to detail.

LETTERS IN RESPONSE TO AN AD

Accounting Manager

From: Your Name [Your e-mail address]
To: Recipient e-mail address
Cc:
Subject: Accounting Manager job posting

Dear Recipient Name:

Re: File No. 213

I have six years of accounting experience and am responding to your recent posting for an Accounting Manager. Please allow me to highlight my skills as they relate to your stated requirements.

Your Requirements	**My Experience**
• A recognized accounting degree plus several years of practical experience.	• Obtained a C.A. degree in 2001 and have three-plus years' experience as an Accounting Manager.
• Excellent people skills and demonstrated ability to motivate staff.	• Effectively managed a staff of 24 including two supervisors.
• Strong administrative and analytical skills.	• Assisted in the development of a base reference library with Microsoft Excel for 400 clients.
• Good oral and written communication skills.	• Trained four new supervisors via daily coaching sessions, communication meetings, and technical skill sessions.

I believe my background provides the core professional skills you require. I would welcome the opportunity for a personal interview to further discuss my qualifications and have enclosed my resume for your consideration.

The position sounds interesting and I would welcome the opportunity for a personal interview to further discuss my qualifications. I also sent my resume via e-mail; I wanted to be sure you saw my credentials.

Yours truly,

Your Name
(555) 555-1234
Attachment: resume

Administrative Investment Banker

Dear Recipient Name:

I am responding to the Administrative Investment Banker job posting on your company's website. My 12+ years' experience as an administrative investment banker and assistant to a Vice Chairman seem a good match for your stated needs.

Some things not mentioned in your posting that I know will be important considerations: In bank administration we do what needs to be done to keep the engine running smoothly. In addition to all your stated requirements, administration responds to the legal and political polemics that conscribe the banker's world. I have had a seat on the legal committee for 7 years, and spent 4 years as a PAC representative.

My years as a line and administrative professional have also provided me with an unusual sensitivity to the needs of senior professionals. I have substantial computer experience and am fully computer literate. I have been told my verbal and written communication skills are exceptional.

I know of your company, and my colleague _____ is a VP in the systems area; we tend to be happy in similar environments, so I would be eager to talk with you about this position.

Based on the responsibilities and opportunities you describe, and the industry norms for this job, you'll find my salary requirements reasonable and negotiable. I have attached my resume for your consideration in both MS Word and as a PDF. And as I'm a guy who likes to cover all bases, I also pasted an unformatted version after my signature.

Sincerely,

Your Name
(555) 555-1234
Attachment: resume

Health Care Administrator

From: Your Name [Your e-mail address]
To: Recipient e-mail address
Cc:
Subject: Administrator Healthcare Services, RN, program director, school nurse, operating room circulator, and charge nurse in clinic, ER, OR

Dear Recipient Name:

I am a registered nurse and native of this area with a background as program director, school nurse, operating room circulator, and charge nurse in clinic, ER, OR, and hospital floor environments. The following skills and characteristics are reason to take a closer look at my credentials. I am:

- *Strong in handling multiple tasks and multifaceted situations while maintaining satisfactory interpersonal relationships with staff, physicians, patients, students, and families.*

- *An expert at ensuring compliance with regulations while keeping costs within budget.*

- *Talented in prioritizing issues and tasks and visualizing the "big" picture when considering the long-term effects of my decisions.*

- *An outcome-oriented self-starter with superior organizational and administrative skills.*

After reviewing my attached resume, you will discover that my qualifications are a good match for this position. You may reach me at (555) 555-1234 to schedule an appointment at your convenience. In the meantime, thank you for your time and consideration.

Sincerely,

Your Name
(555) 555-1234
Attachment: resume

Aerospace Construction

From: Your Name [Your e-mail address]
To: Recipient e-mail address
Cc:
Subject: Aerospace Construction job posting

Dear Recipient Name,

When I saw your announcement for a skilled laborer at ____, I made writing this letter my first priority.

I think you deserve to see the contributions I can make to the ____ team at once. That's why you'll find my resume different from others you may have run across. In place of the usual "objective statement," you'll read about four productivity-building capabilities I can bring to the job. And right below them are seven examples of the kinds of contributions I've made to my employers.

But I am concerned that you may think I am "overqualified," that I will be bored by the job. In fact, your position fits in nicely with the goal of getting my degree in Aerospace Engineering. I can't think of a better opportunity to see the OT&E process at work than being "in the trenches" on a project like yours.

I do best when I can learn about my employer's special needs. My resume is attached for your review; may I call in a few days to explore how I might fit best into your team?
Sincerely,

Your Name
(555) 555-1234
Attachment: resume

Assessment Coordinator

From: Your Name [Your e-mail address]
To: Recipient e-mail address
Cc:
Subject: Assessment Coordinator job posting

Dear Recipient Name:

Your posting on the *New York Times* website, on June 9, for an **Assessment Coordinator** seems to perfectly match my background and experience. As the International Brand Coordinator for _____, I coordinated meetings, prepared presentations and materials, organized a major off-site conference, and supervised an assistant. I believe that I am an excellent candidate for this position, as I have illustrated below:

YOUR REQUIREMENTS	MY QUALIFICATIONS
A highly motivated, diplomatic, flexible, quality-driven professional on every project.	Successfully managed project teams involving different business units. The defined end results were achieved.
Exceptional organizational skills and attention to detail.	Planned the development and launch of the _____ Heritage Edition bottle series. My former manager enjoyed leaving the "details" and follow-through to me. Coverdale project management training.
College degree and minimum 3 years' relevant business experience.	B.A. from _____ College. 5+ years' business experience in productive, professional environments.
Computer literacy.	Extensive knowledge of Windows & Macintosh applications.

I'm interested in this position because it fits well with my new career focus in the human resources field. Currently, I am enrolled in _____'s adult career planning and development certificate program and working at _____.

My resume is attached for your review. If you believe that there is a match, as I do, please call me. Thank you for your consideration.

Sincere regards,

Your Name
(555) 555-1234
Administrator Healthcare

Campus Director

From: Your Name [Your e-mail address]
To: Recipient e-mail address
Cc:
Subject: RE: PIN 1826 Campus Director, Library, _____ Campus

To whom it may concern,

I am responding to your job postings on _____ and _____ for a Library Director for the _____ Campus. I have completed a job application and uploaded my resume and graduate degree transcripts for your consideration.

I am interested in this position for two main reasons. First, I have had the pleasure of working with _____ students across the Information Services Desk at _____ Library for a number of years. Secondly, becoming your Library Director is the right place for me to land after my more than fifteen years of professional experience with increasing levels of responsibility. I would greatly enjoy the opportunity to ensure your students receive outstanding library services in every place they gather— online, and on or off campus.

I believe I am an excellent candidate for this position as I have illustrated below:

Your Requirements	My Qualifications
• Five years of progressively more responsible professional/technical experience in area assigned.	• 15+ years of library experience with increasing responsibility in innovative, customer-focused environments.
• Leadership and supervisory experience.	• 7 years of successful staff management in multiple departments. Proven ability to inspire a shared vision.
• Master's Degree in Library/Information Science from an ALA-accredited university.	• MLS from University of _____ in 1994. Continued professional education in leadership and technology.

An extensive listing of my core competencies in management, relationship building, technical areas, and technology are featured in my resume along with a few performance highlights for your review. I would welcome the opportunity to meet with your selection team for an in-depth interview to discuss the results you can expect from me as your Library Director. Thank you for your time and consideration. I look forward to an e-mail or phone call from you soon.

Sincerely,

Your Name
(555) 555-1234
Attachment: resume

Director of College Housing

From: Your Name [Your e-mail address]
To: Recipient e-mail address
Cc:
Subject: Director of College Housing job posting
Re: Reference Code: TC-E-5556E2

Dear Recipient Name,

In response to your posting on the _____ website for an Assistant Director of College Housing, I have attached my resume for your review. The following gives you a snapshot of how my experience matches your needs:

Your requirements	My qualifications
• Bachelor's Degree or four years of experience in lieu of degree.	• Master's Degree in Clinical Counseling.
	• Eight years of combined experience in residence hall administration and counseling capacities.
• Promote and develop educational programming and maintain extensive budget.	• Plan, develop, and implement educational programs, and manage an operational budget.
• Administration of three to five residence halls housing approximately 1,000 students.	• Administration of residence halls housing up to 500 college students.
• Supervise, develop, and evaluate three to five full-time residence hall directors.	• Supervise, develop, and evaluate 26 Resident Advisors with direct responsibility for four RA's and a Head Resident Advisor (HRA).
• Develop departmental policies and procedures, manage area office including billing, occupancy, and facilities records.	• Direct all aspects of front desk management and facilities maintenance operations.
• Assist in the development and leadership of departmental committees, and serve as manager for student conduct cases.	• One year as VP of Committees and Organizations for the Student Government with the State University of _____ at _____.

Thank you for your review and consideration of my attached resume. I look forward to hearing from you soon.

Sincerely,

Your Name
(555) 555-1234
Attachment: resume

Director of Database Engineering

From: Your Name [Your e-mail address]
To: Recipient e-mail address
Cc:
Subject: Director of Database Engineering job posting

Dear Recipient Name,

14 years' experience in data warehousing, database administration, and business systems development are the essential assets I bring to your Director of Database Engineering position. As a senior-level employee of _____, Inc., I have established a track record for successfully managing complex projects. One example:

Managed $10 million development project for _____, building and implementing first enterprise data warehouse and certain downstream divisional data marts. Within three months of implementation, established as the source for accurate company data for all _____ business units. Met service-level commitments over 97% of the time and experienced no downtime due to programming error.

I bring competency in correlating data warehousing functions with overall company goals, am skilled in providing counsel to senior managers and executives on database issues as they relate to performance imperatives, and am adept at monitoring data warehouse systems to continually ensure their value and usefulness to an organization as a whole.

Please review my attached resume and contact me to schedule an interview. I am excited about this opportunity.

Sincerely,

Your Name
(555) 555-1234
Attachment: resume

Entry-Level Sales

From: Your Name [Your e-mail address]
To: Recipient e-mail address
Cc:
Subject: Sales Associate with verifiable track record

Dear Recipient Name,

If you are searching for a success-driven Sales Associate with a verifiable track record, look no further. Highlights of my achievements include:

- Awarded with 3 plaques and nominated to President's Club for exemplary sales performance.
- Started a business from scratch and grew customer base using multiple marketing approaches.
- Paid college expenses while working full-time in sales.

Although I will not graduate with a BA in Communications until December, I am eager to start work as soon as possible—either full- or part-time. I can balance the responsibilities of a Sales Associate position with my final studies, because I have done so with a full course load for the past four years.

As a sports nut with proven closing ability in B-to-C sales, I know that I can make a positive contribution to _____ _____. My resume is attached for your review and I will call you next week, hopefully to arrange an interview. Thank you for your consideration.
Sincerely,

Your Name
(555) 555-1234
Attachment: resume

Heavy Equipment Supervisor

From: Your Name [Your e-mail address]
To: Recipient e-mail address
Cc:
Subject: Heavy Equipment Supervisor job posting

Dear Recipient Name,

Please accept the attached resume in response to your Heavy Equipment Supervisor position posting.

My experience includes 10+ years of experience operating and maintaining heavy equipment. In my current position, I operate backhoes, loaders, lulls, Gallion cranes, Ditch Witch trenchers (large and walk-behind), forklifts, street sweepers, and bucket trucks. In addition, I supervise the troubleshooting, maintenance, and repair of all of the department's equipment.

Of equal importance are my supervisory and leadership skills; I have managed crews of up to 40 employees. Being extremely diligent, I have assumed responsibility for overseeing and monitoring various projects and issues that affect the daily operations, efficiency, and profitability of the company. I am recognized by senior management for consistently completing projects on time and within budget.

My transition through several trades during my career has developed my strong multi-tasking abilities, which have proven to be an asset in a business where everything needs to be done yesterday.

Assuming my skills match your needs, I would welcome the opportunity to meet with you and determine what contributions I can make to your company. Thank you for your consideration. My resume is attached for your review.

Sincerely,

Your Name
(555) 555-1234
Attachment: resume

Hydrologist

RE: Position of Hydrogeologist/Groundwater Modeler, Company Job ID: ACHZ4121-234059, AJB Reference Number: 4950495, Job ID #0000BZ/BBBB

Dear Recipient Name:

I learned about your need for a Hydrogeologist/Groundwater Modeler with great interest, as my qualifications match your requirements for this position almost exactly. Please accept my attached resume for your review and allow me to explain briefly how I can contribute to ____.

With an MS Degree in Hydrologic Sciences and over 7 years of research experience, I have developed a strong background in advanced theories of solute transport modeling; consequently, I have developed effective quantitative skills and a practical understanding of the fundamental principles and concepts associated with hydrogeology.

My resume will provide additional details regarding my educational background and professional experience. Beyond these qualifications, it may be helpful for you to know that I have worked successfully in both independent and team project environments, adapt readily to rapidly changing work conditions, and enjoy the prospect of contributing to CRPH's "80-year reputation as a water industry leader" in the advancement of hydrogeologic and groundwater projects.

I would welcome the opportunity to interview for this position and discuss the results you can expect from me as a member of your team. Thank you for your time and consideration.

My resume is attached for your review.

Sincerely,

Your Name
(555) 555-1234
Attachment: resume

Legal Administration #1

From: Your Name [Your e-mail address]
To: Recipient e-mail address
Cc:
Subject: BAR COUNSEL LEGAL SECRETARY

RE: OFFICE OF BAR COUNSEL LEGAL SECRETARY

Dear Recipient Name:

It is with continued interest and enthusiasm that I respond to your recruitment posting for Legal Secretary to the Ohio Bar Association's Office of Bar Counsel.

Although a relative newcomer to the field, I have earned my degree in Paralegal Studies, graduating with Magna Cum Laude distinction. With more than two years of experience after graduation providing administrative and clerical support in private practice, I am confident that I possess the expertise and dedication that will make an immediate and significant contribution to the efficiency and organization of the Office of Bar Counsel.

It has long been my dream to associate with the top professionals in the field. Where better to continue my professional development than within the heart of the organization as a provider of administrative support to members of the Ohio Bar Association itself!

If you are looking for a legal support professional who is committed to the highest standards of performance, relates well to others, is self-directing and highly motivated, and is looking for a long-term employment relationship, please contact me to arrange an interview. I will make myself available at your earliest convenience. My resume is attached for your consideration.

Sincerely yours,

Your Name
(555) 555-1234
Attachment: resume

Legal Administration #2

From: Your Name [Your e-mail address]
To: Recipient e-mail address
Cc:
Subject: Legal Administration job posting: mgmt, mktg, cmptr, acctg, planning, personnel

Dear Recipient Name:

I am writing in response to your job posting on Hotjobs.com for a legal administrator. I have been a legal administrator for two twenty-one-attorney law firms. Additionally, I have also been a medical administrator for over ten years. I believe that this experience might be of interest to a law firm with such a significant malpractice caseload.

I possess the management, marketing, computer, accounting, budgeting, financial planning, personnel, and people-management skills you would expect from someone who has been in professional practice administration for 15 years.

I will be in the area later in the month. Hopefully, we can meet at that time to discuss how well my skills and personality might fit your needs and company culture. I am very interested in this position and have attached my resume for your consideration.

Thank you for your time and consideration.

Sincerely,

Your Name
(555) 555-1234
Your e-mail address

Logistics

From: Your Name [Your e-mail address]
To: Recipient e-mail address
Cc:
Subject: Warehouse pro: 26 yrs' inventory control, import/export, shipping, tracking, organization

Re: Warehouse Manager posting

Dear Recipient Name,

You are seeking an experienced and self-motivated warehouse manager. For 26 years I have been successfully working in manufacturing and warehouse settings. I have been a warehouse manager for 12 years and am dedicated to the principles of quality, continuous improvement, and customer satisfaction.

I like to make a difference when I go to work, and always look for ways to improve productivity, efficiency, and accuracy. In my current position I have identified ways to reduce downtime and waste, as well as methods to increase productivity. Performance reviews have noted my "excellent attendance and dependability" and praised me as "reliable and highly motivated."

Throughout my career, I have demonstrated my loyalty, commitment, and a solid work ethic. If you need a warehouse manager who can hit the ground running, I am confident that, since I am a professional at the top of his professional stride, our meeting would be time well spent. My resume is attached as a PDF.

Sincerely,

Your Name
(555) 555-1234
Attachment: resume

Office Administrator

From: Your Name [Your e-mail address]
To: Recipient e-mail address
Cc:
Subject: Office Administrator job posting
_____

Dear Recipient Name,

Your posting for an **Office Administrator** on _____ caught my attention because my background appears to parallel your needs.

I am **self-sufficient** and able to **work independently with little supervision,** as my references will confirm. I am regarded as **an information resource** and enjoy sharing my knowledge to help others. I always listen to understand what others need, I don't just wait my turn to speak; and then, with a full grasp of the issue, I solve the problem.

Process streamlining is a strength. I have **developed** software-based **systems and processes** to automate production reporting, notify customers of changes, and inform field staff of corporate directives. When supervising clerical staff, I always try to **plan ahead** to make the best use of their time.

I **work well with executives, sales representatives, customers, vendors, _and_ coworkers, and demonstrate strong interpersonal communication skills and good judgment**. I also have extensive experience **managing projects and planning meetings, trips, and special events**.

I am confident that I can deliver similar results for _____. My resume is attached for your review. Thank you for your time and consideration; I look forward to speaking with you soon.

Sincerely,

Your Name
(555) 555-1234
Attachment: resume

Operations Manager

From: Your Name [Your e-mail address]
To: Recipient e-mail address
Cc:
Subject: Hi-Performance Operations Manager job posting

Dear Recipient Name,

The job posting on CareerBuilder says you need an Operations Manager who can impact the bottom line. Adding a season operations guy like me to your staff will increase productivity because "no one has money to burn in a tough economy."

The match between your needs and my talents is ideal. My strengths lie in leveraging the labor and manufacturing operations that design, build, install, and manage equipment for environmental and production improvements. I am a leader both by example and through effective management of individuals and teams.

My attached resume will identify a dozen projects (and their impact) that have been successfully implemented. The work performed under my direction has always come in at or below budget, and my teams always meet project deadlines.

The resume summarizes my qualifications and achievements. Because "proven skills" are best verified in person, I look forward to our conversation and will call early next week to schedule our meeting. Thank you for taking the time to review my resume, and for your consideration.

Sincerely,

Your Name
(555) 555-1234
Attachment: resume

Peace Officer

From: Your Name [Your e-mail address]
To: Recipient e-mail address
Cc:
Subject: Peace Officer application

Dear Recipient Name:

I am submitting my attached resume in application for the position of Peace Officer. I have recently completed necessary educational requirements, and I am enthusiastic about the possibility of interviewing for this position.

My degree from _____ _____ in Criminal Studies provided me the opportunity to analyze the key concepts, principles, and practices associated with human behavior and criminal justice. I demonstrated in-depth knowledge of law enforcement and social science issues through excellent work in class assignments and projects.

I realize that there is a significant difference between academic studies and field experience, but I am confident that my knowledge and commitment to criminal justice will ensure my ability to perform effectively within your department.

I worked through college, earning recognition from my managers for my leadership and organizational skills. For example, as a Certified Trainer at _____, I trained a staff of eight bussers and contributed to improved team performance by building great relationships with team members and guests.

My resume is attached to provide you with full details concerning my background and achievements. Thank you for your time and consideration.

Sincerely,

Your Name
(555) 555-1234
Attachment: resume

Production Supervisor

Dear Recipient Name:

I am writing in response to the job posting on your company's website. Please consider my attached resume in your search for a Production Supervisor.

I am presently responsible for the coordination of production in three assembly and test areas that employ 35 union personnel. With a hi-tech background in *Fortune* 500 companies, I feel well-qualified for the position you describe.

Supervising production of union personnel in three dispersed facilities requires my being able to function independently, but with clear lines of communication and immediate response with sales, operations, HR, and legal. Constant negotiations with union employees and all levels of management have fine-tuned my interpersonal skills.

I am accustomed to a fast-paced environment where deadlines are a priority and multitasking is the norm. I would like very much to discuss with you how I could contribute to your organization.

Thank you for your time and consideration.

Sincerely,

Your Name
(555) 555-1234
Attachment: resume

Professional Practice, Billing

From: Your Name [Your e-mail address]
To: Recipient e-mail address
Cc:
Subject: Re Medical Biller job opening. ICD-9, CPT coding, ebilling, superbilling

Dear Recipient Name,

I am very interested in the Medical Biller job opening you have posted on _____ and believe I have the qualifications to successfully fulfill your requirements.

I have a solid 3 years in administration of professional practices, and have just completed intensive training in medical billing policies and procedures with _____.

Coursework emphasized the international classification of diseases (ICD-9) and complex CPT coding for insurance purposes, and included instruction in standard billing procedures to produce invoices or superbills within the office, utilization of outside billing services, and electronic billing.

From my prior experience in a law office, I know how to deal diplomatically with confused and difficult clients, not unlike the patients at a doctor's office who do not understand the provisions of their healthcare plans. I am equally comfortable in close working relationships with physicians and other professional staff.

I attach my resume for your review and look forward to discussing how I may be able to contribute to your efficiency, patient relations, and profitability.

Sincerely,

Your Name
(555) 555-1234
Attachment: resume

Senior PR Professional

From: Your Name [Your e-mail address]
To: Recipient e-mail address
Cc:
Subject: _____ consumer PR

Dear Recipient Name,

As a high-tech PR professional with 15 years' technology experience, I possess both the proven skills and drive that you seek and _____ is known for. My specific experience includes:

Point of Strategic Counsel
Primary contact for creation, execution, and delivery of messaging and launch strategies for both companies and C-level executives. This has resulted in superb client-management skills at the highest levels, demonstrated by repeat business as loyal clients stay with me over the years.

Manage High-Level Influential Relations with Key Press
Having developed long-term relationships as well as forging critical new relationships with key media, I understand the importance of managing those relationships with integrity, respect, reliability, and discretion. This has enabled me to craft and place stories in hundreds of outlets ranging from ___ to ___.

Coach Team and Account Staff
I learned over the years that a team is only as good as its leader. And, it's more rewarding to be on the winning team. I lead by example, believe in positive reinforcement and recognition, and keep team members focused on our client's goals and objectives: our ultimate prize.

The attached resume will give you further insight into my capabilities. I feel confident that a meeting would demonstrate that my hi-tech public relations expertise would be a worthy addition to your team. I look forward to speaking with you soon.

Regards,

Your Name
(555) 555-1234
Attachment: resume

Tutor

From: Your Name [Your e-mail address]
To: Recipient e-mail address
Cc:
Subject: SAT Tutor

Dear Recipient Name,

I am writing in reference to your opening for an English and SAT tutor. I am a dedicated student of literature and, more generally, intellectual history, and I believe I can make a real contribution to your company, for a number of reasons.

- As someone who has himself taken the SAT, ACT, and AP English and History exams in the not-so-distant past, I am familiar with not only the tests themselves but also the mental and emotional strains involved in preparing for them.
- The nature of my two areas of expertise has engendered a collateral familiarity with related disciplines, such as history, as well as a facility in acquainting myself with the rudiments of unfamiliar Humanities disciplines on short notice.
- Through my work with mentally challenged children at _____, I have become well-versed in the patience and tact required of an educator, as well as empathetic to the challenges facing students for whom the promise of academic excellence is not compelling, or not viable.
- Because I intend to go on to graduate school and become a professor, I have a profound commitment not only to excel in teaching but to inspire in students the devotion to learning that informs every aspect of my own life. Through tutoring, I hope to learn every bit as much as students will potentially learn from me.
- Through my work as an editor and copy-editor, I have had ample experience using my knowledge of English grammar, syntax, and argument structure to improve the work of even professional authors, and doing so in a way that is both encouraging and sensitive to the feelings of the writer.

I appreciate your taking the time to review these credentials and my attached resume, and hope that we can talk soon. I am available at any time at the telephone number below.

Sincerely,

Your Name
(555) 555-1234
Attachment: resume

Voice & Articulation Adjunct Faculty

From: Your Name [Your e-mail address]
To: Recipient e-mail address
Cc:
Subject: Voice & Articulation adjunct faculty

Dear Recipient Name:

Your posting for **Voice & Articulation** adjunct faculty captured my serious interest. My 25 years' experience as a Speech Therapist in the ___ provides me with all the skills you seek.
Some key points you may find relevant include:

✓ *Experience assessing needs of, and providing instruction to, the disabled. In my current position, I work one-on-one with students with hearing loss, emotional disorders, ADHD, autism, and other physical disabilities impacting their ability to acquire speech. I also develop IEPs and participate in the CSE process to define students' needs and implement instruction plans.*

✓ *Excellent leadership skills, with experience mentoring co-workers. Currently, I mentor speech therapists and teachers working with hearing-impaired students, as well as direct the activities of two other speech therapists.*

✓ *A Master's Degree in Speech Pathology, plus NYS Certification as a Speech & Hearing Handicapped Teacher. In addition, I have attended workshops in Phonemic Awareness, Autism, and Pervasive Developmental Disorders.*

In my current role, I am accountable for addressing the needs of approximately 300 elementary and secondary school students with various speech deficiencies. I believe that my knowledge and expertise would allow me to effectively serve your students in this Voice & Articulation instructional role.

Thank you for your time and consideration. I look forward to speaking with you soon. Please contact me via phone or e-mail to arrange a mutually convenient date and time for us to meet. My resume is attached.

Sincerely,

Your Name
(555) 555-1234
Your e-mail address

DIRECT APPROACH TO POTENTIAL EMPLOYERS

Accountant—MBA

From: Your Name [Your e-mail address]
To: Recipient e-mail address
Cc:
Subject: Accountant, AR/AP/AUDITS/MBA

Dear Recipient Name:

Just completing my MBA in Accounting at _____ __ _____. Some of the key experiences I can bring to an entry-level position with your firm include:

- **Administering Accounts Receivable and Payroll for an engineering firm that was also engaged in construction and some custom manufacturing.**

- **Preparing individual tax returns as part of a volunteer program in conjunction with CIT.**

- **Serving as Treasurer of a campus organization, Delta Beta Gamma, which encompassed maintaining financial records and providing financial reports to the auditing CPA and to the national organization.**

- **Proficiency with basic Windows and Microsoft Office applications, as well as a keen interest in technology and high-tech businesses.**

I hope to join an organization where I can learn and grow, following the traditional paths to CPA and partnership. I would enjoy speaking with you to discuss the possibilities that exist and how I might best serve the needs of your firm and your clients. Please call me at **(555) 555-1234**, I look forward to opening a dialogue with you soon.

Very truly yours,

Your Name
(555) 555-1234
Attachment: resume

Accounting Management

Dear Recipient Name,

With proven capabilities in financial analysis and accounting management, I hope that my education and experience could benefit your company. For this reason, I have attached a resume for your review. Some key qualifications:

- 7 years' experience providing timely and accurate financial reports utilizing a variety of applications and procedures. I manage accounting functions for a manufacturing firm with over $100 million sales. I advanced quickly in the finance department and have gained a wide range of experiences, primarily focusing my efforts on analyzing, reporting, and planning.

- Absolute reliability and dedication to efficiency. I work closely with controllers and managers in monitoring financial input/output, streamlining financial reporting processes, and meeting aggressive deadlines for delivering information and analyses. I am also knowledgeable and current on legislative and regulatory requirements.

- Planning and budgets. I participate in both strategic planning for long-term marketing, and in annual budget preparation. My analyses and input have contributed to the successful outcomes of external audits, annual reviews, and budgeting processes in domestic operations.

- Proficiency in current business applications, including CODA, DCS, 4TH Shift, FAS1000, MP 2, FOCUS, and Microsoft Office.

I have a strong desire to move into a business environment where my skills can be fully utilized in a more secure environment. I am confident that my track record, along with my dedicated professionalism, would allow me to make a significant contribution. I would enjoy meeting with you to further discuss the possibilities.

Please review the attached resume. Thank you for your time and consideration. I look forward to speaking with you soon.

Sincerely,

Your Name
(555) 555-1234
Attachment: resume

Career Change to Teaching

From: Your Name [Your e-mail address]
To: Recipient e-mail address
Cc:
Subject: Japanese-Speaking English Teacher

Dear Recipient Name,

With this letter, I would like to introduce myself and share my sincere motivation to teach English in Japan. My experience as a substitute middle school teacher has helped me to understand methods of student interaction and reach a level of comfort in the classroom.

I strive to build relationships with students and to facilitate classroom activities and inspire the learners. It is something I truly enjoy.

The _____ website encourages "all outgoing, dynamic, and flexible people to apply." In my current position as a flight attendant for Hawaii Wings Airlines, I am required to demonstrate these characteristics daily. Communication and quick-thinking skills are a must onboard an aircraft full of passengers. Flexibility is essential in the areas of customer service, in interaction with colleagues, and in work scheduling.

My motivation is indeed genuine. I speak conversational Japanese and I look forward to the possibility of discussing the opportunity with you. I will gladly make myself available for a telephone or videoconference interview. My resume is attached for your review.

Respectfully,

Your Name
(555) 555-1234
Attachment: resume

Career Change—Marketing to Finance

From: Your Name [Your e-mail address]
To: Recipient e-mail address
Cc:
Subject: Finance: Accounting Manager/Director, Controller/Treasurer

Dear Recipient Name,

I have ten years' successful experience within financial services marketing, and will receive my CPA within two months. With this unique combination of skills and awareness, I now hope to segue into a more distinct financial management position such as accounting Manager, Controller, or Treasurer.

As an Account Manager in financial services, I know many different industries, and my marketing savvy would be of unusual benefit to any company seeking someone with these titles.

My understanding of the revenue generating function *and* the revenue protection and leveraging function, especially of financial services companies, gives me a very special frame of reference on my chosen path. As an executive recruiter, I am sure you can appreciate this.

I have attached my resume, which will flesh out my unusual and desirable background; I would appreciate your input. I am available for interviews, and can be reached at 555.555.1234. Please consider me available as a resource for your other searches within my profession.

Yours truly,

Your Name
(555) 555-1234
Attachment: resume

Career Change to Railroad Industry

From: Your Name [Your e-mail address]
To: Recipient e-mail address
Cc:
Subject: 2o years in transportation

Dear Recipient Name,

    With 20 years' experience in transportation, I am seeking a job opportunity that will help me achieve my long-time goal of working in the railroad industry.

    Attached for your review is a resume that briefly outlines my relevant qualifications. Some of the key skills that I believe make me a strong candidate for a position with your rail line include:

- **Significant experience as an Equipment Operator and Truck Driver.**

- **Experience dispatching for the New York State Dept. of Transportation.**

- **An excellent aptitude and desire to learn new tasks.**

- **An enjoyment of and willingness to work outdoors - in all weather conditions.**

- **Exceptional attention to detail and accuracy in my work.**

- **Responsible worker who is dedicated to consistently exceeding expectations.**

    I understand the structure of the rail industry and am more than willing to accept an entry-level position (and all the challenges that go with it) in order to get the opportunity to break in with a railroad line. I would enjoy speaking with you in person about how I could fill a need for your company. I look forward to talking with you soon, please email or call me at (555) 555-1234.

Sincerely,

Your Name
(555) 555-1234
Attachment: resume

Career Change to Pharmaceutical Sales

From: Your Name [Your e-mail address]
To: Recipient e-mail address
Cc:
Subject: Pharmaceutical Sales

Dear Recipient Name,

I currently hold a sales management position for a very successful retail company. My talents at achieving high sales volume, working cooperatively with diverse personalities, and providing exceptional customer service have allowed me to excel in customer relations and succeed in sales and marketing.

I want to extend my experience to the pharmaceutical sales field. I thoroughly understand the importance of developing customer relations, generating revenue from sales potential within a designated territory, and maintaining accurate customer information. Pharmaceutical sales have been an interest of mine for some time, and I am confident that my background will allow me to make the transition without difficulty.

I have the aptitude and willingness to learn the necessary technical and medical materials to promote your products intelligently. What I may lack in specific experience, I more than make up for with my dedication, energy, and determination.

Your time in reviewing my attached, confidential resume is greatly appreciated. I will follow up next week to answer any questions you may have regarding my qualifications. At that time, I would like to discuss the possibility of setting up a personal interview at your convenience. Please contact me if you would like to speak sooner.

Very truly yours,

Your Name
(555) 555-1234
Attachment: resume

Chief Financial Officer

From: Your Name [Your e-mail address]
To: Recipient e-mail address
Cc:
Subject: CFO, global and boardroom performer

Dear Recipient Name,

As a Chief Financial Officer, I have built a reputation for strategic business and financial planning for global corporations. My ability to identify challenges to, and capitalize upon, opportunities to expand revenue growth, reduce operating costs, and improve overall productivity has always been one of my strongest assets.

My strengths in financial and accounting management as well as my thorough understanding of finance operations have vastly contributed to my career and success as a leader. I maintain the self-confidence, credibility, and stature to make things happen with colleagues. Just as significant are my abilities to develop rapport among subordinates, coworkers, executive management groups, and the board.

My objective is to secure a position as a CFO or Vice President, and to pursue new opportunities with an organization providing new and exciting challenges. Having a complete picture of my expertise and experience is very important. As you will note in my resume, I have made significant contributions to my employers, and take my job very seriously.

I appreciate your time and consideration, and will be in contact next week to see if we are able to schedule a meeting date for an interview. I look forward to speaking with you soon. My resume is attached for your review.

Regards,

Your Name
(555) 555-1234
Attachment: resume

Credit-Collections

From: Your Name [Your e-mail address]
To: Recipient e-mail address
Cc:
Subject: Credit/Collections applications job posting

Dear Recipient Name,

I bring 18+ years of accounts receivable experience in addition to being involved in all processing stages of collections, resolving payment issues, and collecting on past due payments. The scope of my experience includes, but is not limited to, commercial, automotive, and manufacturing environments.

I focus on delivering results and providing superior service by quickly identifying problem areas in accounts receivable and developing a solution strategy to ensure issues are resolved. My expertise lies in my strong ability to build rapport with clients, analyze accounts, and manage all aspects related to my appointed position and areas of responsibilities.

Due to circumstances beyond my control, I was unable to continue my employment as a cash applications analyst with a well-known automotive industry leader. My objective is to secure a position in accounts receivable and credit collections with an established company.

My attached resume details my skills, experience, and the contributions I have made to employers. I look forward to speaking with you soon and answering any questions you may have regarding my background, and I will follow up with you next week.

Regards,

Your Name
(555) 555-1234
Attachment: resume

Customer Service

From: Your Name [Your e-mail address]
To: Recipient e-mail address
Cc:
Subject: Customer Service Specialist, organized, calm, analytical, solution-oriented

Dear Recipient Name,

Are you looking for a Senior Customer Service Specialist who is:

* A team player able to achieve results through coordination with employees in all functional areas?
* An effective communicator with excellent writing, training, and telephone skills?
* Able to learn quickly, analyze complex information, and find solutions to problems?
* Organized, thorough, and precise?

If so, you will be interested in my qualifications. I have a bachelor's degree in Business Administration and 7 years' experience in the insurance/financial indus-tries, serving as Customer Relations Advisor and Calculations Processor.

I consistently receive the highest rating in my unit despite the fact that the difficult cases frequently find their way to my desk. I also contribute to my team by putting in extra time to clear backlogs and analyzing existing procedures to devise more efficient methods of operation.

My resume is attached for your review. If you think that I can make a positive contri-bution to _____, I look forward to meeting with you to discuss my qualifications in detail. Thank you for your time and consideration.

Sincerely,

Your Name
(555) 555-1234
Attachment: resume

Dedicated Assisted Care

From: Your Name [Your e-mail address]
To: Recipient e-mail address
Cc:
Subject: Your dedicated assisted care mission

Dear Recipient Name,

I was captivated by your company's mission statement when I visited the website. Your dedication of resources within assisted care facilities grabbed my attention because, as my attached PDF resume indicates, it is precisely my area of expertise.

I am currently employed by one of your major competitors, I have 7 years' experience in dedicated assisted care, and I am looking to make a strategic career move. I hope we might find time to discuss possibilities.

Sincerely,

Your Name
(555) 555-1234
Attachment: resume

Direction Shift Within Sales

From: Your Name [Your e-mail address]
To: Recipient e-mail address
Cc:
Subject: B-to-B sales professional

Dear Recipient Name,

Having spent 5 years as an executive recruiter, I realize how many resumes you receive on a daily basis. I also remember how valuable a few always turned out to be.

My background, skills, and talents are in all aspects of sales and sales management. As job search is the only field of sales where the products talk back, I am confident that my skills will readily translate into less complex sales environments. My research indicates that your expertise is in this broad Sales/Marketing area.

I have attached my resume, which highlights my skills and supports my objectives. I would appreciate the opportunity to meet and exchange ideas. I will call you over the next few days to make an appointment. If you prefer, you may reach me by e-mail or in the evening at (555) 555-1234.

Thank you; I look forward to speaking.

Sincerely,

Your Name
(555) 555-1234
Attachment: resume

EMEA Account Management

Dear Recipient Name,

It has been said, *"in today's world there are two kinds of companies—the quick and the dead."* I propose the same is true of managers. I am a dynamic sales management professional with extraordinary team-building and interpersonal skills, and thrive in a global market.

I've held direct responsibility for commercial dealings with the UK, Ireland, and Germany; bilingual, my translation skills are strong in both languages. I also have conversational knowledge of French. I have a remarkable knack for capturing key client relations with diverse cultures and people. I would like to bring my business savvy and management/marketing skills to your company.

My experience spans Real Estate Development, International Affairs, and Procurement, a frame of reference relevant to any company with global aspirations. I never run from a difficult situation. If you want a successful outcome, you can count on it—accurately, timely, and right the first time.

Dedicated to doing whatever it takes to achieve outstanding results, I will lead your team to meet tight deadlines. In short, I will not let you down. Outstanding references will verify these claims.

Please see my attached resume. I look forward to meeting with you to discuss your needs and the immediate impact I can make.

Best regards,

Your Name
(555) 555-1234
Attachment: resume

Entry-Level Chemical Engineer

From: Your Name [Your e-mail address]
To: Recipient e-mail address
Cc:
Subject: Entry-Level Chemical Engineer

Dear Recipient Name,

Following my recent graduation from _____ University with a **Bachelor of Science Degree in Chemical Engineering**, I am currently seeking an entry-level position in the Energy Industry. I offer more than two years of hands-on experience, a strong work ethic, and commitment to personal and company success.

Representative of my qualifications and accomplishments:

- Graduated with honors, including being named to the *Engineering Dean's List*.

- Gained valuable hands-on laboratory experience as a Lab Assistant for two years in the *Dow Chemical Engineering Lab*, working on nanoparticle suspension projects.

- Completed a summer internship with _____ *Nutrition*, where I experienced and managed real-world corporate challenges and honed team-based communication skills.

I work hard, contribute, collaborate, and strive to deliver strong and sustained contributions to organizational goals. I learn quickly, thrive on challenges, and am flexible in adapting to new environments. I am always willing to go the extra mile, no matter what the task.

While my resume provides an overview of my past performance, I look forward to a personal meeting at which we can discuss my desire to start at the bottom and earn the right to become a respected member of your team. Thank you for your consideration.

Sincerely,

Your Name
(555) 555-1234
Attachment: resume

Entry-Level Entertainment

From: Your Name [Your e-mail address]
To: Recipient e-mail address
Cc:
Subject: Entry-Level Entertainment Industry

Dear Recipient Name,

If you are looking for a highly motivated recent college graduate, with a BA in Communications and work experience with production companies, who understands that you start at the bottom, then we should talk.

I offer a combination of creative talents and a strong work ethic as well as the following qualifications:

- BA in Communications from the University of _____.

- Hands-on experience directing, acting in, and producing short independent and student films.

- Realistic understanding of the demands of the entertainment industry, gained through internships for TV production companies.

- Operating knowledge of a wide variety of audio and video equipment.

Please review my attached resume. I will call you next week to schedule a meeting; you can contact me at this e-mail address or the number below. Thank you for your time and consideration.

Sincerely,

Your Name
(555) 555-1234
Attachment: resume

Entry-Level Media Production

From: Your Name [Your e-mail address]
To: Recipient e-mail address
Cc:
Subject: Entry-Level Media Production

Dear Recipient Name,

Do you need a tenacious and driven Production Assistant? Having completed classes, I will be granted a BA in Journalism from _____ in December, but I am eager to start my career now. I held two jobs while attending school, and will have completed my degree in three years. It is with the same passion, integrity, and energy that I intend to pursue my career.

"I would rank Ms._____'s work in the top 10% of students I have taught; she is not afraid to tackle tough projects; I believe she has the ability to quickly make positive contributions."
**** *******, Ph.D., Chairperson, Department of Communications, _____ College

"_____ was an exemplary Journalism major. She took charge of the tasks given to her and performed them in a superior manner. I admire her strong enthusiasm and her attention to detail."
****** ****, Assistant Director of Television Technical Operations, _____ College

I possess the talent for a career in media and an understanding of how demanding it can be. But unlike most, I am willing to "pay the price" of hard work, rough work schedules, and the total availability that the industry requires.

I am eager to learn more about the challenges facing your organization and to discuss how I can make a difference. Please review my attached resume, and thanks so much for your consideration.

Regards,

Your Name
(555) 555-1234
Attachment: resume

Entry-Level Network Administrator

From: Your Name [Your e-mail address]
To: Recipient e-mail address
Cc:
Subject: Entry-level Network Administrator

Dear Recipient Name,

With my **MCP Certification**, and imminent **A++ Network Certification**, I am seeking an **entry-level Network Administrator** position. A brief highlight of the skills and values I would bring to your organization includes:

- Knowledge of installation, configuration, troubleshooting, and repair of sophisticated, state-of-the-art software and hardware.

- Acquired analytical, research, troubleshooting, interpersonal, and organizational skills developed through on-the-job training within an IT environment.

- Proven success in prioritizing time, completing projects, and meeting deadlines under time-sensitive circumstances, achieving stellar results.

- An energetic, enthusiastic, and "people-driven" communication style.

I would welcome a personal interview to further explore the merging of my training and knowledge with your **IT** needs. My resume is attached, and I thank you for your consideration.

Very truly yours,

Your Name
(555) 555-1234
Attachment: resume

Entry-Level Pharmaceutical Sales

From: Your Name [Your e-mail address]
To: Recipient e-mail address
Cc:
Subject: Entry-Level Pharmaceutical Sales

Dear Recipient Name,

Since you are one of the most respected pharmaceutical companies in the industry, I am eager to make a contribution to your team as a Pharmaceutical Sales Representative.

As a recent graduate with a BA in Marketing, my professional experience is limited. However, I believe you will find that I exhibit intelligence, common sense, initiative, maturity, and stability. I would also like to bring these three relevant points to your attention:

1. As the daughter of a physician, sister of a nurse, and cousin of a surgeon, I have had a lifetime of exposure to the medical community, and this gives me a greater than expected grounding in healthcare and its terminology compared to most candidates.
2. It also gives me insight into the way physicians think, evaluate, and make decisions. For example, I know product presentations must be made in a timely, succinct, and caring manner for successful sales in this industry.
3. In the last 18 months, since I made my decision to join the pharmaceutical industry, I have had intensive tutoring from family members.

I believe you will be impressed with my grasp of the sales process, and very pleasantly surprised with the depth of my understanding of the people who make up the target customer base.

After reviewing the attached resume, please e-mail or contact me at (555) 555-1234 to arrange an interview. I look forward to discussing how my qualifications can meet your personnel needs and contribute to your company's important mission.

Sincerely,

Your Name
(555) 555-1234
Attachment: resume

Executive Chef

From: Your Name [Your e-mail address]
To: Recipient e-mail address
Cc:
Subject: Executive Chef

Dear Recipient Name,

I am confident that my 23 years' experience as an executive chef and hotel/restaurant manager would become an asset in your organization.

I have been the General Manager and Corporate Executive Chef of _____, a division of _____, since its opening in 1999. Responsible for menus, staffing, liquor, publicity, on- and off-site event catering (up to 7,000), and many _____ ____ City premiers.

Beyond the obvious, I deliver all the skills you would expect of an executive chef in the nation's most competitive market. I have prepared food and special events for heads of state, celebrities, and society. I am responsible for all financial reporting and control systems to the parent company, and am experienced in all aspects of new construction and kitchen design.

Prior to this, as Vice President of Operations and Executive Chef for _____ Country Club, I oversaw all profit and loss functions for a 165-seat à la carte restaurant and a 1,000-seat banquet facility. I managed the club's 18-hole Championship Golf Course, which had an active membership of 1,000 members.

Thank you for your consideration. I look forward to speaking with you personally regarding my qualifications and how I can contribute positively as a member of your management staff. My resume is attached for your review.

Sincerely,

Your Name
(555) 555-1234
Attachment: resume

Facility-Maintenance Mechanic

From: Your Name [Your e-mail address]
To: Recipient e-mail address
Cc:
Subject: Facility/Maintenance Mechanic

Dear Recipient Name,

As a Facilities and Maintenance Mechanic with 16 years' experience, I understand that the timely maintenance and repair of machinery, supervision of maintenance programs, and monitoring of outside contractors have a real impact on company reputation and success.

Throughout my career, I have always been promoted and successfully assumed increasing responsibilities. In my latest position as a Mechanic for _____ Foods, I had a reputation for excellent machinery knowledge and a keen attention to detail.

_____ Foods is downsizing the plant in ____, __, and I have accepted a voluntary separation package. I would like to continue my career with a new company offering me new challenges.

Thank you for your consideration. I hope that this letter and my attached resume grab your attention so that we may discuss how I can make a positive contribution to your team. I look forward to hearing from you.

Sincerely,

Your Name
(555) 555-1234
Attachment: resume

Finance Intern

Dear Recipient Name,

Are you looking for a driven, overachieving intern committed to excelling in business and finance?

As a junior at _____ University, I am pursuing a BS with a major in Finance. My passion for financial markets and economics has steadily increased over the last five years, and I am committed to following a career path as a business leader within a major corporation. I am enthusiastic about working at _____ .

I approach all of my work with discipline and focus; and as an intern with _____ , I have the energy and commitment to make a meaningful contribution to your program goals. _____ University, Cushing Academy, and The Boys Club of New York have acknowledged my academic and leadership achievements for excellence in academic studies, volunteerism, and peer mentoring.

Please review my attached resume and feel free to contact me at _____ . Thank you for your consideration.

Sincerely,

Your Name
(555) 555-1234
Attachment: resume

Finance Management

From: Your Name [Your e-mail address]
To: Recipient e-mail address
Cc:
Subject: Finance Management with CPA

Dear Recipient Name,

As a Certified Public Accountant with solid experience as a **Chief Financial Officer** and a **Vice President of Finance**, I understand that success depends on the bottom line, with special attention to financial and managerial teamwork. I believe that my background and accomplishments have proven to be a productive combination.

Throughout my career, I have been assigned increasing responsibilities and significantly contributed to corporate growth in Architectural, Engineering, and Construction sectors. Here are some accomplishments:

- Increased shareholder distribution from zero in _____ to $1.3 million and $1.5 million in _____ and _____, respectively, in spite of a 20% revenue shrinkage over the same time period.
- Improved cash flow more than $3 million in 6 months.
- Grew profit margin from 3% to 10% for 3 consecutive years, *the best in company history*.
- Reduced overhead from 170% to 120% in direct labor.
- Trimmed DOS 21% from 85 to 67 days.

Thank you for your consideration. Please see my attached resume. I look forward to speaking with you to discuss how I might make a positive contribution to your operation.

Sincerely,

Your Name
(555) 555-1234
Attachment: resume

Financial Planner

From: Your Name [Your e-mail address]
To: Recipient e-mail address
Cc:
Subject: Financial Planner

Dear Recipient Name,

The Rock, a corporate symbol supported by the slogan "Growing and Protecting Your Wealth," is a premier brand that can only be sustained through principled management, effective investment strategies, and ethical financial planners. I am a financial planner who strictly adheres to these same principles.

As an accomplished, credentialed, and ethical financial planner, my qualifications include:

* Series 7 and 66 Licensing.
* Registered Investment Advisor.
* BA in Economics.
* Consultative and needs assessment approach.
* The communication and presentation skills necessary to articulate product benefits.
* Outstanding time management and organizational ability.
* A willingness to "go the extra mile" for client and corporation.

I am skilled at new business development, cold calling, and seminar presentations. Employers and colleagues have consistently praised my attention to detail, strong work ethic, and ability to deal with the most complex client engagements.

I am confident that upon review of my attached resume you will find I possess the solid combination of experience and achievement that _____ looks for in its representatives.

I look forward to hearing from you.

Sincerely,

Your Name
(555) 555-1234
Attachment: resume

HR Generalist

From: Your Name [Your e-mail address]
To: Recipient e-mail address
Cc:
Subject: HR Generalist, M&A and re-org experienced

Dear Recipient Name,

Your recent growth might require someone acclimated to working with new subsidiaries and maintaining corporate policies and procedures. If your organization seeks someone to ensure the integrity of human resource programs with new subsidiaries, please consider my track record:

* 15 years' diverse HR experience.
* 5 mergers and reorganizations.
* 9 years advising senior decision-makers on employee matters.
* 5 years in benefits administration for $1B company and 5 affiliates.
* 15 years delivering HR presentations.
* Open enrollment/benefits processing for professional employees.
* 13 years' grievance/disciplinary meeting involvement.
* 10+ years' training/development, entry through professional levels.

If you need a seasoned HR generalist who can interface with decision-makers and keep you 100 percent compliant with federal regulations, I am awaiting your call.

However, I know how busy you must be right now, so I will initiate contact on Monday at 11.30 a.m. Central. My resume is attached for your review. I look forward to talking, meeting, and, given your needs and our having chemistry, perhaps joining the team.

Sincerely,

Your Name
(555) 555-1234
Attachment: resume

Inside Sales

Dear Recipient Name,

My first job in sales management was right out of college, running a beach bar. My competitors were like pesky flies—they kept popping up everywhere, opening with lots of glitz, taking all the customers, and then crashing and burning after six months. But during those six months they were trying to take all <u>my</u> customers!

These were serious challenges, to which I responded with the best strategies and tactics I could coordinate—free pool playing, fruity drinks for girls, sports TV for the guys. I even gave away free beer one night.

Today I am the same aggressive, ambitious sales professional I was then. OK . . . these days I wouldn't give away free beer, but I <u>do</u> respond to sales challenges with all the competitiveness, creativity, and customer concern in my heart. In my last sales position, I was quite successful selling vacation packages by telephone for several reasons:

- I qualified my targets well.
- I was knowledgeable about the product and customer's motivators for that product.
- I think well and profitably on my feet.
- I'm honest and a natural rapport-builder.

The point of my attached resume is that I would like to talk with you about putting my sales, problem-solving, and customer service skills to work for your organization. When can we meet? My resume is attached for your review.

Sincerely,

Your Name
(555) 555-1234
Attachment: resume

International Relations Intern

From: Your Name [Your e-mail address]
To: Recipient e-mail address
Cc:
Subject: International Relations Intern

Dear Recipient Name,

I am interested in being considered for an internship. I am currently a senior at the University of _____ majoring in International Studies with a concentration in Latin America and a minor in Political Science. I speak and write Spanish.

Previous internships have increased my knowledge of International Relations and have enabled me to make use of my education in a professional environment. I am very serious about my education and future career, and am eager to learn as much as possible throughout my internship.

My references will confirm that I tackle any task, no matter how humble or complex, with skill and enthusiasm. As a highly motivated professional, I enjoy the challenge of complex, demanding assignments. My well-developed writing and communication skills are assets when dealing with such challenges.

I would welcome the opportunity to discuss how I could make a contribution to your organization as an intern. Please review my attached resume; I look forward to talking with you soon. Thank you.

Sincerely,

Your Name
(555) 555-1234
Attachment: resume

IT Consultant

Dear Recipient Name,

- Is your organization fully prepared to safeguard its technology services, information, and facilities in the event of disaster?
- Are you taking full advantage of high-value and cost-effective vendor agreements?
- Do you benefit from high team performance and low turnover?

If you have answered "No" to any of the above questions, then allow me to introduce myself and the expertise I can offer your organization.

My expertise is delivering results. I design, implement, manage, and optimize comprehensive enterprise-class disaster recovery and information security systems and procedures.

- **Expert in Disaster Recovery, Information Security, and Business Continuity—** expertise includes planning, protection, and off-site recovery of technology services, databases, and facilities.
- **Superior contract procurement, negotiation, and vendor management capabilities—**proven record for negotiating agreements that improve service quality and save millions in vendor costs.
- **Strong, decisive, and motivational leader—**reputation for building and leading high-performance teams to breakthrough achievement.

These abilities have saved millions in vendor negotiations and third-party service agreements, optimized and secured company performance, and led a variety of cross-functional teams consistently to achieve and exceed organizational mandates.

If this interests you, I invite you to review the attached resume. I am available for full-time, part-time, contract, and consulting assignments. I thank you for your consideration, and I look forward to speaking with you soon.

Sincerely,

Your Name
(555) 555-1234
Attachment: resume

IT Project Manager

From: Your Name [Your e-mail address]
To: Recipient e-mail address
Cc:
Subject: IT Project Manager

Dear Recipient Name:

Information technology expertise, combined with steady leadership and the ability to motivate cross-functional teams and develop cost-effective solutions, are key to creating long-term customer satisfaction and loyalty.

As a seasoned **Project Manager** experienced in providing strategic direction in the design and deployment of technology solutions, I have:

- Successfully managed customer accounts from defining project requirements through implementation.

- Engineered e-commerce business solutions for myriad organizations from start-up ventures to *Fortune* 500 companies.

- Completed all of the coursework, including specialized electives, to obtain the Microsoft Certified Systems Engineer designation.

- Developed comprehensive RFIs and RFPs; selected the most qualified, cost-effective vendor; and directed cross-functional teams to ensure on-time, on-budget implementation.

- Efficiently prioritized projects, developed realistic timelines, and consistently met deadlines.

- Compiled and driven ratification of product requirements.

- Provided technical expertise to sales teams to assist them in closing the sale.

Could your company use a high-achiever with a thirst for growth and new challenges? If so, I would like to discuss how my skills and experience could benefit your organization. I have attached my resume for your consideration, and look forward to speaking with you.

Sincerely,

Your Name
(555) 555-1234
Attachment: resume

Logistics

Dear Recipient Name,

An industry association referred to your organization as an active and selective executive search firm because of your work in logistics. I liked that referral and think my experience might be of interest.

I have a 7-year career using logistics to cut costs and improve profits, usually in concert with other parts of the business. For example:

- I supervised the start-up of several remote offices to assist our plants in improving their distribution operations. By offering customized service, and through sharp negotiations, we saved over $500 million in operations and warehouse costs.

- I directed the efforts of sizeable computer resources in the design and installation of a major application that saved $2.5 million in carrier costs. The application became the standard throughout the company's 46 locations.

- Working with International Sales, I established Quality Control programs that have improved the timeliness, accuracy, and speed of product delivery. Customer complaints plummeted to virtually zero, and remain there today.

A recent reorganization has reduced the number of growth opportunities within my company. I have concluded that another firm may offer a position and career advancement more in line with my personal expectations.

Please see my attached resume; I would like to talk with you about options. I suggest next week, the week of October 29, when you have a free minute. Please e-mail or call my cell number below. I look forward to hearing from you.

Sincerely,

Your Name
(555) 555-1234
Attachment: resume

Mental Health Care

From: Your Name [Your e-mail address]
To: Recipient e-mail address
Cc:
Subject: Mental Health Care

Dear Recipient Name,

Throughout my 17-year career within the mental health profession, I have held increasingly complex positions, gaining extensive experience in working both with patients and in administrative functions. My particular areas of expertise are:

- Physical Medicine and Rehabilitation
- Adult Intervention
- Family Counseling
- Legal Issues
- Government Regulations
- Child Evaluation

Working with patients, physicians, legal officers, and family members has enabled me to be a highly effective therapist and an advocate for the patient and the patient's family.

As a Veterans Administration official, I understand the intricacies of the federal bureaucracy, and know how to navigate the workings of government agencies as they relate to mental health, including the Social Security Administration, Department of Veterans Affairs, Department of Defense, and other entities.

I desire to *return* to a more focused health care organization, and would welcome an opportunity to interview with you in person. I feel my knowledge and strengths would be best applied as a consultant somewhere within Mental Rehabilitation Therapy.

I look forward to speaking with you at your earliest convenience, and appreciate your time in reviewing my credentials and qualifications. I am confident that my professional knowledge and strengths, combined with my dedication, work ethic, and energy, will add measurable value to your organization. Thank you for your consideration. Please review my attached resume.

Sincerely,

Your Name
(555) 555-1234
Attachment: resume

Military to Civilian

From: Your Name [Your e-mail address]
To: Recipient e-mail address
Cc:
Subject: RN, emergency/post-op/medical/infectious disease/oncology/end-of-life/crisis

Dear Recipient Name,

In anticipation of completing my military service in April 2011, I am seeking a civilian position that will capitalize on my experience and training as a US Navy Registered Nurse. I believe that my clinical background and specialized training in emergency response and crisis management would make me an asset to your nursing staff. With this in mind, I have attached a resume for your review that outlines my credentials.

Some key points you may find relevant include:

- **Caring for a broad array of patients, ranging from infants to senior citizens, and including post-operative, medical, infectious disease, oncology, and end-of-life scenarios.**

- **Developing rapport with diverse cultural groups, both in clinical and social settings. The patients I have dealt with cut across the full spectrum of ethnic and socioeconomic strata, from enlisted personnel to flag officers and their dependents.**

- **Completing training and engaging in field exercises that have prepared me for disaster response in a civilian community.**

I am confident that my dedication to caring for patients, and desire to become an integral part of a treatment team, would allow me to make a significant contribution to the health and well-being of your patients.

Please contact me via phone or e-mail to discuss how I might fulfill your needs in a clinical nursing role. Thank you for your time and consideration. I look forward to speaking with you soon.

Sincerely,

Your Name
(555) 555-1234
Attachment: resume

Mutual Funds Advisor

Dear Recipient Name,

I am an investment professional with unique experience as both a financial advisor and someone who has sold to financial advisors. I also have considerable complementary experience in mutual fund research and work with high-net–worth investors.

With 16+ years' experience in asset management, mutual fund analytics, sales, marketing, research, client relationship management, financial advising, and more, my experience gives me unusual insight into the nuances of investment strategy and client relationship management—assets *consistently recognized* by my employers.

At _____, as a Senior Sales Consultant, I have developed a solid reputation for raising the bar and establishing greater visibility and credibility for our team's professional role. I am interested in talking with you about opportunities at _____, involving investment analysis, product management, mutual fund investment strategy analysis, and product and platform analytics and research.

I have attached my resume to furnish you with specifics regarding my background, skills, and experience, and I am confident that you will find sufficient merit in my qualifications to warrant further investigation.

Thank you for your courtesy in reviewing my qualifications. I look forward to the opportunity of discussing my ability to make a meaningful contribution toward your goals.

Sincerely,

Your Name
(555) 555-1234
Attachment: resume

Production Assistant, Publishing

From: Your Name [Your e-mail address]
To: Recipient e-mail address
Cc:
Subject: PA Publishing

Dear Recipient Name:

In the interest of exploring opportunities in the publishing industry, I have enclosed my resume for your review. Over the last two years, I have gained valuable knowledge and experience in many aspects of personnel assistance, office procedures, and administrative operations.

Recently I volunteered my time to edit a cookbook, and have been responsible for editing the newsletter for my sorority. I consider myself a good writer and an avid reader, and have always wanted to get into publishing.

With my considerable energy, drive, and ability to work long hours, I believe I could make a positive contribution to your organization, and I would appreciate the opportunity to discuss my qualifications at your earliest convenience.

Thank you for your time and consideration. I look forward to meeting with you. My resume is attached for your review.

Respectfully,

Your Name
(555) 555-1234
Attachment: resume

Physician's Assistant

Dear Recipient Name,

As a Physician's Assistant with 2 years of clinical experience in an emergency department setting and 20 years in other aspects of emergency medical services, I hope to utilize my skills in an emergency medicine position at your hospital.

In addition to a BS from _____ Institute of Technology, I have extensive training and experience in emergency medicine. Some of the highlights of my background include:

➤ Over twenty years' experience as a volunteer and as paid staff for the Henrietta Volunteer Ambulance Corps in suburban _____. In addition to logging over 7,600 active duty hours, I served as Vice President/General Manager for this busy service, which answers over 4,700 calls each year. In this position, I was responsible for all operational aspects of the services provided.

➤ Three years' experience as a Flight Paramedic for Mercy Flight. I provided critical care to patients being transported by this air medical service that covers an 11-county region, transporting patients to critical care facilities.

➤ Nearly two years' experience in _____ General Hospital's Emergency Department, treating a wide array of patients, from infants to senior citizens, with cases ranging from acute injuries and medical conditions to routine, non-acute cases.

I hope you will agree that my education, training, and experience have prepared me to contribute effectively to the care of your patients. I would enjoy speaking with you about opportunities that may exist and how I can best serve your needs. Please e-mail or call me at the number below to arrange a time for us to meet. I have attached my resume and look forward to speaking with you soon.

Sincerely,

Your Name
(555) 555-1234
Attachment: resume

Purchasing Manager

From: Your Name [Your e-mail address]
To: Recipient e-mail address
Cc:
Subject: Smart Purchasing Choice

Dear Recipient Name,

Do you cringe at the high costs your company incurs for goods and services?

Do you need someone who will maximize vendor resources, working hard to secure lower-cost, longer-term contracts?

Do you need someone who will immediately slash supply costs and streamline purchasing operations?

With more than 20 years in purchasing, retail sales management, store expansions, and new product research and market launch, I believe I may offer just what you're missing.

In my career with _____, a premier auto parts and accessories distributor, I have:

- Directed procurement of over $200M of goods and services, accounting for 60% of _____'s total purchasing budget.
- Launched 3 private label programs, garnering $500K in additional profits during the first year of distribution alone.
- Recouped $300K in stolen merchandise and prosecuted the employees responsible.
- Generated $3M in savings by cultivating partnerships and negotiating long-term contracts with key suppliers.

If you're tired of seeing your company's profits slip through your fingers, please review my attached resume and call me today to schedule a meeting. I can't wait to discuss how I might benefit your purchasing operation right away.

Very truly yours,

Your Name
(555) 555-1234
Attachment: resume

Radiation Safety Officer

From: Your Name [Your e-mail address]
To: Recipient e-mail address
Cc:
Subject: Radiation Safety Officer

Dear Recipient Name,

    Please accept this letter and the attached resume as an expression of my interest in the Radiation Safety Officer position you are currently seeking to fill. I am confident that my education, experience, and familiarity with the University of _____ Research Center facilities provide me with the necessary skills to meet or exceed your expectations in this role.

    For the past year, I have been a Health Physicist with the university, with responsibility for a variety of functions, including:

- Testing & Monitoring Equipment
- Training Medical Staff
- Ensuring Compliance with NYS Regulations
- Monitoring Staff Exposure
- Achieving CRESO Certification
- Supervising Four Technicians
- Serving on Various Committees
- Consulting with Physicians
- Maintaining Updated Technical Knowledge

    I held a similar position at University of _____'s School of Medicine and Hospital. There I trained and supervised the work of a six-person technical team. I ensured that all equipment, materials, and supplies were in compliance with state regulations. State inspection results were always outstanding. *My commitment to health and safety has resulted in a perfect safety record.*

    I hold two master's degrees, one in Nuclear Engineering from _____ State University, the other in Nuclear Physics from _____. In addition, I speak three languages (English, Portuguese, and Russian).

    I thoroughly enjoy working at U of ___, and would welcome this opportunity to make an even more significant contribution to the success of its mission. I would enjoy discussing my qualifications with you in person, and after reviewing my attached resume, invite you to contact me to arrange an initial interview. Thank you for your time and consideration.

Sincerely,

Your Name
(555) 555-1234
Attachment: resume

Relocation for Application Developer

From: Your Name [Your e-mail address]
To: Recipient e-mail address
Cc:
Subject: Application Developer

Dear Recipient Name,

As an Application Developer I am very interested in joining your software development team. You have long been on my radar as a major innovator. You have a reputation for quality products, customer support, and being a great employer, and I want to work in an environment in which application development is critical.

My current position is Application Developer for _____. The job has provided me with 3 years' hands-on experience in Visual Basic and other languages. However, I am eager to jump into actual software writing, as well as return to the _____ area.

I have a Bachelor's Degree in Computer Science and am getting close to completing my Master's Degree.

My resume is attached for your review. I'll be back in _____ in three weeks, so I am going to call you to arrange a meeting for when I visit. In the meantime, please feel free to e-mail or call for further information. Thank you for your consideration. I look forward to meeting you in the near future.

Yours truly,

Your Name
(555) 555-1234
Attachment: resume

Research–Reference Librarian

From: Your Name [Your e-mail address]
To: Recipient e-mail address
Cc:
Subject: Research/Reference Librarian

Dear Recipient Name,

Are you looking for an **Entry-Level Research or Reference Librarian or Cataloguer**? My experience with Internet resources and navigational tools, combined with my experience with library databases, affords you the opportunity to hire an entry-level library professional with proven librarianship success.

With my recent MLIS, 3.95 from _____, as well as internship experience in the reference department of academic and state government libraries, perhaps I can be of service.

My resume is attached for your review; in it you will find information on my education, training, and work experience. I would like to draw your attention to credentials that are out of the norm:

- ✓ Fluent Polish, Russian, Slovak, German, Latin
- ✓ Taught English and Civics, pass rate of 100% over 8-year period: 2000 foreign students
- ✓ Voyager Module, AACR2r, LC classification scheme, MARC format, and OCLC, as well as Lexis-Nexis, Dow Jones, Dialog Web, and Classic

Providing high-level customer service and efficiency is my goal in library services. Can we meet soon to discuss your needs? I will call your office next week to schedule a mutually convenient appointment. Thank you for your time and consideration.

Sincerely,

Your Name
(555) 555-1234
Attachment: resume

Sales

Dear Recipient Name,

I want to add zeros to your bottom line. Specifically, I'd like to become your newest sales professional. Perhaps the best way to link those two ideas is with this graph that shows how I'm performing right now.

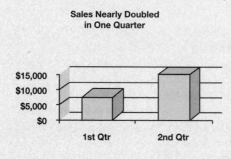

Sales Nearly Doubled in One Quarter

What I do isn't magic. I just work harder and smarter than my competition by finding some profitable way to say "yes" to every customer and potential customer.

In the following resume I believe you will see something more than the usual recitations of job titles and responsibilities. You'll find six capabilities I want to put at _____'s disposal at once. Backing them up are a dozen examples of those sales capabilities in action.

My company values what I do. And, if I thought our market was growing as fast as yours, I would stay with them. While I cannot control market conditions, I am interested in making even greater contributions to my employer. That's why I'm "testing the waters" with this confidential application.

I do best using the consultative approach to sales. So, as a first step, I'd like to hear about _____'s sales needs in your own words. May I call in a few days to arrange time to do that? My resume is attached for your review.

Sincerely,

Your Name
(555) 555-1234
Attachment: resume

School Board Member

Dear Recipient Name,

I am very interested in the vacated seat on the _____ City School Board. My motivation for seeking this position is public service. Because I have a deep commitment to community service and an in-depth knowledge of how a community works, I recognize that a public education system is critical to overall community success.

After retiring from law enforcement after thirty years of service, I returned to public service two years ago. I currently work as the Substance Abuse Prevention Coordinator for the City of _____ Health Department. Perspectives in the areas of substance abuse and public health would be beneficial to the school board.

In today's world, we fear for the security of our homeland. Our students and teachers need to be in a safe environment. Parents need to be confident that their children are secure at school and school-sponsored events. From my life experiences and training, I also bring expertise to the school board in this area.

Public service has always been my calling. An appointment to the _____ City School Board would allow me to use the skills gained from a 32-year career in public service to make a difference in people's lives. Though my children are grown, I look forward to a strong school system for my grandchildren.

I have the time to devote to the task and the drive, energy, experience, and vision to make a positive contribution as a board member. I ask you to consider not only my qualifications but also my desire to serve. My extensive community involvement is outlined in the attached resume.

Sincerely,

Your Name
(555) 555-1234
Attachment: resume

Senior Account Manager

From: Your Name [Your e-mail address]
To: Recipient e-mail address
Cc:
Subject: Senior Account Management

Dear Recipient Name,

Capitalizing on a career that encompasses substantial IT project management experience and extensive sales/marketing experience, I am seeking a new professional challenge that will combine these skills in a senior account management, project management, or technical leadership role. With this goal in mind, I have attached a resume that outlines my qualifications.

Some experience you may find relevant:

- Managing the technical deployment of six different releases of _____ _____.
- Ensuring that hardware platforms in the field are prepared to receive new releases, and resolving technical issues impacting end-user training for 6,000 users at 34 sites across the U.S.
- Pre- and post-sales support to key account decision-makers at _Fortune_ 500 companies, delivering logistics solutions for import and export.
- Hands-on experience providing desk-side support to end-users; configuring hardware and installing software in the field; and delivering training to end-users and IT specialists.

I would enjoy speaking with you about how my capabilities might match your needs, and will contact you soon to arrange an appropriate time for an initial meeting. Please review my attached resume. Thank you for your time and consideration.

Sincerely,

Your Name
(555) 555-1234
Attachment: resume

Senior Customer Service

From: Your Name [Your e-mail address]
To: Recipient e-mail address
Cc:
Subject: Senior Customer Service

Dear Recipient Name,

Are you looking for a Senior Customer Service Specialist who is:

- A consistent top performer with a strong desire to get the job done?
- A team player able to achieve results through coordination with employees in all functional areas?
- An effective communicator with excellent writing, training, and telephone skills?
- Able to learn quickly, analyze complex information, and find solutions to problems?
- Organized, thorough, and precise?

I have a Bachelor's Degree in business administration and 7 years' experience in the insurance/financial industry, serving in such diverse roles as customer relations advisor and calculations processor.

I consistently receive the highest ratings in my unit despite the fact that the difficult cases *frequently* find their way to my desk. I also contribute to the team by putting in extra time to clear backlogs and by analyzing existing procedures to devise more efficient methods of operation.

I believe that I can make a positive contribution to _____ _____, and look forward to discussing my capabilities with you in detail. Thank you for your time and consideration. My resume is attached for your review.

Sincerely,

Your Name
(555) 555-1234
Attachment: resume

Senior EMEA Marketing

From: Your Name [Your e-mail address]
To: Recipient e-mail address
Cc:
Subject: Senior EMEA Marketing

Dear Recipient Name,

I am a Senior EMEA Marketing professional with stellar Asian sector successes who has leaped over cultural barriers to forge some of the most profitable technical opportunities in the telecommunications and construction fields.

I received 3 promotions in the last 4 years due to my success in managing contacts, motivating staff, and implementing marketing campaigns that tripled ROI. My work in strategic partnering, developing alliances, creating new opportunities, and exceeding multinational clients' expectations has helped my employers more than double their sales. Some repeatable highlights:

- Market data and voice communication services to multinational corporations and Internet service providers in Japan, Southeast Asia, Canada, and Western Europe.
- Delivered 28 global accounts representing up to a 250% sales increase.
- Created the first transcontinental ATM circuit.
- Added $1.5M in sales, with an add-on service option.
- Partnered parent company with Japan-based joint venture interests that enabled the first US-built airport in Japan. Landed 2 additional opportunities for a total of $10M in business in one year.

Reviewing my attached resume, you will note Doctoral, Master's, and Bachelor's degrees—quantifiable results and extensive technical training that serve only to enhance my drive and enthusiasm. I will gladly set aside time to meet with you and discuss how my knowledge of technology, client relations, and strategic partnering can become your biggest asset.

Sincerely yours,

Your Name
(555) 555-1234
Attachment: resume

Senior PR Professional

From: Your Name [Your e-mail address]
To: Recipient e-mail address
Cc:
Subject: Olympic performance in PR

Dear Recipient Name,

Saw you quoted on the _____Newswire blog last week, and your comments made me smile: "everyone sees the gleaming results, no one sees the blood, sweat, and tears that lead to them." I believe I might have something of interest to say.

An Olympic gold-medal winner and 12-year high-tech public relations professional, I am passionate about achieving results for my clients and team. My track record for delivering successful strategic PR, executive communications, and leadership positioning is demonstrated by ten years of client loyalty. I am a dynamic professional with extraordinary team-building and interpersonal skills, and I thrive in the competitive environment that is PR.

My complementary experience as a television commentator, coupled with 20 years as a professional public speaker, give me real validity when advising, coaching, and media-training clients and C-level executives.

In my attached resume you will find proof points for my PR acumen including:

* Demonstrated track record of strategic communications and influential public relations

* Accomplished media relations/story placement, from ABC News to ZDNet

* Team, account, budget, client, and C-level executive management

* Client loyalty and satisfaction

* Considerable network of high-tech industry players

* New business success

* Self-motivated team player

Thank you in advance for reviewing my resume. Please contact me at your earliest convenience to schedule an interview.

Best regards,

Your Name
(555) 555-1234

Technical Services Marketing Professional

From: Your Name [Your e-mail address]
To: Recipient e-mail address
Cc:
Subject: Technical Sales

Dear Recipient Name,

As a seasoned Technical Services Marketing Associate, I've generated considerable new business for my previous employers, and now I'd like to do the same for you. For the past 15 years I have pursued an increasingly successful career in telecommunications sales and marketing. Among my accomplishments are:

SALES
Competent with the entire sales-cycle management process, from initial client consultation and needs assessment through product demonstration, price and service negotiations, and closing. Sales increased 230% over last five years.

MARKETING
Success in orchestrating all aspects of marketing strategy, from competitive market intelligence and trend analysis, through product development and positioning to launch, channel management, and customer care.

TELECOMMUNICATIONS & NETWORK SOLUTIONS
Recognized for pioneering technology solutions that meet the needs of complex customer service, logistics, and distribution operations. Able to test operations to ensure optimum systems functionality and availability, guide systems implementation across multiple platforms, and deliver user training and support programs that outpace the competition.

Please see my attached resume. I look forward to learning about opportunities in your corporation.

Sincerely,

Your Name
(555) 555-1234
Attachment: resume

Transportation Manager

From: Your Name [Your e-mail address]
To: Recipient e-mail address
Cc:
Subject: Transportation Manager

Dear Recipient Name:

How big is that gap between what leadership wants from its production function and what production delivers to the customers in a timely manner? If you'd like to shrink that gap, you should consider adding me to your team as Transportation Manager.

In the attached resume, you'll see more than a half-dozen cost, process, and time-saving contributions I have made in this area. They illustrate the five profit-building capabilities I list right at the top of my resume. I'd like to put those advantages to work for you right away.

Over the last year, the failing health of parents guided my relocation from Knoxville to Montgomery and made great demands upon my time. Now, with their passing behind me, I am eager to return to work in the town where I grew up.

If my credentials in the attached resume appeal to you, I would like to hear about your needs and how I might fulfill them. Thanks for your consideration; I look forward to hearing from you.

Sincerely,

Your Name
(555) 555-1234
Attachment: resume

Veterinarian

From: Your Name [Your e-mail address]
To: Recipient e-mail address
Cc:
Subject: Veterinarian

Dear Recipient Name,

My 15 years' experience addressing the health and performance needs of race horses at major tracks makes me a strong candidate for the opening you recently advertised at the AAEP website. Accordingly, I have attached my resume for your consideration and review.

Some key points include:
- Strong capacity to function independently and make critical decisions without direct supervision. My knowledge of horses and experience at several major tracks means that I will need minimal orientation to "hit the ground running."
- An excellent track record maintaining the health of thoroughbreds and quarter horses, as well as assisting trainers in enhancing the performance of horses by improving their respiratory and general health and dealing with lameness issues (references can be provided).
- The ability to effectively evaluate young horses prior to purchase, through observation and diagnostic testing. I routinely produce quality repository radiographs and review radiographs in a repository setting. I also accompany buyers to auctions (Keeneland, etc.) to assess horses under consideration.
- Experience assisting trainers setting up effective farm-based training programs, as well as helping breeders address reproductive health issues for horses in breeding farm settings.

I believe that I can be an asset to your organization, and would enjoy discussing further how my knowledge, expertise, and professional dedication can address your needs. Please feel free to contact me to arrange either a phone or in-person interview at a mutually convenient date and time.

Thank you for your time and consideration. I look forward to speaking with you soon. My resume is attached for your review.

Sincerely,

Your Name
(555) 555-1234
Attachment: resume

Warehouse Logistics

From: Your Name [Your e-mail address]
To: Recipient e-mail address
Cc:
Subject: Warehouse Manager, assembly/expediting/scheduling/shipping/receiving/order fulfillment/ customer service

Dear Recipient Name,

If you are in need of a Warehouse Manager/Inventory Control Specialist/Production Manager or Assembly Order Fulfillment Supervisor, please consider my track record: 15 years' experience in assembly, expediting and scheduling, shipping and receiving, order fulfillment, customer service, sales, supervision, and training.

I have a verifiable track record of meeting deadlines in demanding situations:

- ✓ Efficiently scheduled assembly, material handlers, and warehouse personnel, and closely monitored interplant transfers of raw materials from 20 warehouses. Assembly production and distribution procedures yielded high levels of productivity: 90% on-time delivery, including emergency orders, of up to $1 million in SKUs per week.

- ✓ As final assembly and inspection member of 4-person team, met heavy production schedule (35 to 60 complex, fabricated units per day) with 6% or less error rate.

- ✓ Working as part of a team, created, tested, packaged, and directed to shipping custom ship sets of complex hose assemblies, meeting deadlines 99-plus% of the time.

It is hard-working and cooperative people who deliver results. My focus on teamwork and productivity has always proven successful in past assignments. I am competent, enthusiastic, with a strong work ethic, dedicated, and dependable – I get the job done right.

May we meet soon to discuss your needs? Please review my attached resume. Thank you for your consideration.

Sincerely,

Your Name
(555) 555-1234
Attachment: resume

DIRECT APPROACH TO RECRUITERS

Corporate Attorney

From: Your Name [Your e-mail address]
To: Recipient e-mail address
Cc:
Subject: Corporate attorney searches

Dear Recipient Name,

Do you have a technology or telecommunications client looking for a savvy, commercially oriented C-level corporate attorney and executive with over 20 years' experience in law and business, as well as recognized expertise in corporate governance and M&A transactions?

As a lawyer and business executive, I have worked with both public and private companies, from venture capital and private start-ups to global public companies. I have provided significant details of my contributions and work experience in the attached resume. By way of highlights:

❑ Headed the legal group and was the right-hand man to CEO and a key advisor to board, navigating them through strategic planning, SEC, Sarbanes-Oxley, and other corporate governance issues. I also closed over 50 M&A deals over an 8-year period, advised the board on our acquisition and disposition strategy, and managed investor relations for the company.

❑ Held a corporate development role at _____ as Director of Ventures & Alliances, responsible for managing joint venture interests and supporting the merger implementation programs. Before taking on this role, I was a lawyer in the consumer markets group, acting as the lead attorney supporting the company's initial efforts at launching consumer Internet products.

❑ 15+ years of technology/Internet experience in private practice and industry, have delivered advice in all aspects of technology practice, and provide a superior broad-based knowledge in intellectual property protection programs and commercialization, including IP sale agreements, licensing and development deals, IP-sharing joint ventures, and distribution agreements.

❑ A graduate of _____ School of Law and Graduate School of Arts & Sciences, and member and contributing author, _____ *Journal of International Law*. At _____ Law, awarded the *Order of the Coif.* My undergraduate degree (BA) was from _____, where I graduated *magna cum laude* and was elected to *Phi Beta Kappa* honor society.

I bring a level of maturity, significant international experience, and a mix of legal and business experience and an entrepreneurial outlook. I am willing to relocate as required. I am seeking an opportunity with an emerging or rapidly growing technology or communications firm; I thrive in the chaotic environments of aggressive entrepreneurship. If you believe there is potential for a strong fit with a client, please contact me.

Sincerely,
Your Name
(555) 555-1234
Attachment: resume

Engineer to Programmer

From: Your Name [Your e-mail address]
To: Recipient e-mail address
Cc:
Subject: Programmer Analyst

Dear Recipient Name,

My certification in computer programming, along with my experience in electromechanical engineering, is among the primary assets I would bring to a programmer/analyst position, perhaps with one of your clients who specialize in website development.

As part of my training at _____, I designed, wrote the code for, edited, and modified numerous e-commerce websites. These projects succeeded not only because of my skill in applying my technical knowledge but also because of my strict attention to detail, and understanding of computer architecture, fostered by my 6 years of engineering experience.

Currently I'm employed at _____ in _____, ___, executing experiments on electrical/mechanical testing equipment to ensure conformance to customer specifications.

I am committed to continuing my professional education and success as a programmer analyst. I love the work. Please review my attached resume; I look forward to hearing from you to schedule an interview.

Sincerely,

Your Name
(555) 555-1234
Attachment: resume

Executive Computer Specialist

Dear Recipient Name,

My experience installing and maintaining computer networks, hardware, and software, along with my skills in training users and developing cost-saving applications, are the assets I would bring to the position of Executive Computer Specialist.

I am a Certified Novell Administrator, and my technical skills include expertise in Novell Netware, MS DOS, and Windows, as well as experience with hardware including Cabletron, and software including the Microsoft Office Suite. My computer expertise has saved my employers production time and costs. As a Senior Computer Specialist, I:

- Installed a Personal Computer LAN utilizing the Novell Netware Networking System. I saved $35,000 and used the savings to upgrade the equipment installation.
- Designed and implemented a system to cut printing costs. The system is projected to save the government $4 million over four years.
- Developed software packages, including "point of sale" software and mortgage software, for commercial applications.

I believe my skills and experience will make me succeed in the position of Executive Computer Specialist. Please review my attached resume, which details my experience and achievements, and then I look forward to talking technology solutions with you.

Sincerely yours,

Your Name
(555) 555-1234
Attachment: resume

Health Management

From: Your Name [Your e-mail address]
To: Recipient e-mail address
Cc:
Subject: Health Management Professional

Dear Recipient Name,

With a 20-plus-year track record in the pharmaceutical industry, I believe I have unique talents that could benefit one of your HMO clients. Some of the key capabilities I bring include:

- Design and implementation of health management programs. First-hand experience developing programs for asthma management, and directing programs that have delivered substantial savings to client firms.
- Managing the development and implementation of web-based services that are new revenue streams for my firm and value-added services to its physician customer base.
- Exceptional account relations skills. I currently call on and maintain business relationships with key client contacts at the highest levels.
- A broad understanding of the health care industry, which includes pharmaceutical sales and extensive interaction with health care professionals at all levels.
- National certifications from the University of Wisconsin in Quality Management and from the National Heart, Lung & Blood Institute.

I am confident that my knowledge and expertise will allow me to deliver successful results for one of your clients in the health care industry. I would enjoy speaking with you to explore potential client opportunities.

Please review my attached resume. You can call or e-mail me to arrange a convenient time for us to meet. As my employer is unaware of my job search, I trust that you will hold this correspondence in strict confidence and consult with me before releasing my materials to a prospective employer. Thank you for your time and consideration.

Your Name
(555) 555-1234
Attachment: resume

International Operations

From: Your Name [Your e-mail address]
To: Recipient e-mail address
Cc:
Subject: International operations and project management

Dear Recipient Name,

Over 12 years, I have built a successful career in **international operations and project management.** I have extensive experience in **diplomacy and international public affairs,** dealing with foreign government officials, Heads of State, and Ambassadors, as well as *Fortune* 100 senior executives. I am particularly adept at living and working effectively in foreign countries and with diverse cultural imperatives.

Feasibility studies, crisis resolution, and international risk assessment are areas where I excel. Unit construction and operations, mining/drilling and industrial equipment procurement, and sales and distribution are areas where I may be of particular assistance, but my skills are transferable to virtually any industry.

I look forward to hearing from you to discuss any mutually beneficial opportunities that you may be aware of. Please feel free to send my resume to others who may have a need for a professional of my caliber. I am willing to explore interim assignments and consulting projects as well as senior management opportunities.

My attached resume details some of my accomplishments and credentials.

Sincerely,

Your Name
(555) 555-1234
Attachment: resume

IT Design and Implementation

From: Your Name [Your e-mail address]
To: Recipient e-mail address
Cc:
Subject: IT design and implementation

Dear Recipient Name,

Capitalizing on my success managing IT design and implementation projects for _____, I am seeking a professional opportunity where my project management, customer relations, and organizational skills can benefit one of your clients.

Some of the skills and experience I bring to the position include:

- *Defining project parameters, including interviewing clients to assess goals and objectives, and developing specifications and project deliverables.*
- *Serving on leadership teams that have managed project budgets of up to $10 million to consistently meet customer timeline requirements and budgetary constraints.*
- *Coordinating activities of programmers, Web developers, software engineers, network engineers, graphic artists, and customer representatives to meet project goals.*
- *Testing and validating applications during development stages and upon completion to ensure client objectives are met.*

I am open to relocation anywhere in the United States and would eagerly accept either contract assignments or permanent employment. Thank you for your time and consideration, and please review my attached resume. I look forward to speaking with you soon.

Sincerely,

Your Name
(555) 555-1234
Attachment: resume

IT Management

From: Your Name [Your e-mail address]
To: Recipient e-mail address
Cc:
Subject: IT Management, needs/evaluations/vendors/systems development/beta/quality/documentation/multisite

Dear Recipient Name,

Information technology projects for high-growth companies are my area of expertise. Throughout my career I have been successful in identifying organizational needs and leading the development and implementation of industry-specific technologies to improve productivity, quality, operating performance, and profitability.

Responsibilities include the entire project management cycle, from initial needs assessment and technology evaluations through vendor selection, internal systems development, beta testing, quality review, technical and user documentation, and full-scale, multisite implementation.

In my current position at _____, I initiated and managed the technological advances, administrative infrastructures, training programs, and customization initiatives that have enabled the company to generate over $3 million in additional profits in the past year.

My technological and management talents are complemented by my strong training, leadership, and customer service skills. I am accustomed to providing ongoing support and relate well with all levels of an organization. Most notable are my strengths in facilitating cooperation among cross-functional project teams to ensure that all projects are delivered on time, within budget, and as per specifications.

Originally hired for a one-year contract at _____, I have been offered a permanent position within the company. However, I am interested in greater challenges and would welcome the opportunity to meet with you to determine the contributions I can make to your client. My resume is attached and I will call you next week to set up an appointment.

Sincerely,

Your Name
(555) 555-1234
Attachment: resume

Marketing Director

Dear Recipient Name,

I recently learned that you have a Marketing Director assignment in process. I am a serious candidate for this position. Please consider:

- After joining _____ as Marketing Director, I revitalized a declining processed-meats product category in less than a year, introducing better-tasting formulas and reducing product costs by over $100,000. Dramatic new packaging and fresh marketing strategies doubled previous sales.
- I have carefully crafted and fine-tuned many new product introductions and line extensions, such as ____, _____, and _____'s _____.
- My sales/marketing experience dates from _____, when I formed a direct sales company to pay for my MBA (now the top-rated program in the U.S.A., I'm proud to say).
- I designed events like the _____ program, and _____'s sponsorship of the Indy 500 _____ racing team.
- I always make joint sales calls with field reps and marketing brokers.
- I am familiar with marketing programs for home and commercial satellite systems, "high-tech" audio/video, and radio communications equipment.

I am bilingual and quickly absorb other languages. If this grabs your attention, please review my attached resume and give me a call.

Sincerely,

Your Name
(555) 555-1234
Attachment: resume

Military to Civilian Transition

From: Your Name [Your e-mail address]
To: Recipient e-mail address
Cc:
Subject: Sys admin/people skills/military background

Dear Recipient Name,

If you seek a new Systems Administrator who is technically proficient and has verifiable interpersonal skills, then we have good reason to talk. Whatever the Sys Admin challenge, I've done it, done it under fire, and can handle whatever you throw at me; that's my military training speaking.

I possess extensive technical skills and experience. My primary focus has been on Windows NT. In fact, I am currently pursuing my Microsoft Certified Systems Engineer designation. My plans are to attain this at about the time I leave the military in two months, when I will be able to bring this added expertise to an employer. My attached resume has all the details.

More difficult to portray on a resume are people skills. My job is to serve as a support person, there to keep the system operating smoothly for end-users, as well as to provide them training. Colleagues, supervisors, subordinates, and end-users will confirm my interpersonal skills during reference checks.

Sys Admin is a team and cross-functional team effort. I have commendations for my abilities as a team player as well as a team leader and a verifiable track record in taking projects and running with them, but the successes are a result of the combined efforts of the whole team.

A meeting at your convenience would be greatly appreciated. I look forward to speaking with you in the near future. Please review my attached resume.

Your Name
(555) 555-1234
Attachment: resume

Product Marketing

From: Your Name [Your e-mail address]
To: Recipient e-mail address
Cc:
Subject: Product Marketing

Dear Recipient Name,

If you are looking for a successful executive to take charge of new product marketing, you will be interested in talking to me.

10 years of experience in every aspect of marketing and sales in different industries gives me experience in ____ and the helpful frame of reference from working in other areas. My search is focused on companies that innovate, because I am particularly effective at new product marketing.

I have successfully managed new product-marketing research, launch planning, advertising, product training, and sales support, as well as direct sales. In my current position with _____, I created several product marketing approaches that other operating divisions adopted for their programs.

My business education includes a Marketing MBA from _____ School of Management, and provides me with a variety of useful analytical tools in managing problems and maximizing opportunities. My superior sales track record guarantees that I bring the reality of the marketplace to each business situation; I know what sells and why.

Currently, my total compensation package is in the _____ range; I am looking for a company that rewards performance consistently. Since I am active in a job search, please contact me immediately if you are conducting any searches that might be a good fit. Relocation is no problem.

Thank you in advance for your consideration. Please see my attached resume.

Sincerely,

Your Name
(555) 555-1234
Attachment: resume

Quality Assurance Technician

From: Your Name [Your e-mail address]
To: Recipient e-mail address
Cc:
Subject: Quality Assurance Technician, Reliability, Critical Thinking, and Attention to Detail

Dear Recipient Name,

If you are looking for a dedicated and competent Quality Assurance Technician, look no further. In 15+ years' experience in quality assurance and quality control, I have designed better consumer-friendly products and improved sales of existing products. Reliability, critical thinking, attention to detail, and focus are a few of the qualities I bring to Quality Assurance work.

Delivering solid productivity increases has been the norm throughout my career in the electronics field. I have achieved superior results at *Continuum Biomedical, HMT Technologies, Wheco Electronics, 3M Healthcare, Irwin Magnetic,* and *Xircom Electronics*; I have the references to back up this claim.

My track record means your client gets a Quality Assurance Technician who is productive from day one. And from day one, my commitment would be to simplify processes, improve products, develop workforce competencies, and boost output while completing projects ahead of schedule and under budget.

Further qualifications are outlined in the attached resume. Given my relevant technical skills, familiarity with the product line, and understanding of electronics manufacturing, I could step into a job and be of immediate assistance. Please contact me by phone or e-mail to arrange a convenient time to meet. Thank you; I look forward to speaking with you soon.

Sincerely,

Your Name
(555) 555-1234
Attachment: resume

Senior Network Control Technician

From: Your Name [Your e-mail address]
To: Recipient e-mail address
Cc:
Subject: Senior Network Control Technician job posting

Dear Recipient Name,

I am excited by your job posting for Senior Network Control Technician/Administrator. My qualifications and technical background, as well as fieldwork, marketing, and customer service experience, match your requirements for this position. The attached resume reflects the experience and technical training needed to provide customized network and hardware and software solutions to meet remote customer needs.

I believe the following are relevant to your needs:

- An accommodating attitude and willingness to work hard at any level to accomplish tasks and meet deadlines.
- The ability to multitask, prioritizing tasks and job assignments to balance customer needs with company goals.
- Strategic planning to head off downtime and restructure company systems to realize major improvement.
- Aptitude for troubleshooting problems, while respecting customers and explaining problems/solutions in accessible language.
- Consultative, straightforward communication techniques that promote development of strong and lasting rapport and trust.
- A work ethic that honors integrity and excellence to enhance company distinction.
- A persuasive, take-charge style seasoned with a sense of humor for a pleasant work environment.
- Psychological insight and a talent for motivating others to work at higher levels to increase productivity.

An interview to further investigate your needs and my qualifications would be of great interest to your clients. I look forward to hearing from you. Thank you for your time and consideration.

Sincerely,

Your Name
(555) 555-1234
Attachment: resume

Senior R&D Engineer

From: Your Name [Your e-mail address]
To: Recipient e-mail address
Cc:
Subject: R&D-to-market problems?

Dear Recipient Name,

If your R&D-to-market time needs a sense of urgency, creativity, and a seasoned coordinator of people and priorities, we should talk. As a Senior R&D Engineer, this is what I do, and have done successfully with 73 new products. Here's why we should talk:

- STRATEGIC PLANNING: Long- and short-term plans that kept a $2B manufacturer ahead of its competition since ____.

- COORDINATED RESOURCES: 20+ years in planning, reviewing, benchmarking technical performance, meeting budgetary goals, and coordinating interlaboratory and interdepartmental efforts.

- ENRICHED KNOWLEDGE: New Product training of sales, marketing, and technical staffs. Worldwide.

- MOVED THE MARKET TO OUR PRODUCT: Expert at using technology to create markets.

- IMPECCABLE RECORD: Achieved 70 to 80 percent first-time success rate in field testing for all products developed; hold ____ US patents; consulted worldwide by engineers and scientists; published; presenter at technical conferences since post-doctoral fellowship.

Reviewing my credentials and past results, you will note they occurred in the _____ field. However, I am confident this core *technical, engineering, analytical, and organizational expertise readily adapts to* _____ , *because in R&D-to-market, while the products may be different, the concerns remain constant.*

If you need *a driven problem-solver who can get staff focused, motivated, and productive*, I am ready to discuss *how I can reignite your R&D efforts and create a flurry of opportunity*. I am the only non-salesperson in my profession ever to get a sales award. Please see my attached resume. I look forward to talking.

Sincerely,

Your Name
(555) 555-1234
Attachment: resume

Systems Integration

From: Your Name [Your e-mail address]
To: Recipient e-mail address
Cc:
Subject: Systems Integration job posting, software, firmware, and hardware

Dear Recipient Name,

My 14 years in electrical engineering, supported by extensive management and product development experience, are key assets that I can contribute to one of your clients' future success. I can contribute significant expertise in systems integration within the telecommunications industry.

I work with cutting-edge technologies, including **embedded microprocessors, RF, telecommunications,** and **wireless,** in the development and manufacture of products for varied industries. Integrating software, firmware, and hardware to create unique applications is a key strength.

Applications that proved marketable include custom instrumentation and a PC-based network for GPS-tracking vehicles in transit. In addition, I have also played an important role in both the sales and customer support process, helping _____ win its largest municipal contract with the city of _____.

I welcome the opportunity to meet with you to explore areas of mutual benefit. Attached is my resume for your review. In order to present my credentials more fully, I will follow up with you to answer any questions you may have. Thank you for your consideration.

Sincerely,

Your Name
(555) 555-1234
Attachment: resume

Technology Professional

From: Your Name [Your e-mail address]
To: Recipient e-mail address
Cc:
Subject: Technology guru with business development & global experience

Dear Recipient Name,

My broad background in all aspects of computers, from design and installation through user training and maintenance, coupled with my business operations expertise, are the assets I would bring to a position with one of your clients.

Currently I hold a management-level position with _____, a firm that designs and builds flight simulators for U.S. and foreign governments. I provide the electronics expertise in completing approximately 12 major projects annually, which means I conceptualize the simulators' computerized mechanisms, direct the design and manufacturing processes, then install and test the systems at clients' sites around the world.

The other major aspect of my job involves aggressively targeting new business. At a point when _____ was facing an essentially saturated U.S. market, I designed and implemented an upgraded Web presence to target international clientele. The site generated 80% of our new business within one year.

Other assets I would bring to one of your clients include skill in relocating entire company IT systems, as well as experience servicing all major brands of PCs. I am familiar with nearly every computer-associated component, program, or operating system on today's market.

Thank you in advance for taking a few moments to review my attached resume. I am confident that the experience you'll find outlined therein will be valuable to one of your clients. I look forward to hearing from you.

Regards,

Your Name
(555) 555-1234
Attachment: resume

Vice President of Asset Liquidation

From: Your Name [Your e-mail address]
To: Recipient e-mail address
Cc:
Subject: Asset liquidation assignment? Get this guy!

Dear Recipient Name,

As the Vice President of Lease Asset Liquidation with _____, I successfully engineered the recovery of $23 million in assets, almost three times the original buyout offer of $8 million.

Throughout my career I have been instrumental in developing and implementing workout and liquidation strategies and have earned a strong reputation as a professional who gets the job done.

My reason for contacting you is simple. I am interested in project opportunities that will serve both to challenge and to utilize my abilities in asset liquidation management. My current project will be completed within the next four to six weeks. I am currently considering offers and intend to make a decision by February 1st.

Please see my attached resume for details. I look forward to hearing from you to discuss any mutually beneficial opportunities.

Sincerely,

Your Name
(555) 555-1234
Attachment: resume

Vice President of Operations–Administration

From: Your Name [Your e-mail address]
To: Recipient e-mail address
Cc:
Subject: VP Operations/Administration

Dear Recipient Name,

In the course of your search assignments, you may have a requirement for an organized and goal-directed VP of Operations, a title I currently hold. I have an MBA degree from _____, and a BBA from _____. Strengths that will contribute to my success in such a position include:

- Direct line operations responsibility improving **gross margin to 8.0%**.
- Planning and developing over **$15 million in new construction projects**.
- Reduction of departmental **operating expenses to 1.1% below budget**.
- Negotiating and developing contractual arrangements with vendors.

I have the ability to define problems, assess both large-scale and smaller implications of a project, and implement solutions.

The attached resume outlines my administrative and business background. My geographic preferences are the Midwest and Southeast regions of the country. Relocating to a client's location does not present a problem. Depending upon location and other factors, my salary requirements would be between $130,000 and $150,000.

If it appears that my qualifications meet the need of one of your clients, I will be happy to further discuss my background.

Sincerely,

Your Name
(555) 555-1234
Attachment: resume

Vice President C-Level Finance

From: Your Name [Your e-mail address]
To: Recipient e-mail address
Cc:
Subject: VP/C-Level Finance

Dear Recipient Name,

Mentored by ___ ___, founder of _____, I successfully progressed within his privately held organization for twelve years, serving on the **Board of Directors of 13 separate companies** and holding positions including **Treasurer, Vice President of Finance,** and ultimately **President**. During my tenure the holding company grew from 7 employees to more than 1,000, while **revenues increased from $3 million to $108 million**. My attached resume gives further details.

I have built my career on my commitment and ability to create open lines of communication between the Board of Directors and senior management to **protect the investments of my organization and assure the attainment of the target return.** I have the experience, talent, and energy to turn around, create, or grow a dynamic organization.

I am interested in exploring any senior management opportunities that may be available through your organization, and would also be interested in interim or consulting roles. Geographically speaking, I have no limitations and am available for relocation throughout the U.S. and abroad.

I look forward to hearing from you in the near future to discuss mutually beneficial opportunities.

Sincerely,

Your Name
(555) 555-1234
Attachment: resume

NETWORKING

Advertising Manager, Networking

Dear Recipient Name,

It was a pleasure speaking with you Monday afternoon regarding my search for a position in Corporate Graphic Design. Thank you for your initial interest.

The position I am looking for is usually found in a corporate marketing or public relations department. The titles vary: Design Manager, Advertising Manager, and Publications Director are a few. In almost every case the job description includes management and coordination of the corporation's online and print marketing materials, whether they are produced by in-house designers or by an outside advertising agency or design firm.

I would like to stay in the area; at least, I would like to search this area first. My salary requirement currently is in the $__,___ range.

My professional experience, education, activities, and skills uniquely qualify me for a position in Corporate Graphic Design. My portfolio documents over eight years of experience in the business, and includes design, project consultation, and supervision of quality printed material for a wide range of clients.

I hope you will keep my resume in your files for future reference. If I come across anyone suitable to your needs, I'll certainly give you a shout.

Sincerely,

Your Name
(555) 555-1234

Animation Technology, Networking

Dear Recipient Name,

Moshimoshi. Since meeting earlier this year at the Korean Film Festival we have exchanged e-mails and met several times. We have discussed our mutual interest in the Japanese movie industry and its future in the global entertainment business. You know well my vision of integrating Japanese gaming and animation technologies into filmmaking.

Over the course of our conversations, you mentioned that there might be an opportunity for an internship or, possibly, employment at _____. I am very interested.

I offer negotiation, persuasion, and liaison abilities, plus leadership and communication skills. I have also proven that I can use my bilingual proficiency to enhance business understanding. Please see my attached resume for examples of how I have used these abilities in the past.

I believe that my unique strengths can contribute to the growth of the _____ program, particularly if you are able to secure departmental status. I welcome the opportunity to discuss my continued involvement in your program.

Sincerely,

Your Name
(555) 555-1234
Attachment: resume

Benefit Administration, Networking

From: Your Name [Your e-mail address]
To: Recipient e-mail address
Cc:
Subject: Great to talk to you again

Dear Recipient Name,

It was a pleasure to speak with you on the telephone recently and, even more so, to be remembered after all these years.

As mentioned during our conversation, I have just recently re-entered the job market and have ten years of experience with a 3,000-employee retail organization in the area of employee benefit administration. My experience includes pension plans and dental, life, and disability insurance. I have been responsible for all facets of management of the company plan, including accounting, maintenance, and liaison with both staff and coverage providers.

My goal is to become a Benefits Manager in a larger organization, and my preference is to remain in the Metropolitan area.

For your information, my resume is attached. If any situations come to mind where you think my skills and background would fit, or if you have any suggestions as to others with whom it might be beneficial for me to speak, I would appreciate hearing from you. I can be reached at the telephone number listed below.

Good luck with the start of the school year.

Sincerely,

Your Name
(555) 555-1234
Attachment: resume

Construction Management, Networking

From: Your Name [Your e-mail address]
To: Recipient e-mail address
Cc:
Subject: Lunch on Friday?

Dear Recipient Name,

We had the opportunity to speak briefly at last week's Chamber of Commerce meeting concerning the Construction Management position you are seeking to fill in ___. I appreciate you filling me in on the details of the project, and have attached my resume as you suggested.

As we discussed, I am well acquainted with ___'s brand and store concept, and I was excited to learn of the company's expansion plans. With my background in construction, maintenance, and project management, as well as operations and strategic leadership, I believe I am primed to play a key role in this growth.

I am currently in the process of selling the company and have been exploring opportunities with dynamic, growth-oriented organizations that could benefit from my broad-based expertise in operations, organizational management, finance, and business development. Your opportunity is something special.

As Chief Executive Officer of _____, I have been instrumental in leading the company to phenomenal success within a very short time, building the organization from start-up into a solid revenue generator reputed throughout the region as an aggressive competitor in markets crowded by multimillion-dollar, nationally recognized companies.

Complementing my diverse leadership background is expertise in all the fundamentals of construction management, including the ability to see projects through to completion while exceeding quality standards. One of my strongest assets is my ability to cultivate long-lasting relationships with clients through attentive, direct communication.

I have been highly successful at defining complex project plans, establishing budgets, outlining scope of work, and directly soliciting qualified contractors utilizing the bid process. I also offer extensive experience navigating through the paperwork and bureaucracy, forging productive alliances with key regulatory agencies to streamline permits and licenses for expedited project starts.

I would enjoy the opportunity to speak with you again in greater detail. Could we meet for lunch on Friday? I'll call your assistant in a few days to confirm the appointment.

Sincerely,
Your Name
(555) 555-1234

Database Administration, Referral

From: Your Name [Your e-mail address]
To: Recipient e-mail address
Cc:
Subject: 6 Years' Intranet implementation 15K users

Dear Recipient Name,

Our mutual colleague, _____ _____, suggested that I send you my resume. I am looking to make a change and he mentioned that your department is looking for a Database Administrator with experience in Intranet implementation and management.

As my attached resume demonstrates, I have done that type of work for six years with a regional organization on a platform of 15,000 users.

This sounds like exactly the kind of work I could sink my teeth into. I would welcome the opportunity to discuss my expertise in relation to the specific deliverables of your job.

After you have reviewed my resume, can we talk?

Sincerely,

Your Name
(555) 555-1234
Attachment: resume

Education Administration, Networking

From: Your Name [Your e-mail address]
To: Recipient e-mail address
Cc:
Subject: Thanks for the referral

Dear Recipient Name,

I enclose my resume as requested during our telephone conversation yesterday afternoon regarding the *Adjunct Adult Education* position currently available. I appreciate your offer to forward these credentials to Ms. _____ _____.

With a Master's Degree in Education Administration, and a Principal of Administration and Supervision certification through the state of _____, plus four years of cumulative experience in the classroom, I possess the hands-on expertise and educational credentials that are critical to guiding adult students in pursuit of their educational goals.

What do I offer _____ Community College students?

- Effective listening and communication skills—a demonstrated ability to provide individualized instruction based on students' interests and needs.
- Encouragement and motivation—an empowering atmosphere of interaction and participation.
- Sincere desire to reach each student on a level s/he can understand, no matter the skill level or cultural background.

I am excited at the opportunity to work with adult students, because I recognize that they are in that classroom because they want to be there. The adult population brings a unique flavor of enthusiasm and motivation that energizes and inspires me as an instructor.

My resume is attached for forwarding to _____ ____. I would welcome the opportunity for an interview to discuss this job and a place on your educational team. Thank you for your consideration.

Sincerely,
Your Name
(555) 555-1234

EMEA Administration, Referral

From: Your Name [Your e-mail address]
To: Recipient e-mail address
Cc:
Subject: EMEA Administrative Assistant
_____

Dear Recipient Name,

_____ of _____ suggested that I contact you in regard to your need for an **Administrative Assistant.** I have 3 years' experience in office administration, customer service, sales, training, and marketing, and my German and French fluency will be an asset with your European commitments.

My resume is attached for your review. Highlights include
- ✓ I consistently focus on creating and maintaining excellent client relationships, and training others in successful techniques to do the same.
- ✓ A resourceful problem-solver with a track record of getting positive results, such as a 75% collection rate on accounts 90 days past due.
- ✓ Ability to build confidence and trust at all levels, and demonstrated experience in supporting cooperative, results-oriented environments.
- ✓ Proven communication skills, including fluency in French and German.

My career success has been due in large part to supporting teams, as well as internal and external customer relationships, and tackling persistent problem areas with creative approaches.

Should my qualifications meet with your needs, I would be available to schedule a meeting immediately. Thank you for your consideration. I look forward to a conversation.

Sincerely,

Your Name
(555) 555-1234
Attachment: resume

Executive Assistant, Referral

From: Your Name [Your e-mail address]
To: Recipient e-mail address
Cc:
Subject: Executive Assistant referral

Dear Recipient Name,

I was very pleased to learn of the need for an Executive Assistant in your company from your colleague _____. I believe the qualities you seek are well matched by my track record:

Your Needs	My Qualifications
Independent Self-Starter	• Served as company liaison between sales representatives, controlling commission and products. • Controlled cash flow, budget planning, and bank reconciliation for three companies. • Assisted in the promotion of a restaurant within a private placement sales effort, creating sales materials and communicating with investors.
Computer Experience	• Utilized Lotus Notes in preparing financial spreadsheet used in private placement memoranda and Macintosh to design brochures and flyers. • Have vast experience with both computer programming and the current software packages.
Compatible Background	• Spent 5 years overseas and speak French. • Served as an executive assistant to four corporate heads.

A resume is attached that covers my experience and qualifications in greater detail. I would appreciate the opportunity to discuss my credentials in a personal interview.

Sincerely,

Your Name
(555) 555-1234
Attachment: resume

Financial Consultant, Networking

From: Your Name [Your e-mail address]
To: Recipient e-mail address
Cc:
Subject: Be thankful you're not me, Charlie ;-)

Hi Recipient Name,

Just found an original Thurston Iasia, what a poster, the colors are still really fresh! Sadly can't justify the expense right now, c'est la guerre! You interested?

Hope all is well with you and yours and that you aren't going through the upheaval of job change like I am. I am no longer with _____, and am actively seeking my next career opportunity.

I would welcome any advice/input/support/kick in the pants and look forward to returning the favor immediately or at any time in the future.

Most recently as a Financial Consultant, I worked on long-term projects at leading companies such as _____, _____, and _____. I designed and implemented business office practices, refined reporting deadlines, streamlined efforts and provided recommendations for departmental efficiencies. My successes in these roles were based on my 20 years in Finance & Accounting, my analytical skills, being a team player, and commitment to the company mission.

Please take a look at Ye Olde resume, which is attached—actually it's all new and up-to-date—and advise me of any options/avenues you think I should explore; names of Director/CP/C-level guys would be much appreciated. Is there anyone among your friends or colleagues with whom I might speak?

I hope you'll scratch your head for me. If anything comes to mind, please let me know. Thanks in advance for your thoughts; I'll give you a call next week, if for nothing more than to catch up on your poster collection. No pressure on this, Charlie, just help if you can.

Sincerely,

Your Name
(555) 555-1234
Attachment: resume

Financial Professional, Networking

From: Your Name [Your e-mail address]
To: Recipient e-mail address
Cc:
Subject: _____ suggested I contact you re Finance Associate position

Dear Recipient Name,

I recently spoke with ___ _____ from _____ _____, and he strongly recommended that I send you a copy of my resume. I am very pleased to learn of the need for a **Finance Associate** and I believe the qualities you seek are well matched by my track record:

Your Needs	My Qualifications
3–5 years of experience building and maintaining complex financial models	Four years of experience at a top-performing hedge fund
	Built and maintained complex financial models to support investment theses in private equity transactions and coverage of over 30 stocks, $100M of portfolio value
	Created matrices in Excel to analyze model sensitivity to risk factors
Background of exceptional academic performance	BS in Economics with Honors from _____
Ability to manage multiple projects and meet deadlines	Delivered 15–20 research reports and notes per month in a fast-paced work environment

My greatest strength lies in my ability to clearly communicate complex financial information. This has enabled me to summarize the results of models and in-depth due diligence into concise investment theses for the portfolio managers of ___ _____, resulting in many profitable investments.

I am confident that my dedication, enthusiasm, and creativity would allow me to make a real contribution to your team. I hope to speak with you further and will call the week of August 2nd to follow up with you. Hopefully you'll be so fired up by the attached resume that you'll call or e-mail me sooner.

Sincerely,
Your Name
(555) 555-1234
Attachment: resume

HR Professional, Networking

From: Your Name [Your e-mail address]
To: Recipient e-mail address
Cc:
Subject: Congratulations on the nomination!

Dear Recipient Name,

Congratulations on your nomination for the _____ Award; the nomination demonstrates the high degree of professional excellence you have achieved.

It's been a while since we've chatted, and I wanted to bring you up to date on what I've been doing. After leaving _____, I explored several options before accepting a position as Director of Human Resources for ____ ____. Unfortunately, the daily drive to _____, among other factors, proved to be untenable—particularly during the winter months—and I have left that position.

This puts me back in the job market, and I am writing to inquire if you are aware of any HR positions that would capitalize on my skills. I am flexible regarding specific job responsibilities and am most interested in making a meaningful contribution to an organization's success. With these goals in mind, I have attached an updated resume.

Reiterating some of the key capabilities that I can bring to a position, consider the following:

- Excellent team-building and leadership skills.
- Superb interpersonal skills and supervisory experience.
- Developing and implementing human resource policies.
- Recruiting and hiring a variety of hourly and salaried employees.
- Extensive knowledge and experience in the healthcare arena.

I am convinced that my experience and professional diligence could be an asset to one of the IMC's member firms, and would appreciate any referrals you may be able to give me for potential employment opportunities.

Feel free to pass my resume on to anyone who may have an appropriate opportunity, or give me a call at (555) 555-1234 so that I might follow up on any suggestions you may have.

Thank you in advance for your much-appreciated assistance. I look forward to talking with you soon.

Sincerely,
Your Name
(555) 555-1234
Attachment: resume

International Consumer Sales, Referral

From: Your Name [Your e-mail address]
To: Recipient e-mail address
Cc:
Subject: International Consumer sales
_____

Dear Recipient Name,

I know and use your brand religiously. I spoke with _____ _____ recently. ____felt my 8 years' experience in international consumer sales would be of interest and suggested contacting you; he also wished to send his regards.

As a sales professional, I appreciate the ease with which I can sell your product line, because as a woman, I appreciate the high standards of quality that define your brands.

My experience working overseas has brought me a greater understanding of international cultures and traditions, as well as a better understanding and appreciation of how our own culture impacts others', insights that can impact success in the international marketplace.

I would very much like to discuss career opportunities with you and I will be calling you within the next few days. In the meantime, if you have any questions, I may be reached via this e-mail address or at the number below. Thank you for your consideration.

Sincerely,

Your Name
(555) 555-1234
Attachment: resume

International Sales Manager, Referral

From: Your Name [Your e-mail address]
To: Recipient e-mail address
Cc:
Subject: International Sales Manager referral

Dear Recipient Name:

I was recently speaking with _____ _____ from your firm and he strongly recommended that I send you a copy of my resume in reference to the above position. Knowing the requirements, he felt that I would be an ideal candidate. For more than eleven years, I have been involved in international sales management, with seven years directly in the aerospace industry. My qualifications for the position include:

♦ Establishing sales offices in France, Great Britain, and Germany.
♦ Recruiting and managing a group of 24 international sales representatives.
♦ Providing training programs for all of the European staff, which included full briefing on our own products as well as competitor lines.
♦ Obtaining 42%, 33%, and 31% of the French, German, and British markets, respectively.
♦ Dealing with all local engine and airframe manufacturers.
♦ Generating more than $32 million in sales with excellent margins.

My BS in electrical engineering was obtained from the University of _____ and my languages include French and German.

I feel confident that an interview would demonstrate my expertise in setting up rep organizations, and training and managing an international sales department; given my interest in your company, this could be time well spent. I look forward to meeting with you and will give you a call to follow up on this letter the week of ___ .

My resume is attached for your review.

Yours truly,

Your Name
(555) 555-1234

Local Services, Networking

From: Your Name [Your e-mail address]
To: Recipient e-mail address
Cc:
Subject: Thanks for the advice

Dear Recipient Name,

Congratulations on your reelection. I hope this letter finds you and your family well, and that you are having an enjoyable holiday season.

I am writing to update you on my job search. You may recall from our last conversation that I am now focusing on obtaining an hourly position with basic benefits that will sustain me until such time as I am ready for retirement (in three to five years).

As you recommended, I have applications on file with the Town of _____ for various positions, and have corresponded with various department heads, in each case indicating my flexibility and strong interest in making a meaningful contribution to smooth operations within one of their departments.

_____, I genuinely appreciate the advice and assistance you have offered to date. Once again, I am requesting that if you are aware of any other avenues I should be pursuing, please forward the attached resume and let me know.

I believe I have skills and experience to offer and can be an asset to someone in just about any position requiring maturity, reliability, and dedication. Thank you, again, for all your help, and Merry Christmas.

Sincerely,
Your Name
(555) 555-1234
Attachment: resume

Networking at Church

From: Your Name [Your e-mail address]
To: Recipient e-mail address
Cc:
Subject: I bumped into Father _____ at church

Dear Recipient Name,

Talk about coincidences. I bumped into Father _____ at church this past Sunday and learned that St. _____ is opening a new foster care division this coming March. One thing led to another, and he told me that Little Lamb Foster Care & Adoptive Services is in desperate need of social workers and foster/adoptive care counselors to fill several positions.

You might not recall my name, but hopefully I can help you to remember our meeting. I participated in an interview with you in early May of 2010 for the position of Foster Care Counselor with Little Lamb _____ facility.

We discussed my involvement with _____ Youth & Family Counseling Program at great length, and agreed I would be well suited for a similar position with Little Lamb as an Adoptive Care Counselor. Unfortunately, the lack of state and federal funding was reduced that month, leaving you with no other choice but to put a freeze on hiring.

As you can imagine, I am thrilled to learn of Little Lamb's new foster care program, and would welcome the opportunity to meet again to pick up where we left off. For your convenience, I am attaching my resume for your review. Thank you for your reconsideration. I look forward to speaking with you soon.

Sincerely,

Your Name
(555) 555-1234
Attachment: resume

Pharmacist Referral

From: Your Name [Your e-mail address]
To: Recipient e-mail address
Cc:
Subject: Hello from your new clinical pharmacist

Dear Recipient Name,

I was very excited to hear about your clinical pharmacist position from our mutual colleague ____ _____, as this has been a position I have been interested in for some time.

According to the job profile I saw on your website, a good candidate for this job is someone who works well with other health professionals and provides high-quality care and customer service to patients.

I have six years' experience working with the public in a hospital setting, and consequently with an extended team of health care professionals. Importantly, I have complete familiarity with the wide range of medications used in a teaching hospital and the protocols that accompany good pharmacy management in such a setting.

My attached resume will show that I am dedicated to my profession, with education and experience that exactly match your requirements for the clinical pharmacist position.

I am looking forward to speaking with you, and for your convenience have attached my resume as a PDF and also pasted it in beneath my signature in ASCII. I appreciate your consideration of my application, and am confident you will see a close match on evaluation of my resume.

Sincerely,

Your Name
(555) 555-1234
Attachment: resume

Publishing, Networking

From: Your Name [Your e-mail address]
To: Recipient e-mail address
Cc:
Subject: Sincere thanks for the help ;-)

Dear Recipient Name,

It was a pleasure to meet with you for lunch today. I am grateful for the time you took out of your busy schedule to assist me in my job search.

It was fascinating to learn about the new technology that is changing the publishing field; we live in exciting times. I went straight to the bookstore to purchase the book that you recommended.

I will be contacting _____, as you suggested, and will let you know how things are progressing once I have met her.

Thanks again for your help. You will be hearing from me soon.

Yours sincerely,

Your Name
(555) 555-1234
Attachment: resume

VP of Operations, Networking

From: Your Name [Your e-mail address]
To: Recipient e-mail address
Cc:
Subject: VP Operations

Dear Recipient Name,

_____ suggested I contact you after commenting that my background, business philosophy, and style reminded him of a CEO he had heard speak in Houston last year; apparently you were the hit of the conference.

I understand you too started on the shop floor. It has been several years since I took my first job as a machinist back in _____, __, but I have never lost my enthusiasm for finding more efficient and better ways of cutting costs while getting the job done. A machine shop is a great place to train critical thinking skills.

I worked my way up through the ranks from Foreman to Plant Supervisor to Manufacturing Engineer to Director of Operations and finally Vice President of Operations. Taking a swing at every new idea that came my way, I may have missed a few, but overall my batting average has been good. Three examples:

- Led a $340M manufacturing firm to earning ISO9002 certification on first attempt.
- Increased productivity at a plant in Mexico 34%, and reduced downtime 17%.
- Increased profits by 200% by restructuring production and delivery logistics.

I believe strongly in teams and am comfortable working with R&D, engineering, and marketing professionals. My colleagues have expressed appreciation for my direct and honest approach to people and problems.

Between jobs now, I am planning a fishing excursion on the Gulf. I will be arriving in _____ on ____ and would like to get together with you for lunch. I will give you a call the morning of the ____ to see if that can be arranged.

Please see my attached resume. I look forward to meeting you and exchanging ideas.

Sincerely,

Your Name
(555) 555-1234
Attachment: resume

Web Development, Networking

From: Your Name [Your e-mail address]
To: Recipient e-mail address
Cc:
Subject: Web Development

Hello _____,

Perhaps you remember our chance meeting at the Bio Asia-Pacific Conference at the _____ on the 18th and 19th of last month. In our brief conversation, I shared with you the idea of utilizing Web Development as an administrative tool. You expressed interest in the possibility of implementing such a system within the _____ School of Medicine.

May I suggest a formal meeting to explore the idea?

I have some exciting and creative ideas, which may encourage you to take the next step towards realizing the positive impact a content management system would have within the School of Medicine. This would also be a great opportunity for us to discuss your goals and how an administrative Intranet would help you reach them in a more timely and cost-effective manner.

In addition, there has recently been spirited discussion within the IT community on the topic of organizational continuity and its potential vulnerability due to advances in technology. I think you'll find the specific strategies I have to share with you thought-provoking.

If you recall, my background is in Web Planning and Development, with specific skills in developing administrative Intranets and public websites, and designing Web-based software to address the internal and external reporting needs of organizations.

Please see my attached resume attesting to my experience and specialties. I will contact you within the next few days to discuss the possibility of meeting with you.

Respectfully,

Your Name
(555) 555-1234
Attachment: resume

LINKEDIN—NETWORKING

LinkedIn: Career Transition, Networking

___ ____ has sent you a message.
Date: **/**/2012
Subject: FOOD TRUMPS PHARMACEUTICALS

Dear _____:

I have a passion for food. I am working to transition from the pharma industry, where I am a Brand Manager for _____, to the food and beverage industry. I recently heard about a position as an Associate Brand Manager at _____ and see considerable similarity in the brand strategies.

I know that I can make an immediate and long-term contribution to _____. I would love to send you my resume and, if you like what you see (and I believe you will), perhaps we can set up time to speak live.

Regards,

Your Name
(555) 555-1234
you@email.com

LinkedIn: Common Group & Reconnecting

LinkedIn.com Networking Letters

LinkedIn is the leading social networking site for professionals. At LinkedIn, all communications to other members are sent through the site, so every letter has a similar format. As social networking sites exist for people to communicate and reach out to each other, you will notice that these letters, while polite and professional, cut right to the chase.

If you know someone, or have known him or her in the past, you simply send a request to link. This will probably be fairly limited, so you will need to reach out to others that you don't know. The two easiest ways to do this are:

1. Send a request to link through someone you know to the person you would like to know; the site automatically shows you the people who can provide the patch for your introduction.
2. You can join special interest groups: there are hundreds, maybe thousands. Then as a member of a group, you can approach any other member directly for a link, based on your mutual membership of that group.

Here are a few examples of networking letters to and from members of the LinkedIn social networking site.

Linkedin.com Networking Letter to a Member of a Common Interest Group

_____ _____ has sent you a message.

Date: **/**/2012

Subject: Exchange leads?

Hello _____,

I came across your profile on LinkedIn while doing a job search here on LI. We're both part of the SharePoint Experts Group, and thought it might make sense to connect. Let me know if I can be of assistance in your networking efforts here on LI. Perhaps we could talk and exchange leads?

Sincerely,

Your Name

(555) 555-1234

you@email.com

LinkedIn.com Networking Letter Reconnecting with a Past Coworker

_____ _____ has sent you a message.

Date: **/**/2012

Subject: Blast from the past

_____,

I just came across your profile, and thought I'd reach out. We both worked at _____ in the late '90s, and I believe I may have hired you. I'd like to add you to my network, catch up, and see how we might help each other.

Sincerely,

Your Name

(555) 555-1234

you@email.com

LinkedIn: Network Member

Networking letter to a member of your network

____ _____ has sent you a message.
Date: **/**/2012
Subject: Request for Meeting

Hello _____,

I came across your profile on the LinkedIn Resume group. As we are both actively looking for jobs in financial services, I would like to set up a brief meeting with you this week or next to discuss networking strategies, developing contacts, and ways we might otherwise help each other.

To give you a brief background about myself, I am a recent MBA graduate with an emphasis in finance from the _____ School of Management, University of _____.

Prior to pursuing my MBA, I worked at _____ as a public accountant for four years. Recently, for over a year, I worked at the _____ as a fixed income analyst, and currently work as an Associate at a private investment firm.

I want to make a career in financial services (equity research) and recently took my CFA Level II examination. I would appreciate if we could talk for a few minutes; I think your insights could be very helpful. Thank you for your time.

Sincerely,

Your Name
(555) 555-1234
you@email.com

LinkedIn: Request Endorsement

At LinkedIn you can ask people to endorse your work.
Here is an example of an endorsement request.

____ _____ has sent you a message.
Date: **/**/2012
Subject: Can you endorse me?

Dear ____ _____,

I'm sending this to ask you for a brief recommendation of my work that I can include in my LinkedIn profile. If you have any questions, let me know.

Thanks in advance for helping me out. If you have any questions please just call or e-mail.

Regards,

Your Name
(555) 555-1234
you@email.com

LinkedIn: Request Introduction #1

This is a networking letter asking a networking contact at LinkedIn for an introduction to a prominent headhunter, a member of the recipient's network. The letter concludes a sequence of e-mails: Someone looking for a job locates a recruiter with an open requisition.

___ ____

To: Martin Yate
Date: July 28, 2012. 2.09PM

Hi Martin,

I hope things are well. There is a gentleman named ____ _____ that you are connected to on LinkedIn. ____ _____ recruits for the types of jobs that I am looking at, so I was wondering if you could perhaps introduce me to him. If so, I can send a LinkedIn introduction request.

Thank you.
Your Name
(555) 555-1234
you@email.com

From Martin Yate
To: ____ _____
Date: July 28, 2012. 4.15PM

Hi ____ _____,

I know a talented software guy, ____ _____, who is interested in connecting with you. His communication to me is below. May you have fruitful conversations.

Regards,
Martin
(555) 555-1234
you@email.com

From ____ _____
To: Martin Yate
Date: July 28, 2012. 6.18PM

Martin,

Yes, have ____ _____ send me an invite. In fact, he can e-mail me directly.

Is ____ the ____ in Texas? I just looked him up on LinkedIn and there is one in ____, UT and one in ____, TX. The one in TX looks like the guy since he is into database technologies. If he is the one, I think I have a position that he would be interested in: the job is local to ____. This could be ideal timing.

I am always glad to help out anyone you refer.

Your Name
(555) 555-1234
you@email.com

LinkedIn: Request Introduction #2

The following is a networking letter asking a networking contact at LinkedIn for an introduction to a member of the recipient's network. This one anticipates an introduction and includes a letter to the target contact.

_____ _____ has sent you a message.

Date: **/**/2012

Subject: NBI Certified

Dear Martin,

I am asking for an introduction to ____ _____ so that I can pursue a job opportunity with ____ _____, Inc. I would like to speak with ____ _____ to get a little more information about the job and the company. Thank you for taking the time to make this introduction for me. My e-mail to ____ ____ is below the signature.

Sincerely,

Your Name
(555) 555-1234
you@email.com

_____'s note to _____ _____, which is an integral part of the LinkedIn "request for introduction" protocols:

Dear Cari,

I am applying to work at my local branch of ____ _____ Bank and noticed that you work for them. I was wondering if there would be any way that I could ask you a few questions about the company; it would be really helpful to me.

Hoping you can take a few minutes to let me pick your brain, and find out how I might help you in return.

Sincerely,

Your Name
(555) 555-1234
you@email.com

LinkedIn: Request Introduction #3

The following networking letter is a networking introduction request

___ ____has sent you a message.
Date: **/**/2012
Subject: Your advice is working!

Hello Martin,

I am beginning to get some hits and interview requests since I began using your *Knock 'em Dead* books a couple of weeks ago. The American Red Cross is the place I would most like to end up, and I am trying to get past the cyber wall barrier without much luck. You know ___ _____, who might be able to help. Would you feel comfortable passing my introduction request along? It's below the signature. Thanks for all of your help.

Your Name
(555) 555-1234
you@email.com

(___ ____ note to ____ _____ :)

Hello Bob,

I am currently interested in a recovery planning or field ops position with ___ _____and have submitted my resume through the Web, but am having trouble getting any personal contact with the hiring decision-makers to follow up.

Do you have any insight into how the process works or how I might be able to reach out on a personal level to the recruiting department? Thanks for any info you may have.

Sincerely,

Your Name
(555) 555-1234
you@email.com

LinkedIn: Request Introduction #4

The following networking letter is a networking introduction request

____ _____ has sent you a message.
Date: **/**/2012
Subject: Thank you for inviting me into your network

Hi ____ _____,

Thank you for accepting me into your network, Martin! I am currently looking for networking connections with ____ _____ in _____, ___. Please let me know if you are comfortable with forwarding my request following my signature for the introduction to ____ _____.

Thank you,

Your Name
(555) 555-1234
you@email.com

(____ _____ note to _____ _____ :)

Hello ____ _____,

I am a seasoned Operations and Project Management specialist with a proven track record in optimizing operations to achieve maximum production and profit potential, producing new revenues or savings of over $20 million for my employers over the past 7 years.

I am interested in an employment opportunity with ____ _____ in the _____, ___ area, and noticed that you have identified yourself as someone who is willing to be contacted about jobs inquiries.

Please take a moment to review my profile, and let me know if you are interested in an exploratory conversation. I am of course happy to send my resume if you can send me your e-mail address.

I look forward to your response.

Regards,

Your Name
(555) 555-1234
you@email.com

LinkedIn: Target Company Networking

The following networking letter is a direct approach to a LinkedIn contact at a target company, using some good background information

____ ____ has sent you a message.
Date: **/**/2012
Subject: Risk mitigation—related question

Dear Jacqueline,

I was very impressed with what I learned about the _____ program in _____ at the Export-Import Bank Conference in _____ last week. That is why I write. I am interested in, among other things, risk mitigation and energy supplies and sources. I was impressed with your company's work from exactly this perspective.

I am happy to think that the move toward solar and wind is going to give the world not just better and more cost-effective power but also safer power. This is very important. At the Export-Import Bank Conference, for example, delegates from Morocco asked the Secretary of Energy if the United States would work with Morocco to do alternative energy in the south of Morocco and to include Mauritania, and, signally, to include a consortium of universities to do all of this.

I have worked as a Fulbright Scholar and know that this is absolutely critical for Morocco and for the country's relationship with the United States and for Morocco's security with respect to the rest of Africa.

The Secretary of Energy was happy to hear Morocco wants to come to the table to do business in the south of Morocco for alternative energy sources.

All of this is my way of saying that I would like to come up to _____, to explore and learn more. It might be possible to do a write-up for a broader audience that could feature what you are doing, and we might discuss what sort of audience when we meet.

I look forward to hearing from you soon.

Best,
Your Name
(555) 555-1234
you@email.com

LinkedIn: Vendor & Recruiter Networking

A LinkedIn networking letter to connect with an executive at a vendor
with whose product the sender is certified

____ _____ has sent you a message.
Date: **/**/2012
Subject: NBI Certified

Hello _____,

I'm one of _____'s authorized Partners, and would like to add you to my contacts here on
LinkedIn. ____ _____ or _____ _____ can verify my affiliation.

Sincerely,
Your Name
(555) 555-1234
you@email.com

LinkedIn.com Networking Letter to a Recruiter

____ _____ has sent you a message.
Date: **/**/2012
Subject: NBI Certified

Dear _____

____ _____ recommended that I connect with you. I'm a senior-level staffing and recruitment professional who is seeking opportunity in the greater Philadelphia area. While I am
in play with a few companies right now, I'd appreciate your insight into the local market and
players. In this respect, I'm hoping we might chat.

Sincerely,
Your Name
(555) 555-1234
you@email.com

FOLLOW-UP AFTER TELEPHONE CONTACT

Communications Systems, Headhunter Follow-Up

From: Your Name [Your e-mail address]
To: Recipient e-mail address
Cc:
Subject: Communications Systems follow-up

Dear Recipient Name,

As per our telephone conversation, enclosed is my current resume. I believe the one you have is written for another position. Since we last spoke I have been working as a business consultant for the _____ group of companies on projects in a number of different areas outlined below.

- Elected to serve as the Vice Chairman of the _____ Chapter 11 bankruptcy creditors' committee, including the two primary subcommittees reviewing offers to purchase the _____ operations.

- Spearheaded and supervised upgrading of the _____ communications systems, including Internet, printing and copy machines, telecommunications, hardware, software and archival systems, scanning, fax, and Internet access systems.

- Researched, purchased, and installed a bar code labeling program for the company's products, including label set-up and printing systems to allow them to sell their products to _____ .

Most of my projects should be wrapped up by the end of November, and so I will be looking for another company who could utilize my broad range of experience. Please let me know if you think you might have something for me.

Sincerely,
Your Name
(555) 555-1234

Director of Plant Services

From: Your Name [Your e-mail address]
To: Recipient e-mail address
Cc:
Subject: Glad we finally caught up RE: Director of Physical Plant Services

Dear Recipient Name,

I appreciate the time you took yesterday to discuss the Physical Plant Services job. I recognize that timing and awareness of interest are very important in searches of this type.

Your comment regarding an attempt to contact me earlier this summer is a case in point, but an ailing parent trumps all. Because of the situation, I wouldn't have been any good at an interview anyway. Now I am loaded for bear.

Attached, as you requested, you will find my resume. My experiences as a Director of Physical Plant Services are readily transferable to new environments; the horizontal flexibility is one of the appeals of the job.

You can reach me by e-mail or telephone. I look forward to hearing from you. Thank you for your time and consideration.

Sincerely,
Your Name
(555) 555-1234
Attachment: resume

Event Manager

From: Your Name [Your e-mail address]
To: Recipient e-mail address
Cc:
Subject: Our daybreak Event Management conversation

Dear Recipient Name,

I was lucky to catch you at the office so early yesterday morning; my day always gets off to an early start. As you will remember, we discussed, and you asked me to send you my resume in reference to, the Events Management job.

I am a fanatic about planning, execution, attention to quality and detail, and their cumulative result: communication of an image and feeling that appears effortless to event attendees.

I have never held a "nine-to-five" job and would most likely be bored to death if I had one. It's why I find event management such a fulfilling challenge to my gray matter. I am in my element when I am in a position to organize . . . the more details the better! I have the tenacity of a rat terrier when it comes to achieving the impossible.

Please review my attached resume. I'll give you a buzz on Tuesday, March 14th, hopefully to arrange a meeting. Call or e-mail sooner if your schedule permits; I can make the time at short notice now the annual convention is wrapped. I am looking forward to our meeting in the very near future.

Sincerely,
Your Name
(555) 555-1234
Attachment: resume

Fundraising Consultant

From: Your Name [Your e-mail address]
To: Recipient e-mail address
Cc:
Subject: Re: Fundraising Consultant meeting

Dear Recipient Name,

Thank you for making time to explore how I could help _____ as your newest Fundraising Consultant.

I've already starting thinking about how I might be most productive—right from the start. Of course, my ideas must be preliminary; I don't know nearly enough about how your organization works. Nevertheless, in response to your observations, I would value your reactions to these preliminary thoughts:

* Clients need to see the tailored solutions we provide as a rapid, seamless, continuing operation that guides them through the complex world of modern fundraising.

* Position and brand the company as the "sole source" for the resources they must have to grow financially and operationally.

I am modifying my continuing professional development program to concentrate on fundraising from a consultant's perspective; this is where I see the future. I am looking through the literature and contacting my network to learn their feelings about working with fundraising consultants today.

I'll use what I learn to reevaluate my own successes in campaigns done with and without consultants. I think this current competitive analysis, and my frame of reference from the "other side of the street," could be of value in strategic planning for our marketing initiatives.

I appreciate your vote of confidence in recommending that I meet with ____ ___. I want to make that interview just as useful for her as possible. Toward that end, may I call in a few days to get your reactions to the preliminary thoughts I've outlined above?

With many thanks for all your help...

Sincerely,
Your Name
(555) 555-1234

Headhunter Initial Phone Interview Follow-Up

From: Your Name [Your e-mail address]
To: Recipient e-mail address
Cc:
Subject: Tchunamke/Smith quantitative analysis conversion: growth, value, investment analysis, portfolio measurement, risk control

Dear Recipient Name,

Thank you for taking time to speak with me today. Your firm's reputation within the investment management industry prompted my call, and I am happy to learn that you have an active search that might fit my profile.

Working as a Quantitative Analyst at _____ over the past four years, I have gained valuable experience and solid skills that may be an asset, especially with a client such as _____:

* Strong background in growth, value, and quantitative investment strategies.
* Experience in measuring portfolios against various benchmarks.
* Polished communication skills with portfolio managers.
* Quantitative risk control of portfolios.
* Passion for markets and for finding investment solutions for institutional clients.

To focus my skills in quantitative investment analysis, I recently graduated from the University of _____ with an MS in Financial Mathematics.

I would like to speak with you about this or any other similar positions that call for my background and expertise. I look forward to hearing from you about suitable opportunities.

Sincerely,

Your Name
(555) 555-1234
Attachment: resume

Operations Management, Headhunter Follow-Up

From: Your Name [Your e-mail address]
To: Recipient e-mail address
Cc:
Subject: Operations Management pro, thanks for the conversation

Dear Recipient Name,

Thank you for allowing me to tell you a little about myself this morning.

I offer: 10 years' operations management experience, the ABILITY to quickly understand, manage, and build business; EXPERIENCE in domestic and international corporate cultures; INTELLIGENCE and the capacity to grasp essential elements; and the WILLINGNESS to work hard, travel, and relocate.

I have just completed my MBA and would appreciate the opportunity to talk with your client companies that are in need of an experienced and seasoned manager. Whether the need is for general (operational) management, products, marketing, or sales, my substantial background in operational management, marketing, and technical products should be very valuable to your clients.

Realizing that most of your clients aren't looking for VPs, I'm not necessarily looking for fancy titles (but I am promotable). What I am looking for is that special position that will offer not only a challenge but also an opportunity with long-range potential.

I will be happy to discuss details with you once you have reviewed the attached resume. May we work together?

Sincerely,
Your Name
(555) 555-1234

Pre-Law Part-Time Law Office

From: Your Name [Your e-mail address]
To: Recipient e-mail address
Cc:
Subject: RE our conversation about the office administration job

Dear Recipient Name,

Thank you for returning my telephone call yesterday. It was a pleasure speaking with you, and as promised, a copy of my resume is attached.

I have been working in law firms since the end of February, as well as working on weekends and in the evenings for over one year. At present, I am looking for a second or third shift to continue developing my word processing and legal skills while I complete my degree. I also work as Administrative Assistant to Deans and Department Heads, while attending school.

It's a while till I take the bar, and when I do I want to work in litigation. I need to work to pay for school, so the best of all possible worlds is for me to get a permanent part-time job with a litigation firm. You benefit by getting a part-timer with a unique commitment.

Within the next day, I will contact you to arrange a convenient meeting time to discuss the position you now have available. I look forward to meeting you in person.

Sincerely,
Your Name
(555) 555-1234

FOLLOW-UP AFTER FACE-TO-FACE MEETING

401(k) Professional

From: Your Name [Your e-mail address]
To: Recipient e-mail address
Cc:
Subject: James/Culbertson Communication Consultant meeting

Dear Recipient Name,

It was very enjoyable to speak with you about the Communications Consultant position last Wednesday, January 11th. I truly appreciate all the time and care you took in exploring the scope of responsibilities and examining my qualifications.

I will bring my Section 401(k) experience to bear with good effect–directing the brand communications experience from initial conception through execution; positioning strong development, execution, and management experience of 401(k) plan marketing and communication strategies for plan sponsors, plan participants, financial consultants, and investment committees; thoughtfully managing resources and budgets in alignment with overarching communication plans and goals.

I am comfortable interacting with all levels of internal and external clientele, including Client Relationship Managers, Chief Financial Officers, Human Resource Directors, and Investment Committees, one-on-one or during a boardroom presentation.

I always strive to create trust and respect; building solid relationships across an organization and with key external constituencies has always been an essential ingredient in my overall success as a leader.

I am excited about this opportunity and eager to move forward.

Sincerely,

Your Name
(555) 555-1234

Business Administrator

From: Your Name [Your e-mail address]
To: Recipient e-mail address
Cc:
Subject: Anjo/Stevens/Lyndon business administration meeting

Dear Recipient Name,

I want to express my appreciation to you and your team for the time and courtesy extended to me during my interview at 2 PM on Thursday, October 8th. I enjoyed the discussions and am even more enthusiastic about the Director of Business Administration position after hearing about the financial and operational challenges facing the _____ School District.

I am a hard-working, goal-oriented professional who works well with others at all levels. As evidenced by the positions I held at the _____ School District, Educational Testing Services, and _____, I have a diverse business background that enables me to bring a wide frame of references to the challenges we face here at _____.

I recognize the importance of the Director of Business Administration's role and, based on my past successes, am confident that I can meet the challenge. My educational background is strong and includes a Bachelor's Degree in Accounting cum laude, CPA certification, an MBA degree, and many hours of continuing professional education.

Likewise, my work experience and skills in auditing, accounting, budgeting, finance, and management would permit me to make some valuable contributions. Specifically, my experience includes:

- Managing the operating budget process
- Developing multi-million dollar budgets
- Creating business models to budget, forecast, and record revenues and expenses
- Financial reporting to internal and external clients
- Managing financial and operational audits
- Financial analysis, including variances to budgets and forecasts
- Leadership of projects (corporate-wide reengineering, process improvement teams, and system implementation)
- Revenue growth initiatives (including existing and new product growth and contract negotiations)
- Cost management
- Supervising staff auditors and managerial accountants
- Working with internal and external stakeholders (school board, city, and state)

I was impressed by the warm and confident professionalism of your team and look forward to moving our conversations forward to their logical conclusion. I am excited about the opportunity and I want to join the team as your next Director of Business Administration. Please do not hesitate to contact me at 555-555-1234 (home) or 555-555-2345 (mobile).

Sincerely,
Your Name
(555) 555-1234

CEO Personal Assistant

From: Your Name [Your e-mail address]
To: Recipient e-mail address
Cc:
Subject: CEO's P/A interview follow-up

Dear Recipient Name,

The time I spent interviewing with you and _____ this afternoon gave me a clear picture of your company's operation as well as your corporate environment. I want to thank you, in particular, _____, for the thorough picture you painted of your CEO's needs and work style.

I left our meeting feeling very enthusiastic about the scope of the position as well as its close match to my abilities and work style. After reviewing your comments, I think the key strengths that I can offer your CEO in achieving his agenda are:

- Experience in effectively dealing with senior-level staff in a manner that facilitates decision-making.
- Proven ability to anticipate an executive's needs and present viable options to consider.
- Excellent communication skills—particularly the ability to gain feedback from staff and summarize succinctly.

Whether the needs at hand involve meeting planning, office administration, scheduling, or executive access, I bring a combination of highly effective "people skills" and diversified business experience to deal with changing situations.

With my energetic work style, I believe that I am an excellent match for this unique position. I would welcome an additional meeting to elaborate on my background and how I can assist your CEO. I am excited; when can we talk again?

Sincerely,
Your Name
(555) 555-1234

Concierge

Dear Recipient Name,

We met last Thursday at 9 AM to discuss the Concierge Associate opening. Thank you for the opportunity to interview with you, Mr. _____, and Mrs. _____, to discuss the possibility of my joining your hospitality team as Concierge Associate.

As we discussed, The _____ Hotel is the ideal work environment for me to express my enthusiasm for working with people **and** to put my education in psychology and business administration to work.

I feel strongly that my volunteer work experience at The _____ and my personal experiences acquired over the years while traveling worldwide will prove especially valuable in this highly visible position. These things, combined with my ability to speak Spanish, French, and Italian, would allow me to make an immediate contribution.

Please note that my availability is immediate. If you need to contact me, I can be reached at the telephone number below. Thank you again for your time and consideration. I hope to speak with you soon.

Sincerely,
Your Name
(555) 555-1234

e-Marketing Professional

Dear Recipient Name,

I appreciate the time you took today interviewing me for the eMarketing position. I hope our 2-hour meeting did not throw off the rest of the day's calendar. I trust you will agree that it was time well spent, as I sensed we connected on every major point discussed.

My history in hi-tech, manufacturing, and biomedical industries and background in technology solutions seems to be a good match with the opportunities available in your company.

Your insight on e-commerce was intriguing. As I mentioned, at _____ _____, I initiated the eMarketing stratagems that opened our markets to Latin America. What I failed to mention is that I also have contacts with some e-commerce investors developing online portals targeted to the Latin market.

I am very interested in the position and would like to touch base with you on Tuesday to see where we stand. I am excited about moving forward.

Sincerely,
Your Name
(555) 555-1234

Entry-Level Pension Fund Administrator

From: Your Name [Your e-mail address]
To: Recipient e-mail address
Cc:
Subject: Thank you for the meeting

Dear Recipient Name,

I would like to take this opportunity to thank you for the interview this Wednesday morning, and to confirm my strong interest in an entry-level Customer Service position with the _____ department.

As we discussed, I feel that a BA and an internship with a pension fund have provided me with an understanding of the basic business operations and will help me quickly prove to be an asset. Additionally, I have always been considered a hard worker and a dependable, loyal employee. I am confident that I can make a valuable contribution to your Group Pension Fund area.

I look forward to meeting with you again in the near future to take the next steps. I am sincerely interested and enthusiastic about the position.

Sincere regards,

Your Name
(555) 555-1234

Headhunter Follow-Up #1

From: Your Name [Your e-mail address]
To: Recipient e-mail address
Cc:
Subject: Thanks for the meeting

Dear Recipient Name,

It was a pleasure meeting with you last Tuesday afternoon at 4 PM in reference to the Logistics position at _____ . I appreciate the time you spent with me, as well as the valuable insights you offered. As you suggested, I have adjusted my resume to reflect more accurately my relevant skills for this job. I have attached the new version so that your files can be updated.

Recipient Name, please allow me to thank you again for the compliment on my ability to present a strong interview. Please keep this in mind when considering me for placement with one of your clients. If I can be of assistance with other searches in my field, please let me know; in 12 years, I've gotten to know a lot of people.

Sincerely,
Your Name
(555) 555-1234
Attachment: resume

Headhunter Follow-Up #2

From: Your Name [Your e-mail address]
To: Recipient e-mail address
Cc:
Subject: Jane's prediction was right! Great meeting.

Dear Recipient Name,

Thank you for meeting with me this morning. Our associate, Name, assured me that a meeting with you would be productive, and it was. I sincerely appreciate your counsel, insight, and advice.

I have attached my resume for your review. I would appreciate any feedback you may have regarding effectiveness and strength. I understand you may not have any searches under way that would be suitable for me at this time, but I would appreciate any future considerations.

As we reviewed this morning, I seek and am qualified for senior MIS positions in a medium to large high-tech manufacturing or services business. I seek compensation in the $150,000 and above range, and look to report directly to the C-suite. These requirements are intelligently flexible depending on all the obvious factors. My family and I are willing to relocate to any area except _____.

Thanks again, Mr. _____, and please let me know if I can be of service to you in any related searches in my area of expertise; I'm always happy to suggest a referral. I have learned how important networking is. I really appreciate your assistance and wish to reciprocate.

Sincerely,

Your Name
(555) 555-1234
Attachment: resume

HR, T&D, Distance Learning

From: Your Name [Your e-mail address]
To: Recipient e-mail address
Cc:
Subject: Follow-up, today's 3 PM Distance Learning meeting

Dear Recipient Name,

Thank you very much for taking the time to meet with me today. I enjoyed our discussion, and I'm excited about the possibilities inherent in joining your team.

It was great to learn that you are embracing learning technology tools as they relate to the HR and T&D function—both in terms of day-to-day operations and the future delivery of company training programs (e.g., distance learning) to a dispersed client base.

I am very interested in, and have an affinity for, integrating technology into the HR function and then into the day-to-day operations of the company, and would love to be a part of your efforts in this area.

As we established, I have related experience in all of the required areas for the position. Establishing the new system for the delivery of the assessment workshops to your key clients would be an exciting kick-off project, and one that recent experience predicts I will ace in short order.

I am very interested in the position, and I look forward to hearing from you soon. If you require additional information in the meantime, I may be reached at (555) 555-1234.

Sincerely,
Your Name
(555) 555-1234

IT Auditor

From: Your Name [Your e-mail address]
To: Recipient e-mail address
Cc:
Subject: Very motivated by our meeting

Dear Recipient Name,

Thank you for allowing me the opportunity to meet with you at 2 PM on Tuesday the 30th to discuss the IT Audit position. The position sounds very challenging and rewarding, with ample room for growth. I feel my background and qualifications are a very good match for your needs:
* _____
* _____
* _____
* _____

I am committed to the ongoing development of my audit skills and feel I could work well with your focused audit staff. I am very interested in coming in to meet the team and to move to the next step. I look forward to hearing from you.

Sincerely,
Your Name
(555) 555-1234

Library Development

From: Your Name [Your e-mail address]
To: Recipient e-mail address
Cc:
Subject: Monday afternoon's Librarian selection meeting

Dear Recipient Name,

   Thank you for the opportunity to meet with you and the selection committee on Monday afternoon at 4 PM. I enjoyed our discussion of the Associate State Librarian for Library Development opening and I was impressed with the panel's vision for this role.
   Based on our conversation, I believe that I possess the capabilities to successfully meet your expectations for this key position with the State Library.

To reiterate the experiences I bring to this position, please note the following:

- Promoting programs and fostering working relationships with over 1,000 member libraries in all major segments of the field. These activities also encompass extensive community outreach.
- Providing strategic vision and mission, and motivating staff to pursue organizational goals. In countless assignments, I have recognized member library staffs for their focused efforts in ways that have delivered exceptional program results.
- Managing capital projects and spearheading information technology initiatives. These encompassed upgrades to comply with ADA access requirements, renovations that improved space utilization, and leading efforts to incorporate technology into library settings.
- Supervising departments in urban and suburban settings to address a broad range of competing priorities. Among these experiences was the supervision of an Interlibrary Loan department serving 100 individual branches in a five-county area.

I am most interested in this position and am confident that my track record at _____ demonstrates my capacity to "hit the ground running" and apply my leadership, enthusiasm, and expertise to furthering the mission of state libraries in this development role. I look forward to continuing our discussions in the near future.

Sincerely,
Your Name
(555) 555-1234

Loan Processing

From: Your Name [Your e-mail address]
To: Recipient e-mail address
Cc:
Subject: Follow-up yesterday's 2 PM Loan Processor interview

Dear Recipient Name,

Thank you for meeting with me this afternoon. I think _____ Home Mortgage Lending and I are a good match for each other. I want to become your newest loan processor team member.

In fact, as I was driving back to _____, I began to plan how I might be productive for you right from the start. My ideas are, of course, preliminary. But I would value your reactions to this tentative plan:

- ❏ I would start by introducing myself to every "player." I would want them quickly to recognize me as a trusted face for _____ Home Mortgage Lending. I want to find out what their special needs are *before* any rush requirements come up. When they need answers, I would want them to remember three things: my name, my phone number, and my e-mail.

- ❏ I have already started my plan to master FHA requirements; it won't take but a week; I'm a fast study with these things. I want _____ Home Mortgage to be the "provider of choice" in the eyes of buyers, agents, and closing attorneys—in short, anyone who wants quality loan processing services. The result will be that our percentage of revenue for FHA loan processing grows steadily.

As you asked me to, I plan to call on Friday. And I've already thought of the question I would most like to ask. It has two parts and here it is:

Does the plan I've outlined work for _____ Home Mortgage, in the hands of a proven closer such as myself, demonstrate an understanding of both the sales and client relationship-building processes? And, when can I start work?

Sincerely,
Your Name
(555) 555-1234

Manufacturer's Representative

From: Your Name [Your e-mail address]
To: Recipient e-mail address
Cc:
Subject: Our Manufacturer's Representative meeting

Dear Recipient Name,

Thank you for allowing me to interview with you on Friday, February 23rd for the Manufacturer's Representative position. Everything I learned from you about _____ leads me to believe that this is a progressive company where I could fully utilize my skills and make a valuable contribution. In fact, I have not been this determined or excited about a job since I started my career 20 years ago.

As I mentioned to you, I am sales oriented and have a solid technical background in printing. I relate well to printers at any level, from press people to owners. In my sales activities with ____ _____, when he was a printing buyer at _____, I found him to be very demanding and hard to please. One of the reasons why I was successful in acquiring and retaining his business was my constant commitment to customer service. Whenever there were any questions, I never failed to answer them promptly.

During our discussion, you seemed to express a concern about my lack of experience with dealers. I have had long-term relationships with dealers like _____, and have bought approximately $1 million worth of equipment from them, starting with my first press and expanding to 20 over the years. I am certain that with my persistency and follow-through, I can handle dealers at the sales and service end.

Among my major strengths, I am goal-driven, self-motivated, have a strong work ethic, and an ability to learn quickly. My training period would be brief, and I would use my own time to familiarize myself with your equipment and product line. In addition, I am accustomed to long hours and have no objection to the travel requirements throughout the Middle Atlantic States or being away from home four days a week.

Coming from a medium-sized company, it would be an honor to work at _____. I look forward to talking further about my candidacy.

Sincerely,

Your Name
(555) 555-1234

Mental Health Senior Counselor

From: Your Name [Your e-mail address]
To: Recipient e-mail address
Cc:
Subject: Looking forward to next week

Dear Recipient Name,

I would like to thank you for affording me the opportunity to meet with you to discuss the Senior Counselor position with your organization. I have long been an admirer of your services and commitment to the community. I am very confident that my education, experience, and counseling skills will enable me to make an immediate and long-term contribution to your mental health program.

The position we discussed seems well suited to my strengths and skills, because both my counseling and teaching backgrounds include a real emphasis on the family unit and its influence and relationship to each client's therapy.

I genuinely am looking forward to seeing you again next week; it is so stimulating to discuss the needs of our calling with someone similarly committed and with such a tremendous frame of reference. If you require any additional information before then, please feel free to call.

Sincerely,
Your Name
(555) 555-1234

Merchandise Manager

From: Your Name [Your e-mail address]
To: Recipient e-mail address
Cc:
Subject: Re our Merchandiser meeting

Dear Recipient Name,

Thank you for the opportunity to interview for the **Merchandise Manager** position last Tuesday at 11 AM. I was impressed with the warmth and efficiency of your office, and your genuine interest in acquainting me with the company's concepts and goals.

My background is unique—it does not fit into a traditional career mold—yet this diverse exposure delivers a deep understanding in Home Furnishings and Ready-to-Wear. As we discussed, my extensive experience with the type of clientele your company targets prepares me to quickly "come on board" your team.

My sales record of $279,000 in the last year demonstrates that I can produce immediate value, as well as train new sales reps in highly effective merchandising and closing techniques. I am attaching the newsletter that cites these numbers.

What I did not stress is that I have also built an arsenal of skills around the quantitative, technical processes involved in merchandising dollar planning. For example, I have developed six-month dollar merchandising plans for the _____ division of _____, and classification planning with its focus on merchandise categories, prices, styles, sizes, and colors.

I have always strived to achieve results by knowing our customer, anticipating and responding to market trends, and *never forgetting the brand*. Offering wide but well-edited assortments of multiple classifications to facilitate one-stop shopping has been my hallmark.

High standards have been central in my work, whether with a major retail department store, _____ City wholesale showroom, or upscale home furnishings boutique. Your corporate environment and company goals appear to reflect those same high standards, and I am eager to join your team.

Thanks again for the opportunity to interview. I hope you see the match as clearly as I do.

Sincerely,
Your Name
(555) 555-1234
Attachment: sales verification

Program Developer

From: Your Name [Your e-mail address]
To: Recipient e-mail address
Cc:
Subject: The right choice for program development

Dear Recipient Name,

The program development job we discussed at breakfast on Friday is a tremendously challenging one. After considering our conversation and the job requirements for most of the weekend, I know that I can make an immediate contribution with this job.

Since you are going to reach a decision quickly, I would like to reinforce the following points, which qualify me for the job you unknowingly designed to suit my abilities perfectly:

1. My track record of generating fresh ideas and creative solutions for difficult problems.
2. My 9 years of, as you said, "very impressive" achievements in program planning and development.
3. My multitasking abilities, something we share and laughed about at breakfast.
4. My communication management with program stakeholders; remember I am coming from _____.
5. Experience in administration, general management, and presentations; we have colleagues in common who can verify these points.

_____, I have always had an intense desire to do a killer job in anything I undertake; it is why I have travelled so far professionally in so short a time. I can do this job: I can represent you, the department, and the company well. But most of all, I want to work for you, the acknowledged thought leader of our profession. It would be the honor of my career.

What do I have to do to make this happen?

Sincerely,
Your Name
(555) 555-1234

Recycling

From: Your Name [Your e-mail address]
To: Recipient e-mail address
Cc:
Subject: Thanks for the meeting

Dear Recipient Name,

Thank you for the opportunity to discuss the position of Personal Assistant with you yesterday afternoon, Wednesday, September 7th. I came looking for a job and left a convert to the cause.

____ Corporation is involved in one of the most pressing concerns of today: environmentally safe methods of disposing of solid waste materials. I can see now just how critical the creation of proper disposal systems really is. I have a sincere interest in this position. The skills that I have to offer you are:

- Professionalism, organization, and maturity
- Excellent office skills
- Ability to work independently
- A creative work attitude
- Research and writing skills
- Varied business background
- Willingness to learn

I would be:
- A productive assistant to management
- Part of a technologically developing industry
- In a position to learn and grow in the excitement of an expanding company
- Willing to step up, whatever the task

I look forward to being a part of an organization that is making a difference in the world. Again, thank you for considering my qualifications to become a part of your organization. I want the job.

Sincerely,
Your Name
(555) 555-1234

Region Sales Manager

From: Your Name [Your e-mail address]
To: Recipient e-mail address
Cc:
Subject: Thanks for an exciting meeting. Next steps?

Dear Recipient Name,

I thoroughly enjoyed our 8 AM meeting on Wednesday, and was glad to meet another crazy early-morning runner. You're right; it's when I do all my strategizing and problem-solving, too. After learning more about your goals and expectations, the prospect of joining the organization as the Western Region Sales Manager is enticing.

One of the most important things I have learned in my 20+ years in sales is to listen to what the customer needs. I have always taken pride in designing customized solutions that not only meet the clients' objectives but that are also price/value competitive. This philosophy has enabled me to **_exceed corporate expectations for 17 consecutive years_**.

In addition, I have managed to develop about 65% of sales into established accounts; takes a little more time, but boy what a payback. Client development was the objective you indicated was a high priority for company growth. It's always been a high personal priority for me, too: it's the secret to my track record. ;-)

I recognize that the performance of Company Name's Western Region Sales Manager is an important cornerstone in the company's projections and growth plans for the new fiscal year. I have worked this territory for 14 years, I know the client base, and I understand your product line, having sold against it for seven years. I can deliver the numbers: you have a superior product; you just haven't had the right guy selling it.

Thanks again for your time. How about breakfast, lunch, or dinner to talk numbers and dates?

Sincerely,
Your Name
(555) 555-1234

Sales Follow-Up

From: Your Name [Your e-mail address]
To: Recipient e-mail address
Cc:
Subject: Great to meet you on Wednesday

_____,

First of all, thank you. I thoroughly enjoyed our meeting last-thing Wednesday, and greatly appreciate your insight and the time taken to discuss where I might best fit into the _____ team. Your professionalism and willingness to share what you know put me instantly at ease, and I am now even more motivated to be part of _____'s success.

Let me begin by restating how flattered I am that you saw such potential in me. I likewise feel confident that I have the management and leadership expertise, marketing skills, and business development experience to be successful, and I see tremendous opportunities with the company.

However, as we discussed, I understand that my first step is to make my mark as a member of the Road Crew and am equally excited at the opportunity to make an impact on the front line. I realize that you are not currently in the position to make such an offer, but I want to reemphasize my enthusiasm to join the _____ team wherever you feel I could add value.

I'd like to refresh three points:

♦ I possess the drive, commitment, and strong people skills required to make an impact in this industry.

♦ I deliver proven business development, sales, and revenue-building experience.

♦ I know what it takes to get results, both out of myself and others, and have proven again and again to be the "go to" person when results are expected.

I hope that you and I have the opportunity to continue our discussions soon. Once again, I appreciate the time you spent to meet with me. I wish you continued success in all your efforts and look forward to seeing you at the Sales Excellence seminar at the end of July.

Sincerely,
Your Name
(555) 555-1234

Wholesale Banker, Headhunter Follow-Up

From: Your Name [Your e-mail address]
To: Recipient e-mail address
Cc:
Subject: Wholesale Banker, headhunter follow-up

Dear Recipient Name,

I understand that the search is continuing for the Wholesale Market Manager position at _____. As you continue your search, I would like to ask that you keep my accomplishments and experiences in mind:

1. Direct experience in all phases of wholesale commercial banking, including: market segmentation, prospecting, building and maintaining customer relationships, lending, and the sale of non-credit products and services.

2. Captured 24% share of public funds market within 2 years, and captured a 22% share of insurance company funds market.

3. Developed cash management and trust products tailored to the needs of my target market; $55 million in sales in 3 years.

4. Marketed services through e-mail, social networking, investor-specific seminars, and through active participation in target market's industry professional organizations.

5. Maximized relationships and increased balances through the sale of trust and cash management products.

I will call you next week, after you have seen the other candidates, to continue our discussion. In the meantime, please be assured of both my competency and commitment.

Sincerely,

Your Name
(555) 555-1234
Attachment: resume

REFERENCES, ENDORSEMENTS, AND SALARY TEMPLATES

Endorsement Attachment

Professional Performance Commentaries
on

_____ _____

(555) 555.1234 • me@email.com

From last four years of annual performance appraisal reviews:

"___ stands out in her attention to the nuances of a complex operational infrastructure. Strong communication skills, tuned analytical mind, and a team player."

"She proactively seeks out seminars and webinars that keep her professional awareness on the cutting edge."

"If there's a problem, ___ is always the first to step up."

"A by-the-book type of employee, professional in her dealings with vendors and employees."

"A demonstrated ability to multitask and manage her time effectively based on departmental priorities. Unusual ability to make informed decisions on the details based on the imperatives of the big picture."

~ ___ ___, VP Operations and immediate supervisor

From annual performance appraisal reviews at prior employer:

"___ has proven herself adept at accomplishing tasks with individuals throughout the company. She takes care to clarify issues and expectations for delegated tasks."

"Always ready to accept responsibility."

"Willing to work on projects that may not lie directly in her job responsibilities, but which impact the overall productivity of the department."

"Hardworking, ethical, and even-tempered."

~ ___ ___, Director Operations and immediate supervisor

JANE ROCKHARDT

5863 Pine Street • Salt Lake City, UT 12345
Home (555) 555-1234 • Mobile (555) 555-2345 • me@email.com

Senior Software Architect

Solid Leadership – Software Architecture – Mobile Application Development – Internet Marketing

Professional References

Lead Software Architect
MOBILE APPLICATIONS, SALT LAKE CITY, UT   **2008–Present**

Designed and developed iPhone application, iLogMiles, for commercial transportation industry.
Reference: Winston Churchill, VP
Professional Relationship—Immediate supervisor

VP Information Technology
SALT LAKE FEDERAL SAVINGS BANK,
SALT LAKE CITY, UT   **2003–2008**

Led technology department and created tech strategy for bank.
Technology infrastructure, including migration strategies for accounting and loan origination systems.
Reference: Harry Truman, President
Professional Relationship—Immediate supervisor

Software Developer
MORTGAGE PORTFOLIO SERVICES, DALLAS, TX   **1999–2003**

Designed, developed, & deployed mortgage lock platform using CGI and C++.
Reference: John Connally, President
Professional Relationship—Immediate supervisor

Salary History Attachment

PAUL QUARN

86 Concord Street, Apt # 232 • Charlotte, NC 46776

Home (555) 555-1234 • Mobile (555) 555-1234 • me@email.com

SENIOR OPERATIONS/PLANT MANAGEMENT PROFESSIONAL

Continuous Improvement/Lean Six Sigma/Start-Up & Turnaround Operations/ Mergers & Change Management/Process & Productivity Optimization/HR/Logistics & Supply Chain

SALARY HISTORY

UNITED STATES MARINE CORPS AIR STATION, Cherry Point, NC—2008 to 2010

Chief Operations Officer/***** Training School Officer in Charge

Salary—$95,309

UNITED STATES MARINE CORPS AIR STATION, Futenma, Okinawa, Japan—2005 to 2008

******** Maintenance Chief—General Operations Manager/Plant Manager

Starting Salary—$64,484/Ending Salary—$97,500

UNITED STATES MARINE CORPS AIR STATION, Beaufort, SC—2001 to 2005

Plant Manager/Senior Operations Manager

Starting Salary—$49,507/Ending Salary—$64,484

UNITED STATES MARINE CORPS RECRUITING STATION, Jacksonville, FL—1998–2001

Recruiting Manager

Starting Salary—$42,545/Ending Salary—$49,507

RESURRECTION

Headhunter

From: Your Name [Your e-mail address]
To: Recipient e-mail address
Cc:
Subject: Construction Management searches?

Dear Recipient Name,

   I am in the construction management and business management fields, and am writing to follow up on a resume I sent a while back. Perhaps you did not have any active searches that met my qualifications in construction management, or my file was mislaid.

   I am looking for an executive position that leverages the experience and abilities reflected in the attached resume. I am open to relocating in the United States and overseas. If any positions become available, I would be happy to discuss the details. Thanks for your consideration. I'll call in a couple of days to follow up.

Sincerely,
Your Name
(555) 555-1234
Attachment: resume

Lost in the Shuffle

Dear Recipient Name,

I must have been one of the first people you spoke with about the Programmer job posting, because at the time you seemed very interested, as was I. However, when I called back you had received so many calls for the position you didn't know one from the other. That's understandable, so I hope I can stir your memory and, more importantly, your interest.

I have a solid programming and project development background in both the Windows and Macintosh worlds, and have worked in Web applications for 5 years now. What's even better is my hobby: my work.

You had some ideas for children's software and thought having kids would help when working on such software. You had asked if I had children and I do: a four-and-a-half-year-old daughter and a four-and-a-half-month-old daughter.

My oldest uses _____ on my Macintosh at home and double-clicks away without any assistance from my wife or myself. She has learned a great deal from "playing" with it and is already more computer literate than I ever expected. We need more software like _____ to help stir the minds of our kids.

I have attached a resume for your perusal. But in case you don't want to read all the details, here it is in short:

- I have 6 years' programming and development experience in Windows.
- I have 3 years' programming and development experience on the Macintosh.
- I am currently the Senior Developer for Macintosh programming here at _____ Corp.
- I have 2 years' experience working extensively on cloud-based applications.

I look forward to speaking with you again, so please don't hesitate to call me, (555) 555-1234, or hit me with an e-mail.

Sincerely,

Your Name
(555) 555-1234
Attachment: resume

New Skills

Dear Recipient Name,

We met on _____ site on December 23 in the middle of that major snowstorm, and spoke regarding opportunities for Lift Line Operators. Since then I have obtained a **CDL-B Learner's Permit with Passenger and Air-Brake endorsements**.

I am writing to reiterate my sincere interest in a **Lift Line Driver** position, and hope to speak with you soon to learn what my next steps would be in order to further my candidacy. I look forward to talking with you soon.

Sincerely,

Your Name
(555) 555-1234
Attachment: resume

Overlooked at Job Fair

Dear Recipient Name,

Firstly, I want to thank you for the time you spent with me in a recent telephone conversation, when you suggested I reapply for a Stevedore position.

To refresh your memory of the situation: on August 4 I attended the Stevedore Recruiting event at the _____ Convention Center. I submitted my resume and spoke very briefly with a representative.

In the short time I chatted with her I did my best to communicate my interest in, and qualifications for, the job. However, due to the overwhelming number of applicants, there just wasn't sufficient time to convey how qualified I really am.

With that in mind, I have attached my resume for your review. To summarize:

- I have an extensive history of working safely around heavy equipment.
- I am in outstanding physical condition.
- I am a very reliable and dedicated employee.
- I have received first aid, CPR, and terrorism-awareness training.

This resume is only a hint of who I am—words on paper cannot replace a personal conversation. Therefore, would you please consider my request for a face-to-face interview so that you can evaluate my qualifications, abilities, drive, and enthusiasm for yourself?

I will make myself available for any time that you can take out of your schedule. Thank you for your consideration, and I look forward to possibly meeting with you in the near future.

Sincerely,

Your Name
(555) 555-1234
Attachment: resume

Re-Opening a Rejected Opportunity

From: Your Name [Your e-mail address]
To: Recipient e-mail address
Cc:
Subject: You were so right

Dear Recipient Name,

Four months ago you and I discussed an A/R job, and you were kind enough to set up meetings with _____ and _____. Shortly thereafter, as you know, I accepted a position with _____. You warned me about the issues there, but I had to learn the hard way that all that glitters is not gold.

If now or at any time a similar position opens up, I would like to reopen our discussions; please put me first on your list. I've attached my resume and hope we can get together. I'll call to catch up in the next couple of days.

Sincerely,

Your Name
(555) 555-1234
Attachment: resume

Second Place But Not Next Time #1

From: Your Name [Your e-mail address]
To: Recipient e-mail address
Cc:
Subject: Community Empowerment Team Director, thank you _____
_____

Dear Recipient Name,

Thank you for the opportunity to interview for the Community Empowerment Team Director position. I genuinely appreciated the chance to discuss your vision for the CET program.

Although another candidate was ultimately selected for this important position, I was pleased to be among the short list of applicants under consideration.

I believe that my nine years' experience with the City of _____ provides me with a wealth of knowledge and expertise that can be beneficial to the city, perhaps when a similar position becomes available. I continue to be committed to the mission of the CET program, but also wish to offer myself as a candidate for other roles where my capabilities can further the objectives of the city.

Please keep me in mind if other opportunities should arise where my talents would be an asset, particularly as you move ahead with implementation of the _____ program.

Thank you again for your consideration.

Sincerely,
Your Name
(555) 555-1234

Second Place But Not Next Time #2

From: Your Name [Your e-mail address]
To: Recipient e-mail address
Cc:
Subject: Director of Human Resources position

Dear Recipient Name,

Congratulations on the selection of your new Director of Human Resources! I hope this new person meets your expectations, and I wish you every success.

I appreciated the chance to apply for the position and am grateful for the consideration you have given me throughout this process. Although I am obviously disappointed at not being the successful candidate, I remain interested in potential opportunities with the _____. If for any reason or at any time this position opens up again, please be aware that I am still interested.

In the meantime, should there be openings for support positions within the HR Department, or positions in other departments of the town government, I would like to be considered for such opportunities. I know my organization, communication skills, and flexibility would make me an asset to the team. If you hear of other openings, within either governmental agencies or the private sector, I would be most appreciative if you would pass that information on to me.

Thank you for all your time and consideration. I look forward to speaking with you again.

Sincerely,

Your Name
(555) 555-1234

REJECTION

Accepting Another Job Offer

From: Your Name [Your e-mail address]
To: Recipient e-mail address
Cc:
Subject: Job offer for the Director position

Dear Recipient Name,

Thank you for taking the time to meet with me recently to discuss the position of _____ Director. I genuinely appreciated the opportunity to meet with the Board and the Search Committee to learn about the position. I was very favorably impressed with the _____ City Library System and believe that if selected, my contributions would have more than justified your judgment.

However, I am writing to ask that my name be withdrawn from further consideration for the Director's position at this time. I have recently been offered another challenging and rewarding opportunity. The relative time frames involved have made it necessary for me to render a decision without further delay, and I have chosen to accept the offer.

Had circumstances permitted, I believe that it would have been productive to continue our discussions, and am confident that we could have arrived at a mutually beneficial arrangement.

I would be most interested in keeping in touch; we never know what the future will unfold for us. I wish you the best of luck in this current search. Thank you, again, for your time and consideration.

Sincerely,
Your Name
(555) 555-1234

Not This Job, Maybe Something Bigger

From: Your Name [Your e-mail address]
To: Recipient e-mail address
Cc:
Subject: Appreciate your interest

Dear Recipient Name,

Thank you for your e-mail updating me on the status of the telecommunications project we discussed in our recent telephone conversation.

Although I genuinely appreciate your consideration for the Team Supervisor position, at this time I feel my best interests are to pursue a position more closely aligned with my level of experience, achievements, and demonstrated managerial skills.

I remain most interested in opportunities with your company, and would ask that you keep my name in consideration for other positions that would more fully capitalize on my knowledge and expertise. Thank you for your time and interest.

Sincerely,
Your Name
(555) 555-1234

Rejection after Careful Thought

Dear Recipient Name,

I would like to thank you for offering me the position of Accounting Policy Manager at ___ _____. I am extremely grateful for the opportunity and time I had to meet you, _____, _____, _____, _____, and _____ over the last few weeks, and appreciate the time and incredible effort involved in considering me for a position in your organization.

It was quite a challenging decision for me, as I was genuinely impressed by the strong caliber of your organization and the very impressive energy efficiency strategy. Everything reinforced the great experience I had working at your ___ site while on my Federal tax rotation at _____ in 2009. However, after much consideration, I have made a decision to accept an offer that is better aligned with my immediate career goals.

I wish you, the finance organization, and ____ much continued success. I sincerely hope that we stay in touch and that our professional paths cross again. Thank you again for your time and consideration.

Sincerely,

Your Name
(555) 555-1234
Attachment: resume

Thanks, But Just Accepted Another Job

From: Your Name [Your e-mail address]
To: Recipient e-mail address
Cc:
Subject: re: Internal Audit opening

Dear Recipient Name,

It was indeed a pleasure meeting with you and your staff to discuss your needs for a _____;
our time together was most enjoyable and informative.

As we have discussed during our meetings, a primary purpose of preliminary interviews is to
explore areas of mutual interest and assess the fit between the individual and the position. I was
well along in my job search when we spoke, and intimated that I was close to receiving offers.

As I have accepted a position that is well suited to my qualifications and experience,
I must withdraw myself from consideration. Thank you for interviewing me and giving me the
opportunity to learn more about your facility. You have a fine team, and I would have enjoyed
working with you.

Best wishes to you and your staff; look forward to running into you again one of these days.

Sincerely,

Your Name
(555) 555-1234

With Regrets and Great Hope

From: Your Name [Your e-mail address]
To: Recipient e-mail address
Cc:
Subject: With regrets and great hopes for January

Dear Recipient Name,

I would like to take this opportunity to thank you for the interview on Thursday morning, and to express my strong interest in future employment with your organization.

While I appreciate very much your offer for the position of Department Manager, I feel that at this stage of my career I am seeking greater challenges and advancement than the Department level is able to provide. Having worked in management for over four years, I am confident that my skills will be best applied in a position with more responsibility and accountability.

As we discussed, I look forward to talking again in January about how I might contribute to the company in the capacity of Unit Manager. Roll on the New Year!

Sincere regards,

Your Name
(555) 555-1234

ACCEPTANCE

Delayed Start

From: Your Name [Your e-mail address]
To: Recipient e-mail address
Cc:
Subject: Reference _____ job offer

Dear Recipient Name,

I would like to express my appreciation for your letter offering me the position of _____ _____ in your Department at a starting salary of $__, ___ per year.

I was very impressed with the team and facilities in _____, and am writing to confirm my acceptance of your offer. If it is acceptable to you, I will report to work on Date. I need to offer proper notice, and then wish to take two weeks to go see my parents in Chennai. I do hope this is acceptable.

Let me once again express my appreciation for your offer and my excitement about joining your _____ staff. I look forward to my association with _____, and know my contributions will be in line with your expectations.

Sincerely,

Your Name
(555) 555-1234

Happy to Accept Job Offer

From: Your Name [Your e-mail address]
To: Recipient e-mail address
Cc:
Subject: Happy to accept the job offer and join the team

Dear Recipient Name,

I want to thank you for the privilege of joining your staff as _____ _____. Your flexibility and cooperation in the counter-negotiations were much appreciated. Thank you for making every effort to make the pending transition a smooth one.

Per your requests, I am providing this letter, for my official file.

"In that your organization is a competitor of my previous employer, and in that this organization seeks to maintain goodwill and high levels of integrity within the industry, it should be duly noted that neither you nor any representative of your organization sought me as a prospective employee. It was my identification of a possible position, and solely my pursuits toward your company, that resulted in my resignation as Senior Director to join your firm as Managing Consultant."

If I can provide additional clarification on this matter, or assist in protecting the ethics of your company, notify me at your convenience. I look forward to starting with your team on the _____ of _____.

Sincerely,

Your Name
(555) 555-1234

Offer Acceptance and Plan of Attack

From: Your Name [Your e-mail address]
To: Recipient e-mail address
Cc:
Subject: Marketing Research Manager job offer

Dear Recipient Name,

Thank you for your positive response to our meetings and the resulting job offer for the Marketing Research Manager position. I am delighted to accept your offer of employment and look forward to a fast start with the various projects we discussed during the selection process; the sales forecasting and strategic market planning for the core product line is especially intriguing.

I am honored that your organization feels that I am the right person to lead your marketing research efforts, and I will deliver the results we discussed. As I mentioned in our telephone conversation yesterday, I am constantly in touch with what the competition is doing, with the goal of positioning my team's effort in the marketplace to yield maximum results.

Per your instructions, I will contact Name, Human Resources Manager, on Monday morning to arrange an orientation appointment. I look forward to meeting with you after that to start putting together a plan of attack; maybe at lunch after my orientation appointment?

Sincerely,

Your Name
(555) 555-1234

VP of Finance Acceptance

From: Your Name [Your e-mail address]
To: Recipient e-mail address
Cc:
Subject: VP Finance Acceptance

Dear Recipient Name,

This letter will serve as my formal acceptance of your offer to join your firm as Vice President of Finance. I understand and accept the conditions of employment that you explained in the offer letter.

I will contact your personnel department this week to request any paperwork I might need to complete for their records prior to my starting date. Also, I will schedule a physical examination for insurance purposes. I would appreciate your forwarding any reading material you feel might hasten my initiation.

Yesterday I tendered my resignation at Company Name and worked out a mutually acceptable notice time of four weeks, which should allow me ample time to finalize my business and personal affairs here and be ready for work on schedule.

You, your board, and your staff have been most professional and helpful throughout this hiring process. I anxiously anticipate joining the Company Name team and look forward to many new challenges. Thank you for your confidence and support.

Sincerely,

Your Name
(555) 555-1234

NEGOTIATION

A Commission Issue

From: Your Name [Your e-mail address]
To: Recipient e-mail address
Cc:
Subject: Regarding the _____ job offer

Dear Recipient Name,

I have reviewed your letter and the specific breakdown regarding compensation. I believe there to be a few items to clarify, prior to providing you with a formal acceptance. I do not consider any of the items to be "deal breakers" in any way. I also do not perceive them to be issues that cannot be discussed, as we are, in fact, moving ahead.

The primary concern has to do with the commission structure, as opposed to salary plus commission, to which I have grown accustomed. From a practical perspective I need to have some financial coverage for the start-up period: the time it will take me to make sales, collect the money, and the lead time this takes to go through the accounting and payroll system. I also need this because I will be shifting from a biweekly salary schedule to a monthly format.

I am hoping that as per the industry norm, you will absorb some of this start-up cost. I am therefore asking for straight salary for the first two weeks and then a draw against commission up to the end of the 90-day probationary period.

The second clarification revolves around the 401(k) program; the percentages, timeframes, and terms. This is something we can discuss over the course of the next two weeks. You may even be able to pass something specific on to me in writing.

With these two concerns articulated, I want you to know that I will be meeting with the owner of our company tomorrow morning to discuss my plans for departure. In fairness to him and to my current client load, I could not start full-time with you for 21 days.

I would like to set a time for us to have dinner one evening next week, so you can meet my wife and we can talk a bit less formally.

Looking forward to what lies ahead.

Sincerely,
Your Name
(555) 555-1234

Tactful Request to Raise Salary and Benefits Offer

From: Your Name [Your e-mail address]
To: Recipient e-mail address
Cc:
Subject: Regarding offer for Senior Lab Specialist

Dear Recipient Name,

I am excited by the invitation to join the _____ family as a Senior Lab Specialist. The position, responsibility, and location are consistent with my career goals and objectives. I am genuinely excited about the opportunity.

However, prior to my formal acceptance, there are a number of items for clarification. None of these items are necessarily "deal breakers." Items for clarification are:

- Detailed description of insurance benefits.
- Realistic analysis of the corporate stock and 401(k) plans.
- Written explanation of educational reimbursement allowance.
- The mobility plan seems very reasonable, but I would like specifics on the Permanent Work aspect.
- Relocation coverage: is it an allowance or reimbursement of actual expenses incurred in the move? What are my tax obligations, and does the company cover them?
- Detailed explanation of the Variable Pay Plan.

This final item is significant. In our conversations, I communicated to you that I was making $__K while working part-time and going to school. The salary offer is substantially lower and represents a pay cut. My goal is to discern how feasible it will be for me to meet my financial obligations.

I am really interested in the job, but am finding it difficult to give serious consideration to anything less than $__K salary plus benefits. I am hoping to discover a variety of vehicles that will enable you to help me achieve that goal, so that I can join the team, pay my bills, and begin to nibble at college loans.

I look forward to discussing these issues with you in the very near future, and trust that we will soon be working together.

Respectfully Yours,

Your Name
(555) 555-1234

The Devil's in the Details

From: Your Name [Your e-mail address]
To: Recipient e-mail address
Cc:
Subject: Director of _____ job offer

Dear Recipient Name,

I want to thank you for your invitation to join _____. I have reviewed the offer of position and compensation, as presented in your letter dated _____, 2012. I would like to ask for clarification on a few items prior to providing you with a formal acceptance. While none of these items is necessarily a "deal breaker" I believe consideration of them will enable both parties to begin the partnership better informed of mutual goals and expectations.

Per the breakdown provided:
- I accept the 401(k) plan as proposed
- I accept the paid holiday and personal days plan as proposed
- I accept the educational reimbursement plan as proposed
- I accept the Direct Payroll Deposit plan as proposed (if elected)
- I accept the Medical, Dental, Vision, Pharmacy, and Life Insurance benefits as proposed, contingent on factors clarified below

Points of Clarification:
- What is available in regard to "Stock Options"?
- What are the "standard hours of operation" for _____ employees?
- Would it be possible to have a "Performance Evaluation" at the end of 6 months?
- I would like to structure the vacation days as follows: 3 days in remainder of year ____, one week during calendar year ____, two weeks during calendar years ____ to ____, three weeks beginning January of ____.
- In light of the "out of pocket expenses" anticipated correspondent to the medical benefits, how might we agree to get the annual base salary to $__,___? I am open to a number of different options to achieve this goal, including profit sharing, commission, or 5% annual bonus arrangement.

I am excited about the long-term possibilities that exist at _____. As you can see by my level of attention to the details, I intend to partner with you for a long tenure of success. I believe my skills will be an enhancement to the existing leadership. My presence will enable you and others to focus on new aspects of business development and achieve corporate goals and objectives that will be beneficial to us all. Again, I want to thank you for the gracious offer. I look forward to finalizing these minor details very soon.

Sincerely,
Your Name
(555) 555-1234

We Need to Bump the Money

Dear Recipient Name,

Thank you for your offer of employment with _____. Your state-of-the-art company would afford me the opportunity to make a contribution while continuing to grow professionally in an ever-evolving industry. The Product Specialist position promises challenges and demands a high level of professional commitment that I am more than willing to embrace.

As you know from our previous conversations, I have outstanding skills and abilities that I can bring to the job. First and foremost is my hands-on experience doing this job for a direct competitor. I have a proven track record of relating well to other medical professionals and accommodating their needs.

It is my understanding that as Product Specialist, my communication skills will be critical to performance success. With my experience in troubleshooting technical problems, I know that technology can be learned but becomes utilitarian only when it can be translated into user effectiveness. My expertise integrates both of these critical components that are key in the Product Specialist role.

However, based upon the value I bring to the job and the company, plus the knowledge that the salary range for this type of position in our industry normally falls between $__,____ and $__,___, I would like to request that we reconsider the starting offer of $__,____. Of course, I appreciate the generous benefits package that you provide and take this into account.

I am more than happy to assume all of the responsibilities necessary to meet and exceed the expectations of the Product Specialist position at a starting salary of $___,___. I look forward to hearing from you, and hope that we can reach an agreement that will enable me to begin my career with _____ on June 4.

Sincerely,
Your Name
(555) 555-1234

RESIGNATION

291

Gracious Resignation

From: Your Name [Your e-mail address]
To: Recipient e-mail address
Cc:
Subject: Regretfully, my resignation

Dear Recipient Name,

Please accept my resignation from my position as Sales Representative for the metropolitan area, effective January 25. I am offering two weeks' notice so that my territory can be effectively serviced during the transition with the least amount of inconvenience to our clients.

I now have an opportunity to develop my skills in areas that are more in line with my long-term goals. I thank you for the sales training, and have enjoyed very much working under your leadership. It is largely due to the excellent experience I gained working on your team that I am now able to pursue this growth opportunity in Training and Development.

During the next two weeks, I am willing to help in every way to make the transition as smooth as possible. This includes assisting in recruiting and training my replacement. If I can be of assistance to you or my replacement after this time, perhaps in giving insights on particular clients, I am more than happy to do so. Please let me know if there is anything specific that you would like me to do.

Again, it has been a true honor working as a part of your group. I shall remember you especially and the team with fondness for many years. I hope we stay in touch.

Sincerely,

Your Name
(555) 555-1234

MIS Resignation from First Job

From: Your Name [Your e-mail address]
To: Recipient e-mail address
Cc:
Subject: Resignation notification

Dear Recipient Name,

This e-mail is to notify you that I am resigning my position with _____ effective _____.
In order to achieve the career goals that I've set for myself, I have accepted a higher-level
Systems Operator position with another company. This position will give me an opportunity to
become more involved in the technical aspects of setting up networking systems.

I have enjoyed my work here very much and want to thank you and the rest of the MIS
Department for all the encouragement and support you have always given me.

Please know that I am available to help with any staff training or offer assistance in any way
that will make my departure as easy as possible for the department.

I want to wish everyone the best of luck in the future. Thanks again for giving me my start in a
profession I love. I will always hold you in the highest esteem, _____.

Sincerely,
Your Name
(555) 555-1234

Requested Resignation

From: Your Name [Your e-mail address]
To: Recipient e-mail address
Cc:
Subject: Requested resignation

Dear Recipient Name,

   As requested by _____, Nursing Manager, I am submitting this letter as written confirmation of my resignation as a per-diem on-call CCU nurse with _____ Hospital. My permanent part-time employment was scheduled to begin April 7th. However, in the interim, I accepted a permanent full-time position with _____ Hospital.

   On April 3rd I met with _____, Human Resources Administrator, to inform her of my decision. I expressed a desire to honor my commitment with the understanding that the need for flexibility in my schedule would be taken into consideration. _____ contacted _____ to discuss an alternative employment arrangement. Subsequently, my status from permanent part-time was changed to per-diem on-call.

   Immediately upon completion of the mandatory two-week orientation period, I was faced with a schedule conflict. As a result of an apparent miscommunication, I was scheduled to do my floor orientation from April 21st through 25th. I approached _____, Nursing Manager, to resolve the conflict, and learned that she was completely unaware of both my situation and agreement between _____, Human Resources, and myself. As a result, my resignation seemed to be the logical solution.

   _____, it was never my intention to cause problems within your administration; therefore, please accept my apology for any inconvenience experienced. Thank you for the opportunity to be a part of your staff.

Sincerely,
Your Name
(555) 555-1234

294

Resignation after Ten Years

Dear Recipient Name,

After working for so many years for such a great boss and colleagues, it is with some regret that I offer my resignation. Please accept this letter as my formal resignation from the position of Care Coordinator. I have accepted a new position as Supervisor of Client Services at a growing medical center in _____.

My last day of employment will be on Friday, May 9, which should provide sufficient time to complete existing projects and assist with the transition to a new coordinator.

The past 10 years have been both professionally and personally rewarding. Thank you for your trust and support over all these years. I have appreciated the opportunity to expand my skills and work with many talented individuals. I hope that we stay in touch and that you can wish me the same success in the future I wish you and everyone here at the center.

Thank you sincerely,

Your Name
(555) 555-1234

VP Resignation

From: Your Name [Your e-mail address]
To: Recipient e-mail address
Cc:
Subject: Formal resignation

Dear Recipient Name,

As of this date, I am formally extending my resignation as _____. I have accepted a position as Vice President of _____ at a university medical center in _____.

My staff is readily able to handle the institution's operations until you find a suitable replacement. I intend to finalize my business and personal affairs here over the next several weeks, and will discuss a mutually acceptable termination date with you in person.

My decision to leave was made after long and careful consideration of all factors affecting the institution, my family, and my career. Although I regret leaving many friends here, I feel that the change will be beneficial to all parties.

Finally, I can only express my sincere appreciation to you and the entire board for all your support, cooperation, and encouragement over the past several years. I will always remember my stay at _____ for the personal growth it afforded and for the numerous friendships engendered.

Yours truly,

Your Name
(555) 555-1234

THANK YOU

I Landed a Job and You Helped

From: Your Name [Your e-mail address]
To: Recipient e-mail address
Cc:
Subject: I landed a job and you helped, thanks Jack

Dear Recipient Name,

I want you to be among the first to know that my job search has come to a very successful conclusion. I have accepted the position of _____ at _____, Inc., located in _____.

I appreciate all the help and support you have provided over the last several months. It has made this awful job search process much easier for me. I look forward to staying in contact with you. Please let me know when I can be of any assistance to you in the future. Thank you.

Sincerely,

Your Name
(555) 555-1234Your Initials

Sincere Appreciation

From: Your Name [Your e-mail address]
To: Recipient e-mail address
Cc:
Subject: I finally did it!

Dear Recipient Name,

I am happy to tell you that I received and accepted an offer of employment just after Thanksgiving. I am now employed by _____ as a _____.

My duties include responsibility for all _____ software (General Ledger, Accounts Payable, Accounts Receivable, and Fixed Assets) for worldwide plus the first-year training of several entry-level employees. I am enjoying my new responsibility and being fully employed again.

I want to thank you not only for all your help the past several months during my search for employment but also for your understanding and friendly words of encouragement. It really meant something in some dark hours, thanks muchacho.

If there is ever anything I can do for you please call me. I hope you and your family have a wonderful holiday season, and much luck and happiness in the New Year.

Most sincerely,

Your Name
(555) 555-1234

Career Consultants and Resume Writing Services

As part of your job search, you might feel the need to look into getting extra help from a professional resume writer and/or a career counselor. A professional in the field might be able to help you develop a more polished layout or present a particularly complex background more effectively.

As in any other profession, there are practitioners at both ends of the performance scale. I am a strong believer in using the services of resume writers and career consultants who belong to their field's professional associations. They tend to be more committed, have more field experience, and have an all-around higher standard of performance, partly because their membership demonstrates their commitment to the field and partly because of the ongoing educational programs that these associations offer to their members.

The three major associations in the resume-writing field are the Professional Association of Resume Writers & Career Coaches (PARW/CC, *www.parw.com*), the National Resume Writers' Association (NRWA, *www.nrwa.com*), and Career Management Alliance (CMA, *www.cminstitute.com*). All three associations have hundreds of members and provide ongoing opportunities for members to gain mentoring experience and additional training. They all offer resume-writing certification and operate e-mail list servers for members with access to e-mail.

Two important smaller organizations are CertifiedResumeWriters.com and CertifiedCareerCoaches.com. These two websites are designed to connect job seekers with certified career professionals who meet specific resume writing and career coaching needs. All of the resume writers on these two sites are active members of one or more of the three major associations and have taken the time to achieve accreditation in different aspects of the resume-writing and career-coaching process.

Finally, there is the Phoenix Career Group (*www.phoenixcareergroup.com*), a small group of highly qualified and exceptionally credentialed career-management consultants and resume writers spread all over North America. This is a by-invitation-only marketing consortium of independents who all know each other through membership in other groups. Although I do not offer these one-on-one services myself, I am a member of Phoenix solely for the camaraderie and value I receive from rubbing shoulders with a select group of mature and committed professionals.

The following is a list of career consultants and professional resume writers. Most of these have contributed to the *Knock 'em Dead* books and are members of one or more of the groups already mentioned.

Martin Yate, Executive Career Strategist
E-mail: *martin@knockemdead.com*
Martin Yate, CPC
Typically works with C-level and C-level-bound professionals facing challenges in the areas of Job Search, Interviewing, and Career Strategy.

Phoenix Career Group
www.phoenixcareergroup.com
Debbie Ellis, CPRW, CRW
Serving career-minded professionals to senior executives, the Phoenix Career Group is a one-of-a-kind consortium of fifteen industry-leading professionals specializing in personal branding, resume writing, career-management coaching, research, and distribution.

A First Impression Resume Service
www.resumewriter.com
Debra O'Reilly, CPRW, CEIP, JCTC, FRWC
Debra provides job search and career-management tools for professionals, from entry-level to executive. Areas of specialty include career transition and the unique challenges of military-to-civilian conversion.

A Resume For Today
www.aresumefortoday.com
Jean Cummings, MAT, CPRW, CEIP, CPBS
Distills complex high-tech careers into potent, memorable, and valuable personal brands. Provides resume-writing and job search services to executives and managers seeking to advance their careers in technology.

A Word's Worth Resume Writing and Career Coaching Service
www.keytosuccessresumes.com
Nina K. Ebert, CPRW/CC
Serving clients since 1989, A Word's Worth is a full-service resume and cover letter development /career coaching company with a proven track record in opening doors to interviews.

A+ Career & Resume, LLC
www.careerandresume.com
Karen M. Silins, CMRS, CCMC, CRW, CECC, CEIP, CTAC, CCA
Expertise includes career document development, career exploration and transition, assessments, job search methods, networking, interviewing, motivation, dressing for success, and career-management strategies.

Abilities Enhanced
www.abilitiesenhanced.com
Meg Montford, MCCC, CMF, CCM
Helps enable radical career change, as from IT trainer to pharmaceutical sales rep and technical writer to personal trainer. Career coaching and resumes by a careers professional since 1986.

Advanced Resume Services
www.resumeservices.com
Michele Haffner, CPRW, JCTC
Resumes, cover letters, target mailings, interview coaching, and search strategy/action plan development. Specialty is mid- to senior-level professionals earning $75K+. Complimentary critique. More than ten years of experience. Guaranteed satisfaction.

Advantage Resume & Career Services
www.CuttingEdgeResumes.com
Vivian VanLier, CPRW, JCTC, CCMC, CEIP, CPRC
Full-service resume writing and career coaching, serving clients throughout the United States and internationally at all levels. Special expertise in Entertainment, Management, Senior Executives, Creative, and Financial Careers.

Arnold-Smith Associates
www.ResumeSOS.com
Arnold G. Boldt, CPRW, JCTC
Offers comprehensive job search consulting services, including writing resumes and cover letters; interview simulations; career assessments and coaching; and both electronic and direct-mail job search campaigns.

Brandego LLC
www.brandego.com
Kirsten Dixson, CPBS, JCTC
Creates web portfolios for executives, careerists, authors, consultants, and speakers. Includes experts in branding, career management, multimedia, copywriting, blogging, and SEO to express your unique value.

Career Directions, LLC
www.careeredgecoach.com
Louise Garver, JCTC, CPRW, MCDP, CEIP, CMP
Career Directions, LLC, is a full-service practice specializing in resume development, job search strategies, and career-coaching services for sales and marketing executives and managers worldwide.

Career Ink
www.careerink.com
Roberta Gamza, JCTC, JST, CEIP
Offering career marketing and communication strategy services that advance careers. Services include precisely crafted resumes and customized interview training sessions that persuade and motivate potential employers to action.

Career Marketing Techniques
www.polishedresumes.com
Diane Burns, CPRW, CCMC, CPCC, CFJST, IJCTC, CEIP, CCM
Diane is a career coach and resume strategist who specializes in executive-level military conversion resumes and federal government applications. She is a careers-industry international speaker and national author.

Career Solutions, LLC
www.WritingResumes.com
Maria E. Hebda, CCMC, CPRW
A certified career professional, Maria helps people effectively market themselves to employers and position them as qualified candidates. Provides writing and coaching services in resume and cover letter development.

Career Trend
www.careertrend.net
Jacqui Barrett, MRW, CPRW, CEIP
Collaborates with professionals and executives aspiring to ignite their careers or manage transition. The owner is among an elite group holding the Master Resume Writer designation via Career Masters Institute.

CFO-Coach.com (A Division of Executive Essentials)
www.career-management-coach.com
Cindy Kraft, CCMC, CCM, CPRW, JCTC
Prepares professionals and executives to outperform the competition. Top-notch marketing documents, a focused branding strategy, and job search coaching result in a multifaceted, effective, and executable search plan.

Cheek & Associates, LLC
www.cheekandcristantello.com
Freddie Cheek M.S. Ed., CCM, CPRW, CRW, CWDP
Resource for resume writing and interview coaching with twenty-five years' experience satisfying customers and getting results. Creates accomplishment-based resumes that help you achieve your career goals.

Create Your Career
www.careerist.com
Joyce Fortier, CCM, CCMC
Company collaborates with clients as a catalyst for optimum career success. Offerings include resume and cover letter services and coaching services, including job search techniques, interview preparation, networking, and salary negotiation.

ekm Inspirations
www.ekminspirations.com
Norine T. Dagliano, FJST, Certified DISC Administrator
More than eighteen years of comprehensive and individualized career transition services, working with professionals at all levels of experience. Specializes in federal job search assistance, assisting dislocated workers and career changers.

Executive Power Coach
www.ExecutivePowerCoach.com
Deborah Wile Dib, CPBS, CCM, CCMC, NCRW, CPRW, CEIP, JCTC
Careers-industry leader helps very senior executives stand out, get to the top, and stay at the

top. Executive brand development, power resumes, and executive power coaching services since 1989.

Job Whiz
www.JobWhiz.com
Debra Feldman, BS, MPH
Personally arranges confidential networking appointments delivering decision-makers inside target employers. Engineers campaign strategy, innovates positioning, and defines focus. Banishes barriers, accelerating job search progress. Relentless follow-up guarantees results.

The McLean Group
yourcareercoach@aol.com
Don Orlando, MBA, CPRW, JCTC, CCM, CCMC
Puts executives in control of the career they've always deserved. Personal, on-demand support that helps busy managers get paid what they are worth.

Mil-Roy Consultants
www.milroyconsultants.com
Nicole Miller, CCM, CRW, IJCTC, CECC
Creates the extra edge needed for success through the innovative design of dynamic resumes and marketing tools that achieve results.

Prism Writing Services, LLC
www.prismwritingservices.com
Patricia Traina-Duckers, CPRW, CRW, CEIP, CFRWC, CWPP
Fully certified career service practice offering complete career search services, including personalized civilian/federal resume development, business correspondence, web portfolios, bios, CVs, job search strategies, interview coaching, salary research, and more.

ResumeRighter
www.ResumeRighter.com
Denise Larkin CPRW, CEIP
A mount-a-campaign, market-yourself, total-job-search support system. They promise to present your qualifications for best advantage, write an attention-grabbing cover letter, and coach you to ace your interview.

ResumeROI
www.ResumeROI.com
Lorie Lebert, CPRW, IJCTC, CCMC
A full-service career-management provider, offering personalized, confidential support and guidance; moving client careers forward with focused customer service.

Resumes For Results
www.resumes4results.com
Cory Edwards, CRW, CECC, CCMC
Resume writer and career coach currently achieving 98 percent success rate getting clients interviews. Specializing in all resumes, including federal, SES, postal, and private sector from entry-level to executive.

Resume Magic/Guarneri Associates
www.Resume-Magic.com
Susan Guarneri, NCC, NCCC, LPC, MCC, CPRW, CCMC, CEIP, JCTC, CWPP
Comprehensive career services—from career counseling and assessments to resumes and cover letters—by full-service career professional with top-notch credentials, twenty years of experience, and satisfied customers.

Resume Suite
www.resumesuite.com
Bonnie Kurka, CPRW, JCTC, FJST
Career coach, resume writer, speaker, and trainer with more than eleven years' experience in the careers industry. Specializes in mid- to upper-level management, IT, military, and federal career fields.

Resume Writers
100PercentResumes
www.100percentresumes.com
Daniel J. Dorotik, Jr., NCRW
Global career development service specializing in the preparation of resumes, cover letters, and other associated career documents. In addition to traditional formats, prepares online-compatible documents for Internet-driven job searches.

Write Away Resume and Career Coaching
www.writeawayresume.com
Edie Rische, NCRW, JCTC, ACCC
Creates targeted resumes and job search correspondence for clients in every vocation, and specializes in helping others discover their "Authentic Vocation™," shift careers, and resolve issues using QuantumShift™ coaching.

INTERNET RESOURCES

These are really *Knock 'em Dead* Internet resources, with links to websites in twenty-two job search and career-management categories.

You'll find the big job banks; profession-specific sites for eighteen major industries; association, entry-level, executive, and minority sites; and more. You'll discover tools that help you find companies, executives, and lost colleagues, plus sites that help you choose new career directions or find a super-qualified professional resume writer or job or career coach.

To save time, you can come to the knockemdead.com website, where you can click on each of these resources and be connected directly—no more typing in endless URLs!

Association Sites

www.ipl.org
The Internet Public Library. Lots of great research services of potential use to your job search. This link takes you directly to an online directory of professional associations.

www.weddles.com
Peter Weddle's employment services site also offers a comprehensive online professional association directory.

Career and Job Coaches

www.knockemdead.com
Martin Yate, CPC, Executive Career Strategist
E-mail: *martin@knockemdead.com*
Typically works with C-level and C-level-bound professionals facing challenges in the areas of Job Search, Interviewing, and Career Strategy.

www.phoenixcareergroup.com
A private, by-invitation-only association of seasoned and credentialed coaches, of which I am a member. I know all the Phoenix consultants professionally, and I'm proud to know most of them personally. They're the finest you'll find.

www.certifiedcareercoaches.com
A website that features only certified career coaches.

www.certifiedresumewriters.com
A website that features only certified resume writers.

Career Assessments

www.assessment.com
A career choice test that matches your motivations against career directions. I've been using it for a number of years.

www.crgleader.com

www.careerplanning.about.com
Links to career planning and career choice tools. The first free career choice test listed wasn't very helpful, but the site has other good resources.

www.analyzemycareer.com
A well-organized and comprehensive career choice online testing site.

www.careerplanner.com
Affordable RIASEC-oriented career choice testing by an established online presence.

www.careertest.us

www.college911.com
Helps you find colleges based on your interests. No career choice tests; rather a site you might want to visit after you have a general sense of direction.

www.livecareer.com
Home page says it's free, and the free report is okay as far as it goes, which is not very far. To get a full report you will pay $25, and there are also premium options, but you don't know this until you have spent thirty minutes taking the test! Despite this sleight of hand, a good career choice test with comprehensive reports.

www.princetonreview.com
A $40 online test. This is a good solid test and the site is easy to navigate.

www.rockportinstitute.com
Excellent career choice tests for all ages. Although priced on a sliding scale dependent on income, they start at $1,500 for someone earning 40K a year or less.

www.self-directed-search.com
This is the famous SDS test developed by John Holland. An extremely well regarded test, and at just $9.95 it's a great deal.

Career Choice and Management Sites

www.acinet.org
A site that offers career choice and advancement advice via testing for job seekers at all levels. Has good info on enhancing your professional credentials.

www.phoenixcareergroup.com
A premier site featuring deeply experienced and credentialed career counselors available for consultation on an hourly basis.

www.quintcareers.com
Career and job search advice.

www.rileyguide.com
Excellent site for job search and career-management advice. It's been around for years and is run by people who really care.

Career Transition
Military Transition

www.destinygroup.com
A great site for anyone transitioning out of the military. The #1 post–military careers site.

www.corporategray.com

www.taonline.com
Military transition assistance.

Other Transition

www.careertransition.org
For dancers once their joints go.

College and Entry-Level Job Sites

www.aleducation.com
Directories and links for colleges and graduate schools, test prep, financial aid, and job search advice.

www.aboutjobs.com
Links and leads for student jobs, internships, recent grads, expats, and adventure seekers.

www.aftercollege.com
Internships and co-ops, part-time and entry-level, PhDs and post-docs, teaching jobs, plus alumni links.

www.backdoorjobs.com
Short-term and part-time adventure and dream jobs.

www.blackcollegian.com
Premier site for black college students and recent graduates; help and sensible advice in areas of concern for the young professional.

www.campuscareercenter.com
Job search, career guidance, and advice on networking for transition into the professional world.

www.careerfair.com
Career fair directory.

www.collegecentral.com
A networking site for graduates of small and medium-size community colleges.

www.collegegrad.com
A comprehensive and well-thought-out site full of good information for the entry-level job seeker; probably the best in the entry-level field.

www.collegejobboard.com
A top job site for entry-level jobs; includes jobs in all fields.

www.collegejournal.com
Run by the *Wall Street Journal*, it's a savvy site for entry-level professionals, with lots of resources.

www.collegerecruiter.com
One of the highest-traffic sites for students and recent grads with up to three years' experience. Well-established and comprehensive job site.

www.ednet.com
Reports on college aid, college selection, career guidance, and college strategy.

www.entryleveljobs.net
It's been around since 1999, and it does have jobs posted, though much is out-of-date.

www.graduatingengineer.com
A site for graduating engineers and computer careers.

www.internshipprograms.com
A good site if you are looking for an internship.

www.jobpostings.net
The online presence of one of the biggest college recruitment magazine publishers in North America; includes jobs across United States and Canada.

www.jobweb.com
Owned and sponsored by the Association of Colleges and Employers. It's a great way to tap into the employers who consistently have entry-level hiring needs.

www.snagajob.com
For part-time and hourly jobs.

College Placement and Alumni Networks

www.mcli.dist.maricopa.edu
Resource for community college URLs.

www.utexas.edu
Resource for locating college alumni groups.

Diversity Sites

http://janweb.icdi.wvu.edu
Job Accommodation Network: a portal site for people with disabilities.

www.twolingos.com/jobs/index.php
A site for bilingual jobs, in America and around the globe.

www.blackcollegian.com
Premier site for black college students and recent graduates; help and sensible advice in areas of concern for the young professional.

www.bwni.com
Business women's network.

www.christianjobs.com
Full-featured employment website focusing on employment within the Christian community.

www.diversitylink.com
Job site serving women, minorities, and other diversity talent.

www.eop.com
The online presence of the oldest diversity recruitment publisher in America. For women, members of minority groups, and people with disabilities.

www.experienceworks.org
Training and employment services for mature workers, fifty-five and older.

www.gayjob.biz
A job site featuring a resume bank and job postings for gay men and women.

www.hirediversity.com
Links multicultural and bilingual professionals with both national and international industry sectors. Clients primarily consist of *Fortune* 1000 companies and government agencies.

www.imdiversity.com
Communities for African Americans, Asian
Americans, Hispanic Americans, Native
Americans, and women. No jobs or overt career
advice, but lots of links for members of minority
communities on issues that affect our lives.

www.latpro.com
The number one employment source for
Spanish- and Portuguese-speaking professionals
in North and South America The site can
be viewed in English, Spanish, or Portuguese.
Features both resume and job banks.

Executive Job Sites

www.netshare.com
Been around since before the Internet with ten-
ured management; really understands and cares
about the executive in transition. Job banks,
resources, etc.

www.6figurejobs.com
Solid and well-respected site; includes job banks,
resources, etc. A warning: some of their career
advice seems very nonspecific and geared to selling services.

www.online.wsj.com/careers
Run by the *Wall Street Journal* with all the bells
and whistles, this is an excellent executive transition site.

www.chiefmonster.com
Monster's site aimed at the executive area, though
it's difficult to differentiate from the rest of the
brand. Comprehensive job postings.

www.execunet.com
One of the top executive sites (along with Net-
share, 6 Figure, and the WSJ site). Job banks
and resources. Founder Dave Opton has been
around a long time and runs a blog with interesting insights.

www.futurestep.com
Korn/Ferry is the search firm behind the site.
You can put your resume in their database,
which is not a bad idea.

www.spencerstuart.com
Executive site for eminent search firm Spen-
cer Stuart. You can put your resume in their
database.

www.theladders.com
Like pretty much all the executive sites, you pay
for access. Good job board and aggressive marketing means this site has become a player in the
space very quickly.

Finding Companies

www.flipdog.monster.com

www.corporateinformation.com
In addition to accessing an alphabetical listing
of more than 20,000 companies, you can also
research a country's industry or research a U.S.
state. Also, if you register with the site, it will
allow you to load the company profile. Within
the address section, you will find a link to the
company's home page.

www.zoominfo.com

www.goleads.com

www.google.com

www.infospace.com

www.searchbug.com

www.superpages.com

www.wetfeet.com

General Job Sites

www.flipdog.monster.com

www.hotjobs.yahoo.com

www.4jobs.com

www.americasjobbank.com

www.bestjobsusa.com

www.career.com

www.careerboard.com

www.careerbuilder.com

www.careerhunters.com

www.careermag.com

www.careers.org
Good one-stop site for job search resources.

www.careershop.com

www.careersite.com

www.employment911.com

www.employmentguide.com

www.employmentspot.com

www.jobcentral.com

www.job-hunt.org
Excellent site with sensible in-depth advice on job search and career-management issues.

www.job.com

www.jobbankusa.com

www.jobfind.com

www.jobwarehouse.com

www.jobweb.com

www.localcareers.com

www.mbajungle.com
Site for current entry-level-ish and future MBAs.

www.monster.com

www.nationjob.com

www.net-temps.com

www.quintcareers.com

Diversity Job-Seeker Career, Employment, Job Resources

www.snagajob.com

www.sologig.com

www.summerjobs.com

www.topusajobs.com

www.truecareers.com

www.vault.com

www.wetfeet.com

www.worklife.com

Job Posting Spiders

www.indeed.com

www.jobbankusa.com

www.jobsearchengine.com

www.jobsniper.com

www.worktree.com

International Sites

www.ukjobsnet.co.uk
UK Jobs Network: the easiest way to find vacancies throughout the United Kingdom.

www.4icj.com

www.careerone.com.au

www.eurojobs.com

www.gojobsite.co.uk

www.jobpilot.com

www.jobsbazaar.com

www.jobserve.com

www.jobstreet.com
Asia-Pacific's #1 job site.

www.monster.ca
Monster Canada

www.monster.co.uk
Monster UK: England's #1 job site.

www.overseasjobs.com

www.reed.co.uk

www.seek.com.au
Australia's #1 job site.

www.stepstone.com

www.topjobs.co.uk

www.totaljobs.com

www.workopolis.com
Canada's #1 job site.

Job Fairs

www.careerfairs.com
CareerFairs.com is the fastest one-stop Internet site for locating upcoming job fairs and employers. In some cases you can even find the specific positions you desire and the specific positions you are trying to fill.

www.cfg-inc.com
Career Fairs for all levels: Professional & General, Healthcare, Technical, Salary, Hourly, Entry to Senior Level.

www.preferredjobs.com

www.skidmore.edu

Networking Sites

http://network.monster.com

http://socialsoftware.weblogsinc.com
This blog maintains a comprehensive listing of
hundreds of networking sites. If you want to
check out all your networking options, this is
the place to start.

www.40plus.org
Chapter contact information.

www.alumni.net

www.distinctiveweb.com

www.zoominfo.com
Helps you find people and companies.

www.execunet.com
An extensive network of professionals with whom
you can interact for advice, support, and even
career enhancement through local networking
meetings. To locate meetings near you (United
States and the world), check under "Networking"
on their website.

www.fiveoclockclub.com
National career counseling network.

www.rileyguide.com

www.ryze.com
Ryze helps people make connections and expand
their networks. You can network to grow your
business, build your career, and find a job.
You can also join free networks related to your
industry.

www.tribe.net

www.linkedin.com

Newspaper Sites

www.newsdirectory.com
Links to newspapers (global).

Profession-Specific Sites
Advertising, Public Relations, and Graphic Arts

www.adage.com

www.adweek.com
Adweek Online

www.amic.com
Advertising Media Internet Center

www.creativehotlist.com

Aerospace and Aviation

www.avcrew.com

www.avjobs.com

www.spacejobs.com

Agriculture and Horticulture

www.agcareers.com

www.fishingjobs.com

www.hortjobs.com

Broadcast, Communications, and Journalism

www.b-roll.net

www.cpb.org
Corporation for Public Broadcasting

www.crew-net.com

www.journalismjobs.com

www.telecomcareers.net

www.womcom.org
Association for Women in Communications
Online

Business, Finance, and Accounting

www.accounting.com

www.bankjobs.com

www.brokerhunter.com

www.businessfinancemag.com

www.careerbank.com

www.careerjournal.com

www.cfo.com

www.financialjobs.com

www.jobsinthemoney.com

Communication Arts

www.prweek.com
PR Week

Education

www.aacc.nche.edu
American Association of Community Colleges

www.academic360.com

www.academiccareers.com

www.chronicle.com

www.higheredjobs.com

www.petersons.com

www.phds.org

www.teacherjobs.com

www.ujobbank.com

www.wihe.com
Women in Higher Education

Engineering

www.asme.org

www.chemindustry.com

www.engineeringcentral.com

www.engineeringjobs.com

www.engineerjobs.com

www.enr.com
Engineering News-Record Magazine

www.graduatingengineer.com

www.ieee.org

www.mepatwork.com

www.nsbe.org
National Society of Black Engineers

www.nspe.org
National Society of Professional Engineers

http://societyofwomenengineers.swe.org/

Entertainment, TV, and Radio

www.castingnet.com

www.eej.com
Entertainment Employment Journal

www.entertainmentcareers.net

www.showbizjobs.com

www.themeparkjobs.com

www.tvandradiojobs.com

www.tvjobs.com

Health Care

www.accessnurses.com
Travel nursing jobs

http://allnurses.com

www.dentsearch.com

www.healthcaresource.com

www.healthjobusa.com

www.hirehealth.com

www.jobscience.com

www.mdjobsite.com

www.medcareers.com

www.nurses123.com
Nurses can use this site to find nursing jobs across the United States.

www.nursetown.com

www.nursing-jobs.us
Nursing jobs in the United States.

www.nursingcenter.com

www.nurse.com

www.physemp.com

Human Resources

www.hrjobnet.com

www.hrworld.com

www.jobs4hr.com

www.shrm.org

IT and MIS

www.computerjobs.com

www.computerjobsbank.com

www.dice.com

www.gjc.org

www.mactalent.com

www.tech-engine.com

www.techemployment.com

Legal

www.emplawyernet.com

www.ihirelegal.com

www.law.com

www.legalstaff.com

www.theblueline.com

Nonprofit

www.execsearches.com

www.idealist.org

www.naswdc.org

www.nonprofitcareer.com

www.opportunityknocks.org

Real Estate

www.realtor.org

Recruiter Sites

www.kellyservices.com

www.kornferry.com

www.manpower.com

www.napsweb.org
A job seeker can search the online directory
by state, specialty, or by individual. Be sure to
check out the headhunters who are designated
CPCs—the few but the best.

www.randstad.com

www.recruitersonline.com

www.rileyguide.com

www.snelling.com

www.spherion.com

www.staffingtoday.net
Search the database by state, skills, and type of
services you need (temporary/permanent/profes-
sion) and it will tell you about staffing services
companies in your area.

www.therecruiternetwork.com

Reference Checking

www.allisontaylor.com

Researching Companies

www.bls.gov

www.fuld.com

www.industrylink.com

http://iws.ohiolink.edu
A place for getting started with company
research.

www.newsdirectory.com

www.quintcareers.com
The Quintessential Directory of Company
Career Centers, a guide to researching compa-
nies, industries, and countries.

www.thomasregister.com

www.vault.com
Company research

www.virtualpet.com
Teaches you how to learn about an industry or a
specific company.

Resume Creation

Knockemdead.com
E-mail: martin@knockemdead.com

www.phoenixcareergroup.com

http://certifiedresumewriters.com

www.parw.com

Resume Distribution

www.resumemachine.com

Retail, Hospitality, and Customer Service

www.allretailjobs.com

www.chef2chef.net

www.chefjobsnetwork.com

www.coolworks.com

www.hcareers.com

www.leisurejobs.com

www.resortjobs.com

www.restaurantrecruit.com

www.supermarketnews.com

Salary Research

www.jobstar.org

www.salary.com

www.salaryexpert.com

Sales and Marketing

www.careermarketplace.com

www.jobs4sales.com

www.marketingjobs.com

www.marketingmanager.com

www.marketingpower.com

www.salesheads.com

www.salesjobs.com

Science, Chemistry, Physics, and Biology

www.biocareer.com

www.biospace.com

www.bioview.com

www.eco.org

www.hirebio.com

www.medzilla.com

www.microbiologistjobs.com

www.pharmacyweek.com

Telecommuting

www.homeworkers.org

www.jobs-telecommuting.com

www.tjobs.com

Web Resumes/Portfolios

www.brandego.com

www.qfolio.com

For More Information

You can send me your comments and questions about any of the *Knock 'em Dead* books through my website at knockemdead.com, or by:

E-mailing me at *martin@knockemdead.com*

Or writing to me at:
Martin Yate
c/o Adams Media
57 Littlefield Street
Avon, MA 02322

The best of luck to you in your job search, and throughout your career!

INDEX